THE BIG BOOK OF MEDITERRANEAN DIET COOKING

THE BIG BOOK OF
MEDITERRANEAN DIET
COOKING

200 Recipes and 3 Meal Plans for a Healthy Lifestyle

Donna DeRosa

Photography by Thomas Story

ROCKRIDGE
PRESS

For Sam and Kitty with love

For general information on our other products and services or to obtain technical support, please contact our Customer Care Department within the United States at (866) 744-2665, or outside the United States at (510) 253-0500.

Rockridge Press publishes its books in a variety of electronic and print formats. Some content that appears in print may not be available in electronic books, and vice versa.

TRADEMARKS: Rockridge Press and the Rockridge Press logo are trademarks or registered trademarks of Callisto Media Inc. and/or its affiliates, in the United States and other countries, and may not be used without written permission. All other trademarks are the property of their respective owners. Rockridge Press is not associated with any product or vendor mentioned in this book.

Interior and Cover Designer: Jami Spittler
Art Producer: Hannah Dickerson
Editor: Anne Lowrey
Production Manager: Riley Hoffman
Production Editor: Melissa Edeburn
Photography © 2020 Thomas Story.
Food styling by Alexa Hyman.
Art courtesy Shutterstock: cover (lemon) and pages 5–7.

ISBN: Print 978-1-64739-261-1
eBook 978-1-64739-262-8
R0

CONTENTS

Foreword vii

Introduction viii

ONE: Long Live the Mediterranean Diet 1

TWO: The Mediterranean Kitchen 11

THREE: Meal Plans for Everyday Wellness 19

FOUR: Breakfast 33

FIVE: Soups 49

SIX: Salads 65

SEVEN: Meze and Small Plates 83

EIGHT: Vegetables 103

NINE: Pasta, Rice, and Grains 129

TEN: Beans and Legumes 151

ELEVEN: Fish and Shellfish 167

TWELVE: Poultry and Meat 185

THIRTEEN: Breads, Pizza, and Sandwiches 205

FOURTEEN: Snacks and Sips 225

FIFTEEN: Sauces, Spreads, and Seasonings 245

SIXTEEN: Fruits and Sweets 265

Measurement Conversions 277

Resources 278

References 279

Index 280

Foreword

I met Donna several years ago in New York City at a business association for women. Her goal back then was to inspire others to live a lifestyle that incorporated the Mediterranean way of living. Since then, I have been an avid reader and watcher of her YouTube channel. I also enjoy sharing many of her recipes with others.

Donna has been living the Mediterranean lifestyle for some time, so it is no surprise that she wanted to spread her knowledge far and wide. Donna has a way of breaking things down so that they are easy to understand. This is a comprehensive and accessible book on Mediterranean cooking.

As a physician, I have encouraged the Mediterranean diet to my patients in my wellness practice. The Mediterranean diet, which is high in vegetables, fruits, whole grains, beans, nuts, seeds, and olive oil, blends the basics of healthy eating with the traditional flavors and cooking methods of the Mediterranean.

The Mediterranean diet helps with heart health and weight loss and is a delicious way to eat. In fact, many of my patients who switch to this diet say they'll never go back to a typical Western diet.

Whether you have health problems or are drawn to the Mediterranean diet for its healthy reputation, this book covers the diet's many benefits.

I found Donna's vegetable recipes extremely helpful. Many times, we think of vegetables as being bland, but Donna shows us how to create vegetable dishes that are both nutritious and tasty.

Many of her recipes incorporate grains, beans, and legumes, which are heart healthy and full of fiber to help our gut bacteria.

There are fun dishes such as pizza, wraps, and snacks as well as traditional pasta and bread recipes. I found the sauces and seasoning suggestions useful.

Donna's culinary talents make this a must-have cookbook for those who foster wellness in their lives and are looking to delve into Mediterranean cuisine.

Sharon T. McLaughlin, MD FACS
FOUNDER OF SHARONMACKWELLNESS.COM

Introduction

Let's start a new relationship with food.

Let's eat not just because we are hungry or feeling blue, but because it gives us energy, heals our bodies, and tastes delicious.

I want you to adore food. Savor it. Food feeds your brain, makes you smarter, and makes you more beautiful. Food can change your life.

I'd like to introduce you to one of the most studied diets in the world, with proven health benefits.

Before I found the Mediterranean diet, I was overworked, overwhelmed, and overweight. I worked a demanding job in online publishing. My hours were long, and most days I ate lunch in a hurry at my desk while catching up on email. In the evenings, I got home too late to cook, so most of the time I went out to restaurants or ordered takeout. I ate late and then went to bed right after.

This wasn't a sustainable way to live and eventually my body rebelled. I developed high blood pressure. My doctor said that it was mainly because I was overweight and that I could control it by eating more vegetables, reducing my portion sizes, and taking walks. Vegetables, he said, were key.

I had tried many fad diets in the past. They generally left me feeling deprived, weak, and frustrated. I was ready for something new, and I found it in something old—ancient, even.

At the same time, I started doing research into my family tree and became interested in my Italian heritage. I read about the Mediterranean diet and decided to try eating the way my ancestors did.

I eased myself into it at first. I started by making food swaps like olive oil for butter and fish for meat. I felt better. But I wasn't losing weight. I realized that even though I was eating healthy foods, I was still eating too much. That's when I tried an experiment.

For one month I completely immersed myself in the Mediterranean lifestyle. I did so with a male partner. We weighed ourselves and took measurements all over our bodies. For 30 days, we ate healthy Mediterranean meals. We practiced portion control. We moved our bodies more by going to the gym every other day and taking walks after dinner.

At the end of 30 days, our numbers were astonishing. Not only did we each lose about 10 pounds, we also lost inches all over our bodies.

I went to the doctor and had my blood work done. My cholesterol, blood pressure, and all of my other health indicator numbers were dramatically improved. My doctor was so happy for me.

And you know what? It was easy.

The best part was the way we felt. We were energized and had an overwhelming feeling of happiness and positivity. I want you to feel that way, too. This diet and lifestyle can be beneficial on so many levels.

Maybe you are interested in the Mediterranean diet because your doctor recommended it for health reasons, because you've heard a lot of good things about it and are curious, or because you want to lose weight without trying a fad diet. Whatever your reasons for adopting this way of eating, you'll find what you're looking for in this book. I've even designed three two-week meal plans to get you started: one for heart health, one with a focus on weight loss, and one to maintain overall wellness. I wrote the recipes so that they're both easy to prepare and made with ingredients that are readily available.

I believe the Mediterranean lifestyle can change your life for the better. It did for me, and I've never looked back.

The important thing to remember is that this diet doesn't last for a certain number of weeks and then you go back to your old habits. I'll teach you a new lifestyle that will change the way you feel about food. You'll want to eat the Mediterranean way for the rest of your life.

Hungry for more? Let's get started.

one

LONG LIVE THE MEDITERRANEAN DIET

Good news: The Mediterranean diet is not a "diet" in the way we think of restrictive eating in the United States. The word *diet* comes from the Greek *díaita*, which means "way of living." With that in mind, we'll be using the word *diet* in this book to refer to both what and how we eat.

The Mediterranean way of living is to enjoy flavorful dishes that bestow health benefits. I like to think of the Mediterranean diet as a lifestyle of moderate indulgences.

Some strategic planning and preparation is needed, so we're going to give your pantry, refrigerator, and meal plans a Mediterranean makeover. I promise it will be easy and enjoyable.

Remember: We're not going on a diet. We're upgrading our lifestyle.

Arugula and White Bean Salad, p. 74, and
Albóndigas (Spanish Meatballs), p. 93

THE MANY BENEFITS OF THE MEDITERRANEAN DIET

In the second half of the 20th century, the Mediterranean diet began to emerge as the healthiest way to eat to prevent disease.

The Seven Countries Study was the first major analysis of the effects of food and eating habits on our health. The study looked at seven countries with vastly different eating traditions. Citizens of the countries along the Mediterranean Sea, namely Italy and Greece, were found to have the lowest risk of coronary heart disease due to their comparatively low serum cholesterol levels and blood pressure. The study concluded that a healthy diet and lifestyle can help prevent disease, lengthening life spans.

The Mediterranean diet, as it came to be known, consists mostly of vegetables, healthy fats, whole grains, plant-based proteins, and a little red wine. This diet, no matter where in the world it is practiced, can aid in the prevention of heart disease, stroke, hypertension, type 2 diabetes, and cancer.

Further studies have shown that a Mediterranean lifestyle can help prevent cognitive decline and depression as we age; improve liver and kidney function; ease the symptoms of allergies, perimenopause, and mental health issues like anxiety; boost athletic performance; and fight obesity.

It's no wonder the Mediterranean diet and lifestyle is recognized by the World Health Organization and the Mayo Clinic as one of the world's healthiest diets.

EATING THE MEDITERRANEAN WAY

Following a Mediterranean diet is endlessly interesting because there is so much variety in what you can eat.

The Mediterranean diet pyramid is based on local foods of the countries bordering the Mediterranean Sea. These countries' cuisines have their own preferred spices and herbs, but they use the same base ingredients: vegetables, beans, whole grains, and healthy fats. These natural foods are minimally processed to preserve maximum nutritional value.

Here are some of the major food groups that make up this healthy and delightful way of eating.

Fresh Vegetables

Vegetables are the key to healthy eating. They are rich in the vitamins and minerals we need to maintain a healthy body, yet they have very few calories. If you are to reap the many health benefits of the Mediterranean diet, vegetables should make up half of your plate at each meal.

Here are my tips for eating lots of vegetables:

◆ Buy local, seasonal produce whenever you can. As the seasons change, the earth offers up the vegetables we need at that time of year.

- Toss a variety of seasonal vegetables in olive oil, add a few herbs, and roast them in the oven so that you can eat several types of veggies in one meal.
- Use vegetables for seasoning. Shallots, onions, garlic, and herbs like oregano, basil, and parsley can add depth and flavor to your meals.
- Choose a variety of colors. Red, green, orange, yellow, and purple foods all offer specific nutrients that your body needs. Strive to create a multicolored plate.

Beans and Legumes

Beans and legumes provide dietary fiber and are a great low-fat, no-cholesterol source of plant-based protein and iron. They help lower cholesterol and reduce the risk of heart disease, diabetes, and cancer. Beans add substance to meals and can help you feel fuller longer.

Here are my tips for adding beans to your diet:

- Rethink your breakfast meals. Include a serving of lentils, black beans, or chickpeas to promote good intestinal health.
- Add beans, lentils, and peas to stews, soups, pasta dishes, and salads.
- Puree beans to make interesting and healthy dips.

Whole Grains

Whole grains help you feel fuller longer and reduce the risk of heart disease, diabetes, and cancer. Try to add a serving of whole grains to each meal and opt for whole-grain breads. Rye bread is one of the healthiest breads you can eat, and it's delicious.

This book's recipes use the more readily available of these grains: amaranth, barley, brown rice, buckwheat, bulgur, farro, freekeh, millet, oats, quinoa, rye, spelt, teff, wheat berries, and wild rice. These grains can be used as breakfast cereals, incorporated into soups and salads, or eaten on their own.

Fish and Shellfish

Fish such as mackerel, salmon, sardines, and tuna are rich in omega-3 fatty acids. This important nutrient can help lower cholesterol and maintain optimal levels of triglycerides, an important component of heart health.

Fish is best when kept simple. My favorite way to prepare fish is to brush it with a little olive oil, sprinkle it with a few herbs, and roast it in the oven.

Shellfish, like clams, crabs, mussels, and shrimp, are low in calories and rich in lean, easily digestible protein, micronutrients, and omega-3s. They can potentially raise the level of good cholesterol that helps control bad cholesterol in your body, thereby contributing to heart health. Most shellfish can be steamed in just a few minutes.

If you're not used to eating fish, start by adding canned tuna in olive oil to your shopping list. Use it to make tuna salad for lunch. Or try smoked salmon with your breakfast instead of bacon. Then try eating fish at one dinner during the week.

Nuts and Seeds

Nuts and seeds are rich in healthy monounsaturated fats, plus omega-3s, protein, fiber, vitamins, minerals, and complex carbohydrates.

Nut and seed consumption has been associated with a reduced risk of major chronic illnesses such as cardiovascular disease and type 2 diabetes by helping reduce cholesterol levels and improve insulin resistance and blood sugar levels.

Researchers at Tufts Friedman School of Nutrition Science and Policy found that people who ate nuts every day lived significantly longer, and had fewer deaths from cancer, heart disease, and respiratory disease, than those who did not. Even though nuts contain fat, they result in lower rates of obesity. Nuts also help keep you feeling full.

Think about adding a handful of nuts to your daily diet. Good choices are almonds, Brazil nuts, cashews, hazelnuts, macadamia nuts, pecans, and pistachios. (Peanuts are a good choice, too, although they are botanically classified as legumes, not nuts.) Healthy seed choices include chia seeds, flaxseeds, pumpkin seeds, sesame seeds, and sunflower seeds.

Try spreading your favorite nut butter on rye toast, then sprinkle on some of your favorite seeds. Add a piece of fruit and this could be your new favorite healthy breakfast.

Low-Fat Dairy, Poultry, and Meat

Meals in the Mediterranean diet are largely plant-based. Unlike the Standard American Diet, which uses meat as the center of a meal, in the Mediterranean diet, red meat is consumed only a handful of times each month. Poultry is eaten perhaps once a week. This may be the biggest adjustment for most Americans.

Countries around the Mediterranean use meat as a flavor enhancer rather than a main course. A little pancetta, similar to bacon, might be used to flavor a soup or pasta dish. Stews may be made up of mostly vegetables, with a small amount of meat or fish added for flavor.

In order to adjust to this new lifestyle, start by reducing your meat and poultry portions to 3 or 4 ounces, about the size of the palm of your hand, instead of the large servings we typically consume in the United States. Fill that hole on your plate with vegetables, grains, or beans. Then try substituting fish once a week and work up to twice a week. And then move on to plant-based recipes.

Opt for plant-based milks, low-fat versions of dairy products (like Greek yogurt), and small servings of cheese. Try replacing butter with extra-virgin olive oil, and you'll be well on your way to a new, healthy Mediterranean lifestyle.

Fruit and Yes, Wine

Fruit is just as important as vegetables in the Mediterranean diet. When consumed whole (and not in juice form), fruits are filled with vitamins, minerals, and fiber. Keep a bowl of seasonal fruit on your kitchen table for when family members are looking for a snack.

Fresh fruit is also a good choice as dessert when you want something sweet after a meal. It pairs well with cheese or is delicious on its own. Fruit does contain natural sugars, though, so you may want to reach for fruits that are lower in sugar, like kiwis, raspberries, strawberries, and watermelon, if you're trying to lose weight.

Red wine is consumed almost daily in the Mediterranean but always in moderation. You won't find many people in Mediterranean countries binge drinking. Studies suggest that women should limit red wine to one glass a day, and men to two.

Alcohol in general can be beneficial to your health when consumed minimally. Red wine is a good choice because it is delicious and also offers resveratrol, which is found in the skin of red grapes. Resveratrol can improve heart health and protect against certain cancers. If you don't consume alcohol, red grape juice can be just as beneficial, as is a handful of blueberries or raspberries.

EAT SPARINGLY: *Red meat, saturated fat, sweets*

EAT MODERATELY: *Poultry, dairy, cheese, eggs. Red wine (typically with meals). Females: 1 glass per day. Males: 2 glasses per day*

EAT FREQUENTLY *(at least 2x per week): Fish, seafood*

EAT IN ABUNDANCE: *Vegetables, fruits, legumes and beans, whole grains, nuts, healthy fats such as olive oil, herbs, spices, water*

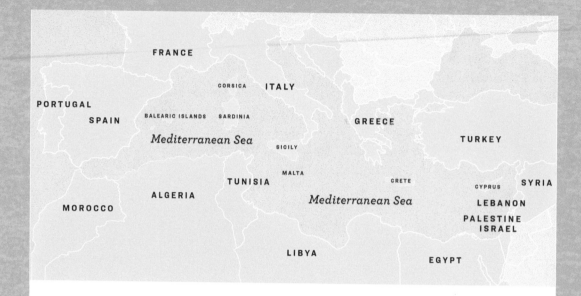

The Origins of the Mediterranean Lifestyle

The Mediterranean diet is based on the eating habits of people who live in the countries bordering the Mediterranean Sea. This area is known for longevity and lower rates of cardiovascular disease, cancers, diabetes, and dementia. People in these areas not only live longer, they also stay healthier and active into their later years.

This diet reaches back to the times of our ancestors, when life was simpler and processed foods were not readily available. People grew their own vegetables, raised their own livestock, and made their own bread and wine. In our modern world, it's possible to get the same health benefits by eating fruits and vegetables in their peak season, reducing meat consumption, and supporting local farmers, bakers, and grocers.

When people think of the Mediterranean diet, they naturally think of the foods of Italy and Greece. But the Mediterranean is made up of many countries, each with its own food traditions. In this book, we'll offer recipes from the many countries along the Mediterranean Sea, including Italy and Greece, but also Algeria, Egypt, Israel, Morocco, Spain, Tunisia, Turkey, and more, as well as islands like Crete, Cyprus, and Sardinia.

Each country follows the same basic premise of eating plenty of fresh vegetables, whole grains, nuts, and healthy fats, but they each prepare their foods in unique ways. Each country has its own favorite spices and flavorings, so meals with similar base ingredients can take on a whole new personality. You're not likely to get bored following a Mediterranean diet. There is good reason this way of living has stood the test of time.

LIVING THE MEDITERRANEAN WAY

To gain the health benefits of the Mediterranean diet, it's important to understand that it's not just about food—it's a complete lifestyle. It's about slowing down, savoring your food, and enjoying good company. Let's delve into what makes the Mediterranean lifestyle so healthy, happy, and sustainable.

Portion Control

People who live in the Mediterranean eat much less food than we are used to in the United States. We are constantly bombarded with advertisements for fast food and offers to super-size it. No wonder our waistlines have expanded and diseases like type 2 diabetes and heart disease are on the rise.

The recommended foods on the Mediterranean diet keep you full longer. While you will be eating smaller servings than you may be used to, the foods are more satisfying. They literally stay in your stomach longer before moving on.

Start by eating a little less than you normally would. Put 25 percent less food on your plate. Eat slowly and give your brain time to catch up to your stomach.

Fill half your plate with vegetables of varying colors. Limit your protein source to 3 to 4 ounces. Add some beans or legumes, some whole grains, and finish with a little fruit. Drink lots of water, and perhaps a small glass of red wine.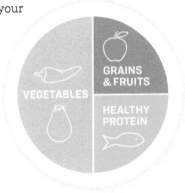

When dining out, be mindful of the ingredients when choosing your meal. Instead of a hamburger, try a portobello mushroom sandwich. Instead of a steak, try Italian sea bass. Instead of spaghetti and meatballs, try shrimp risotto. When in doubt, search the menu for meals inspired by the Mediterranean. There are so many wonderful choices available.

Daily Exercise

Adding some type of movement to your day is also important for maximum health benefits. People in the Mediterranean often spend time outdoors—they walk to the local grocer, ride a bike, or do some gardening. They generally have more active lifestyles, even into their later years.

In Italy, for example, it is customary to take *la passeggiata*, an evening stroll, before dinner. It's not a power walk, but more of a social ritual. People may stop to talk to a neighbor or pick up some bread at the local bakery.

If you're not used to a lot of physical activity, start by moving 15 minutes a day. Take a stroll around the neighborhood, walk the dog, or dance to your favorite tunes while you clean up around the house. Try something meditative, like yoga, or do some simple stretches.

It's important to do some type of movement for strength, balance, and posture, especially as we get older. This will help you maintain an independent lifestyle and keep you feeling good.

Living with Less Stress

Our modern lives have gotten so fast paced. We work late hours, run around with the kids, and get bombarded with news and social media. It's no wonder cases of anxiety and depression have risen in recent years.

A Mediterranean diet can help you feel less stressed because you'll feel better physically and have more energy. But you should also make time for a social life.

The Mediterranean lifestyle is about sharing meals and activities with your friends and family members. Nurturing a sense of community will keep you happier and healthier into your later years. Schedule time with friends, visit your family, and check in on your elderly neighbors. It will add an intangible quality to your life overall.

Managing stress directly relates to our happiness. The Italians have what they call *la pausa pranzo*, the afternoon lunch break. You've probably heard of the Spanish *siesta*. Taking a midday break helps with workday stresses. You may not be able to take a long lunch break, but make sure you do take some time instead of just quickly eating a sandwich at your desk. Make lunch a separate activity from work.

A Harvard study on adult development that spanned more than 75 years has shown that connecting with people may be the most important factor when it comes to longevity. Maintaining friendships and family relationships, having human interaction, and sharing and caring can get us through almost anything. You can withstand hard times and persevere through illnesses and depression by sharing the human experience with others.

Ten Tips for Living Your Best Mediterranean Life

As we've discussed, a Mediterranean lifestyle is about more than food. It's a way of living. It's a little slower, a bit more passionate, and more selective. It goes back to the ways of our ancestors, when life was simpler and revolved around the seasons.

You don't need to live on the Mediterranean Sea to benefit from this lifestyle. Here are 10 tips for living your best Mediterranean life anywhere in the world.

1. **Learn to enjoy cooking.** The only way to really know what is in your food is to prepare it yourself.

2. **Avoid highly processed foods.** Eat as clean and as close to nature as possible.

3. **Choose quality over quantity.** Cook with the best ingredients you can find and afford.

4. **Eat with the seasons.** Each season, the earth offers up the foods and nutrients we need at that moment, like strawberries in spring and apples in autumn.

5. **Spend time with friends.** Invite others to share a meal.

6. **Make time for family.** If you don't have family, make your own out of your best friends.

7. **Slow down.** Savor your food. Enjoy good conversation. Make the most of each moment.

8. **Live passionately.** How you do anything is how you do everything. Be inspired by the world around you and face each day with enthusiasm.

9. **Get out into nature.** Take a walk in the park, or say hello to your neighbors. Get some fresh air and soak up some vitamin D.

10. **Learn to indulge moderately.** Have a glass of wine, not a bottle of wine. You don't need to deprive yourself of the joys of living. When you follow a healthy Mediterranean lifestyle every day, there is room to enjoy your pleasures in moderate doses.

two

THE MEDITERRANEAN KITCHEN

It's time to give your kitchen and pantry a Mediterranean makeover. Living a Mediterranean lifestyle will be a lot easier once you have what you need readily at hand. This will be a simple process—no fancy equipment or exotic ingredients required. The Mediterranean diet is really about getting back to basics, the way your great-grandmother might have stocked her kitchen.

Having the right tools and ingredients is what will help you whip up a Mediterranean meal in no time. A basic pot and pan set will see you through most meals. I'll mention some specialty tools you could use, but they are not necessary for most recipes.

You can really change the essence of a meal by varying the herbs and spices you use. A basic dish can take on a completely different flavor when you use seasoning from Italy versus Morocco or France, for example. A well-stocked pantry will bring variety to your cooking.

PANTRY ESSENTIALS

You'll want to begin by stocking your pantry with healthy fats, whole grains, and interesting spices. We're going to ditch any highly processed ingredients like preflavored rice packets, breakfast bars, "diet" snacks, and supermarket white bread. Anything that has a label with a long list of unpronounceable ingredients gets tossed. We're going back to foods closer to their natural form.

Dry Shelf-Stable Goods

We'll start in the produce section of the grocery store and bring home items that don't need to be refrigerated and can keep for a while in your pantry. Foods like onions, garlic, and shallots can all be used to add significant flavor to your meals.

Nuts and seeds can also enhance your meals or make healthy snacks. A handful of nuts can help keep you satisfied between lunch and dinner.

Don't shy away from pasta and rice. The Mediterranean diet is not a low-carb diet. We'll stay away from highly processed carbs, but semolina pasta and rice are fine, because they are usually consumed in small portions in the Mediterranean. Italians eat pasta almost every day in small amounts. You can use Arborio rice for risotto dishes, a long-grain rice like jasmine for a pilaf, or brown and wild rice for other dishes.

Cans or boxes of good-quality broth are also good to keep on hand. I buy chicken and vegetable broth, and sometimes even seafood broth. I use them to make soups, to flavor rice dishes, and to add moisture to other dishes. And of course you'll need cans of tomatoes and beans and bottles of olive oil and vinegar.

Herbs and Spices

Keeping a variety of herbs and spices on hand allows you to explore the varied flavors of the countries along the Mediterranean Sea. You can visit Spain one day and France the next. Or hop on over to Israel, Algeria, Tangiers, or Morocco and experience completely new tastes.

Herbs and spices also allow you to add flavor to meals without adding too much salt, which can increase hypertension and inflammation.

Dried herbs are more potent than fresh, and there are some herbs I prefer to use dried over fresh. Just a small amount of oregano, marjoram, sage, thyme, and bay leaves can add a lot of flavor. For a more subtle flavor, you can use the fresh version. Fresh thyme, for example, is lovely in soups or cooked with fish. Fresh basil enhances pastas and pizza when sprinkled on top as a garnish.

Here are some of the spice cabinet items I reach for most often:

- black peppercorns
- cayenne pepper
- cumin
- oregano
- red pepper flakes
- thyme

I also like the convenience of spice blends. You can buy blends in the store or make your own, as I'll show you in chapter 15. Maybe you can try your hand creating your own Mediterranean blend.

Fresh herbs are lovely to cook with and easy to grow at home. You can plant them outside or keep them in pots in your kitchen. Some of the herbs I like to grow at home to have on hand for fresh use are:

- basil
- chives
- flat-leaf parsley
- marjoram
- mint
- rosemary

Choosing a Great Olive Oil

Without a doubt, the most important ingredient in a healthy Mediterranean diet is olive oil. People in the Mediterranean pour olive oil over everything. But not all olive oil is created equal.

Choose extra-virgin olive oil. It offers the most health benefits because of its purity and polyphenol content, which are the healthy antioxidants. EVOO, as it is often called, also offers the best flavor. Use it in cooking, when making salad dressings, and for drizzling over food.

Here are some things to look for when choosing an olive oil:

- Check the label for a "produced on" or "harvested" date instead of a "best by" date. This way you know when the olive oil was actually produced. Then try to use the olive oil within 6 months for maximum freshness. That may sound like a short time, but in my house, we go through a bottle of olive oil every few weeks.
- Look on the label for the country of origin. Some olive oils provide only a "bottled in" label. But that doesn't mean the olives were grown and harvested in that country. It could even be a blend. You want to stick to one country, and one farm if possible.

FRIDGE FAVORITES

The most important item I keep in my refrigerator is a pitcher of filtered water. I drink cold water all day long. Sometimes I dress it up with some lemon or cucumber slices. It's the first thing I drink in the morning and the last thing I consume at night.

My crisper drawers are always stocked with fresh vegetables and lettuces. Leafy greens are a must-have on the Mediterranean diet. I love to cook with beet greens, collards, dandelion greens, mustard greens, spinach, Swiss chard, and turnip greens.

Other vegetables I keep in the fridge are celery, carrots, cucumbers, mushrooms, and tomatoes. They are my base ingredients for many soups, salads, and stews. Cucumbers in particular are one of my favorite snacks—I like to use cucumber slices instead of chips for dips and hummus.

My favorite condiments to keep in the fridge are Dijon mustard and hot pepper relish. I also keep jars of hot peppers like whole cherry peppers, peperoncini and jalapeños. I'll often make my own sandwich spread by mixing cayenne pepper and dried herbs into vegan mayonnaise or mayonnaise. I also stock a variety of olives from Greece, Italy, and France to use while cooking, for a garnish, or as snacks.

I always keep a bag of lemons in my fridge. I use them in my water, in salad dressings, and around fish and chicken when roasting. Lemons are very versatile, and a good source of vitamin C and citric acid, which can improve your body's ability to absorb iron.

In addition, I always have farm-fresh eggs in the house. I eat eggs once or twice a week for breakfast, and also use them in recipes.

Last but not least, my meat drawer is usually stocked with smoked salmon and a variety of cheeses. You'll be delighted to discover that each country has unique cheeses to offer. A fruit and cheese plate makes a great after-dinner treat.

The Importance of Seasonal Produce

An important part of the Mediterranean diet is to eat with the seasons, taking advantage of what the earth offers up at different times of year. That means your menu will change throughout the year based on the bounty of the land. Most fruits and vegetables can be found year-round in the supermarket but are at their peak flavor and nutrient content when in season.

Hardy root vegetables keep well over the colder months. You'll find beets, ginger, parsnips, radishes, rutabagas, turnips, and sweet potatoes even in the winter.

In spring, the land comes back to life, offering fruits like apricots, blueberries, cherries, and strawberries, along with vegetables like asparagus, chives, fava beans, fennel, green beans, and leafy greens.

In summer, when we're more active and the weather is hot, we get hydrating fruits with plenty of water content, like berries, mangos, peaches, plums, and watermelon. Summer vegetables include corn, cucumbers, peppers, tomatoes, and zucchini.

In autumn, we celebrate the harvest and the foods change to apples, Brussels sprouts, cabbages, cranberries, pears, persimmons, pumpkins, and squashes.

When shopping for fruits and vegetables, make sure they are blemish-free and unbruised. Colors should be vibrant. Leaves and stems should be firm and not wilted. When possible, support your local farms.

Lastly, don't discount the convenience of frozen fruits and vegetables. They can last longer and are usually frozen at their peak of freshness.

COOKING METHODS

Here are basic definitions of the cooking methods used in this book to help you get started on your journey to preparing foods in the Mediterranean style.

BAKE. Slowly cooking in the oven at a moderate heat, covered or uncovered. This method is used for cakes, breads, and casseroles.

BLANCH. Dunking briefly in boiling water and then quickly draining. This method is used to set the color in greens and remove the skin from tomatoes or fruit.

BOIL. Heating liquid to a temperature at which it begins to change from liquid to gas, producing a rapidly bubbling hot liquid.

BROIL. Cooking rapidly for just a few minutes under a very high heat source. This method works for finishing off dishes or for producing crispy edges.

FRY. Cooking in a pan with a little more fat than when sautéing.

PARBOIL. Boiling for a short time in preparation for further cooking. This method is usually used to soften hard vegetables, such as potatoes, before cooking.

ROAST. Cooking in the oven at a high heat, uncovered. This method can be used for meats, fish, whole poultry, or vegetables.

SAUTÉ. Cooking or browning in a pan with a small amount of fat.

SIMMER. Gently cooking a liquid just below the boiling point, used for slowly cooking soups, stews, and sauces.

WATER FRY. This is my own term for cooking in a pan with a little water instead of oil. This works well with foods than are highly absorbent, like mushrooms and eggplant.

ESSENTIAL EQUIPMENT

In Mediterranean cooking, slow cooking and simmering are emphasized over frying. I recommend having some pans that can go from the stovetop to the oven, as well as baking dishes and baking sheets. This list of kitchen tools will make the cooking process a lot easier.

BAKING DISHES. Baking dishes with deep sides are good for casseroles, baked pasta dishes, or anything you want to keep from overflowing in the oven. They come in glass, ceramic, or metal.

BAKING SHEETS. These usually have a shallow rim and can be used for baking cookies and roasting sliced vegetables, chicken, or fish.

CUTTING BOARDS. It's best to have several cutting boards so that you can keep meat, fish, and vegetables separate. It helps to have several sizes for convenience.

DUTCH OVEN. This can be used on the stovetop or in the oven. I use an enameled cast iron Dutch oven for cooking stews, soups, and chicken in a pot. You can also use a stainless steel saucepan on the stovetop.

FOOD PROCESSOR. I use my food processor all the time for chopping, pureeing, or preparing food quickly. You can also use a blender in many cases.

KNIFE SET. It's essential to have a few good knives for chopping vegetables, butchering meats, and slicing breads. Different blades work better on specific food items.

POTS AND PANS. A variety of pots and pans in various sizes will serve you well. Try to get stainless steel instead of a nonstick coating (unless it has a ceramic coating). Some recipes in this book require a pan that can go from the stovetop to the oven; I use an enameled cast iron braiser.

ABOUT THE RECIPES

In this book, you'll find 202 recipes that are delicious, easy to prepare, and made with readily available ingredients. I designed this book to be practical so you can adopt a Mediterranean lifestyle while still having time for work, play, family, and fun.

These recipes take into consideration why you are choosing a Mediterranean lifestyle. They can be used to help you lose weight, promote better heart health, or generally feel in optimal physical and mental condition. You'll also find meal plans that allow you to choose one of these goals as your focus, if you like.

Each recipe is clearly laid out with the ingredients and instructions you need. I also offer cooking tips, suggestions for ingredient substitutions, and callouts for meals that can be made in advance for added convenience.

I chose these dishes from the cuisines you'll find in the countries along the Mediterranean Sea. Each area offers its own unique flavors. I hope you enjoy eating the healthiest diet on the planet, and also that you'll share the meals you make with these recipes with your family and friends. That is what life is all about.

Let's get started!

three

MEAL PLANS FOR EVERYDAY WELLNESS

Sometimes the hardest part of any new venture is knowing how to take the first step. That's why I've created three easy meal plans so you can learn how to incorporate the Mediterranean diet into your daily life.

The best part of the Mediterranean diet is that it's not about depriving yourself, but rather learning how to look at a plate of food with fresh eyes. Eating whole, healthy foods can feel delicious and satisfying—even indulgent!

Everyone approaches the Mediterranean diet from their individual viewpoint. Whether you are looking to lose weight, improve your heart health, or simply be well overall, this chapter illustrates how to get started by giving you ideas for breakfast, lunch, and dinner for two weeks. The recipes are drawn from this book and combined in ways to make each day interesting and full of flavor.

When you follow these meal plans, you will learn firsthand that the Mediterranean lifestyle will keep you satiated throughout the day and can be maintained for a lifetime. You won't be depriving yourself of good food. You won't go hungry. And you certainly won't get bored.

You can follow these meal plans as written so you won't have to wonder what to eat for the next two weeks. Or you can choose to be inspired by these meal plans and customize further, developing your own Mediterranean eating plan. Either way, you will be supported in this new lifestyle with all of the tasty recipes in this book.

Pizza Dough, p. 214

WEIGHT LOSS

In the weight loss meal plan, you'll find recipes that are low in calories but full of flavor. You will learn that you can eat a satisfying amount of food and still lose weight. There are no diet tricks in this meal plan, just good, wholesome meals full of vegetables, whole grains, and healthy sources of fats and proteins.

When you eat in moderation and control portion sizes, you will slowly begin to lose weight. These meal plans are not quick fixes. You will start to feel small results in a few days, and after two weeks of following these meal plans, you will start to see changes. But it will take longer to see dramatic results. Getting some daily exercise will help greatly.

Creating a new lifestyle takes time. Enjoy the process. You want to build a new healthy lifestyle that can be maintained for the rest of your life. Feel free to create your own meal plans by substituting any of the recipes in the book with the Weight Loss label.

Weight Loss Meal Plan Week 1

MEAL	MONDAY	TUESDAY	WEDNESDAY
BREAKFAST	White Bean Crostini *(page 213)*	Greek Yogurt Parfait *(page 41)*	Oatmeal with Seasonal Fruit *(page 40)*
LUNCH	La Dolce Vita Wrap *(page 217)*	Creamy Carrot Soup with Rosemary *(page 51)*	Sicilian Eggplant with Israeli Couscous *(page 148)*
DINNER	Baked Flounder with Parmesan and Herbs *(page 174)*	Deconstructed Chicken Cacciatore *(page 195)*	Pasta Primavera *(page 132)*

Low in Calories, High in Flavor

I like to use herbs and spices to add flavor to my meals without adding calories or too much sodium. Here are some of my favorites:

DRIED OREGANO: Adds an Italian flair.

FRESH BASIL: Adds subtle freshness to any dish.

FRESH MINT: Adds a cool certain something.

FRESH OR DRIED THYME: Adds wonderful flavor to soups and fish dishes.

GROUND CUMIN: Adds an earthy aroma.

LEMON JUICE: Adds brightness.

RED PEPPER FLAKES: Adds heat and depth.

SMOKED PAPRIKA: Adds subtle heat.

THURSDAY	FRIDAY	SATURDAY	SUNDAY
White Bean Crostini *(page 213)*	Oatmeal with Seasonal Fruit *(page 40)*	Baked Eggs with Roasted Red Peppers *(page 34)*	Greek Yogurt Parfait *(page 41)*
Zuppa di Farro *(Farro Soup)* *(page 50)*	Pesto Vegetable Bread *(page 211)*	Spring Greek Salad *(page 66)*	Ciambotta *(Neapolitan Ratatouille)* *(page 109)*
Chicken in a Pot *(page 192)*	Falafel in Pita *(page 221)*	Mediterranean Stuffed Peppers *(page 105)*	Fishcake Sliders *(page 219)*

Weight Loss Meal Plan Week 2

MEAL	MONDAY	TUESDAY	WEDNESDAY
BREAKFAST	Oatmeal with Seasonal Fruit *(page 40)*	Pesto Vegetable Bread *(page 211)*	Greek Yogurt Parfait *(page 41)*
LUNCH	Mediterranean Chopped Salad *(page 69)*	Three-Bean Salad *(page 154)*	Root Vegetable Soup *(page 54)*
DINNER	Sicilian Eggplant with Israeli Couscous *(page 148)*	Chicken Stuffed with Leeks *(page 190)*	Vegetable Rice Bake *(page 140)*

THURSDAY	FRIDAY	SATURDAY	SUNDAY
Baked Eggs with Roasted Red Peppers *(page 34)*	Oatmeal with Seasonal Fruit *(page 40)*	White Bean Crostini *(page 213)*	Greek Yogurt Parfait *(page 41)*
Shrimp Margarita *(page 178)*	Warm Lentil Salad *(page 159)*	Mushrooms Parmigiana *(page 116)*	Pasta Primavera *(page 132)*
Moroccan Lentil Soup *(page 160)*	Veggie Club Sandwich *(page 222)*	Falafel in Pita *(page 221)*	Portobello Mushroom Sandwich *(page 218)*

HEART HEALTH

Heart disease is the leading cause of death for men and women in the United States. According to the Centers for Disease Control and Prevention, high blood pressure and high cholesterol are key risk factors for heart disease.

The good news is that you can improve your heart health through the foods you eat. Eating a diet low in sodium and cholesterol has been shown to significantly lower the risk of heart disease.

In this heart-healthy meal plan, I've included Mediterranean recipes that keep cholesterol and sodium in check and are made with ingredients that help nurture your heart and cardiovascular system. The meals are mostly plant-based or use fish. Feel free to create your own meal plans by substituting any of the recipes in the book with the Heart Health label.

You should always check with your doctor when you start a new eating plan. I encourage you to talk to your doctor about heart health and how the Mediterranean diet can help.

Heart Health Meal Plan Week 1

MEAL	MONDAY	TUESDAY	WEDNESDAY
BREAKFAST	Toasted Polenta with Mushrooms *(page 94)*	Mediterranean Breakfast Wrap with Roasted Vegetables *(page 39)*	Pan Con Tomate *(Spanish–Style Toast with Tomato)* *(page 46)*
LUNCH	Tuscan Tuna Salad *(page 68)*	Chickpea and Avocado Salad *(page 164)*	Mediterranean Quinoa Salad *(page 81)*
DINNER	White Bean Alfredo Pasta *(page 136)*	Tuna Puttanesca *(page 172)*	Toasted Polenta with Mushrooms *(page 94)*

Heart-Healthy Mediterranean Swaps

To get started on a heart-healthy diet, try these simple food swaps. A few little changes can add up to big results.

- Replace butter with extra-virgin olive oil.
- Instead of red meat, try beans, fish, or portobello mushrooms.
- Instead of white bread, try whole-grain bread.
- Replace French fries with a side salad.
- Replace deli meats with tuna salad.
- Instead of chips, try crudités (cut-up fresh vegetables).
- Instead of chicken or veal Parmesan, try eggplant Parmesan.
- Replace cow's milk with plant-based milk.

THURSDAY	FRIDAY	SATURDAY	SUNDAY
Avocado Toast (page 42)	Pasteli (Greek Sesame Bars) (page 35)	Moroccan Potatoes with Chickpeas (page 38)	Shakshuka (page 45)
Shrimp Salad (page 71)	Arugula and White Bean Salad (page 74)	Classic Niçoise Salad (page 77)	Eggplant Towers (page 112)
Greek Veggie Burgers (page 223)	Mediterranean Snapper with Olives and Feta (page 170)	Moroccan Cod (page 173)	Fish en Papillote (page 175)

Heart Health Meal Plan Week 2

MEAL	MONDAY	TUESDAY	WEDNESDAY
BREAKFAST	Mediterranean Breakfast Wrap with Roasted Vegetables *(page 39)*	Pan con Tomate *(Spanish-Style Toast with Tomato)* *(page 46)*	Toasted Polenta with Mushrooms *(page 94)*
LUNCH	Greek Veggie Burgers *(page 223)*	White Bean Alfredo Pasta *(page 136)*	Classic Tomato Soup *(page 57)*
DINNER	Spanish Salmon with Smoked Paprika *(page 171)*	Moroccan Cod *(page 173)*	Deconstructed Chicken Cacciatore *(page 195)*

THURSDAY	FRIDAY	SATURDAY	SUNDAY
Moroccan Potatoes with Chickpeas *(page 38)*	Avocado Toast *(page 42)*	Shakshuka *(page 45)*	Tunisian Brik Pastries *(page 96)*
Vegetarian Chili *(page 161)*	Chickpea and Avocado Salad *(page 164)*	Cool Cucumber, Avocado, and Radish Soup *(page 56)*	Polenta with Wild Greens *(page 145)*
White Bean Alfredo Pasta *(page 136)*	Mushroom Barley Soup *(page 61)*	Mushroom Barley Soup *(page 61)*	Whole Branzino with Garlic and Herbs *(page 169)*

OVERALL WELLNESS

If your goal isn't to lose weight, but to maintain a healthy lifestyle and feel good for the long term, this meal plan is for you.

The overall wellness meal plan is less restrictive. It focuses less on counting calories and more on offering balanced meals that are flavorful and nutritious. The recipes provide delicious meals inspired by the Mediterranean region. They include lots of fresh vegetables, whole grains, healthy fats, beans, and legumes, and allow for a small amount of meat occasionally. Consider this your maintenance plan.

Following a Mediterranean diet helps you stay active in body and mind into your later years. This is an eating plan that can last you a lifetime—a very long lifetime! Feel free to create your own meal plans by substituting any of the recipes in the book, including those with the Overall Wellness label. If you want to feel good, have energy, and keep a positive outlook, follow these recipes to learn how to eat for overall wellness.

Overall Wellness Meal Plan Week 1

MEAL	MONDAY	TUESDAY	WEDNESDAY
BREAKFAST	Baked Eggs with Polenta and Fontina Cheese (page 36)	Morning Couscous with Raisins, Nuts, and Honey (page 47)	Southern Italian Pepper and Egg Sandwich (page 37)
LUNCH	Lemon Linguine (page 133)	Tortellini in Brodo (Tortellini in Broth with Shrimp) (page 63)	Avgolemono (Greek Chicken and Rice Soup) (page 52)
DINNER	Lamb and Vegetable Stew (page 202)	Seafood Risotto (page 139)	Herbed Salmon with Mashed Potatoes (page 168)

Small Mediterranean Treats

The best part about eating Mediterranean style is that you will want to eat this way all the time, including when you are indulging in snacks. Snacks can be scrumptious and healthy at the same time.

- Fruit is always a good choice. It provides vitamins and energy in a sweet (and often small) package.
- Spice up a handful of mixed nuts with a bit of cayenne and smoked paprika to wake up the flavor.
- Toss some olives in olive oil and fresh herbs. This is also great to serve and share with friends.
- Add a spoonful of chopped hot peppers to a bowl of hummus and dig in with some flatbread or a few cucumber slices.
- Add a pinch of cinnamon to your coffee grounds when brewing for a hint of exotic flavor.
- Enjoy a glass of red wine while watching the sunset in the evening.
- Serve figs with cheese for a nice complementary dessert.
- Try dates dipped in your favorite nut butter for a low-calorie "candy."

THURSDAY	FRIDAY	SATURDAY	SUNDAY
Baked Eggs with Polenta and Fontina Cheese *(page 36)*	Polenta Bowl with Fruit and Honey *(page 43)*	Southern Italian Pepper and Egg Sandwich *(page 37)*	Morning Couscous with Raisins, Nuts, and Honey *(page 47)*
Green Bean and Potato Salad *(page 70)*	Pasta e Fagioli *(Pasta and Bean Soup) (page 59)*	Collard Green Wraps *(page 113)*	Warm Potato Salad *(page 72)*
Roasted Tomato Sauce with Pasta *(page 131)*	Greek Sheet Pan Chicken *(page 187)* and Lemon Linguine *(page 133)*	Shrimp Scampi *(page 177)*	Baked Chicken Paella *(page 141)*

Overall Wellness Meal Plan Week 2

MEAL	MONDAY	TUESDAY	WEDNESDAY
BREAKFAST	Southern Italian Pepper and Egg Sandwich *(page 37)*	Morning Couscous with Raisins, Nuts, and Honey *(page 47)*	Baked Eggs with Polenta and Fontina Cheese *(page 36)*
LUNCH	Shrimp and Polenta *(page 146)*	Panzanella *(page 67)*	Algerian Vegetable Couscous *(page 149)*
DINNER	Lamb Loin Chops with Spaghetti in Tomato Sauce *(page 201)*	Flank Steak with Italian Salsa Verde *(page 197)*	Fusilli Arrabbiata *(page 134)*

THURSDAY	FRIDAY	SATURDAY	SUNDAY
Polenta Bowl with Fruit and Honey *(page 43)*	Southern Italian Pepper and Egg Sandwich *(page 37)*	Moroccan Potatoes with Chickpeas *(page 38)*	Morning Couscous with Raisins, Nuts, and Honey *(page 47)*
Bruschetta Pizza *(page 215)*	Baked Fish Fingers *(page 176)*	Spaghetti with Garlic, Olive Oil, Red Pepper *(page 130)*	Lime Chicken and Shrimp *(page 194)*
Baked Rice with Swordfish and Mussels *(page 143)*	Barley Risotto with Vegetables *(page 147)*	Lime Chicken and Shrimp *(page 194)*	Farro with Porcini Mushrooms *(page 144)*

four

BREAKFAST

Baked Eggs with Roasted Red Peppers 34

Pasteli (Greek Sesame Bars) 35

Baked Eggs with Polenta and Fontina Cheese 36

Southern Italian Pepper and Egg Sandwich 37

Moroccan Potatoes with Chickpeas 38

Mediterranean Breakfast Wrap with Roasted Vegetables 39

Oatmeal with Seasonal Fruit 40

Greek Yogurt Parfait 41

Avocado Toast 42

Polenta Bowl with Fruit and Honey 43

Shakshuka 45

Pan con Tomate (Spanish-Style Toast with Tomato) 46

Morning Couscous with Raisins, Nuts, and Honey 47

Greek Yogurt Parfait, p. 41

BAKED EGGS WITH ROASTED RED PEPPERS

Serves 4 / Prep time: 10 minutes / Cook time: 15 minutes

Baking eggs in a muffin tin makes them look neat and pretty. Try these eggs when you're feeling like something fancy. Each person gets two cups, but you are eating only one egg total.

WEIGHT LOSS

4 Italian bread slices

¼ cup chopped roasted red peppers

½ cup shredded Fontina cheese

4 large eggs

2 tablespoons whole milk

Freshly ground black pepper

1. Preheat the oven to 350°F.

2. Using a cookie cutter or knife, cut 2 rounds from each bread slice to fit into the bottom of 8 cups of a standard muffin tin. Place the bread pieces in the muffin tin cups.

3. Scatter a few roasted red pepper pieces on top of each bread piece and sprinkle 1 tablespoon of cheese on each.

4. In a bowl, whisk together the eggs and milk.

5. Pour the egg mixture into the cups, until about three-quarters of the way full. The eggs will expand, so you want to leave a little room. Grind some black pepper on top.

6. Bake for 12 to 15 minutes, until a toothpick inserted in the center comes out clean.

INGREDIENT TIP: You can substitute any type of milk you prefer in this recipe, such as low-fat milk or almond milk.

COOKING TIP: A silicone muffin tin makes it easier to pop each egg cup out.

PER SERVING (2 EGG ROUNDS):
CALORIES: 198; Total Fat: 11g; Saturated Fat: 5g; Protein: 13g; Total Carbohydrates: 12g; Fiber: 1g; Sugar: 1g; Cholesterol: 206mg

PASTELI (GREEK SESAME BARS)

Serves 20 / Prep time: 15 minutes / Cook time: 10 minutes

The recipe for these sesame-honey bars dates back to ancient Greece. Sesame seeds are a good source of healthy fat, protein, and iron. Raw honey contains polyphenols, which can lower inflammation and reduce the risk of heart disease and certain cancers.

HEART HEALTH

Extra-virgin olive oil, for brushing

1 cup sesame seeds

½ cup raw honey

1 teaspoon freshly squeezed lemon juice

1 tablespoon pumpkin seeds (optional)

1 tablespoon sunflower seeds (optional)

1. Line a rimmed baking sheet with parchment paper, brush with olive oil, and set aside.

2. In a dry skillet, toast the sesame seeds over low heat for about 3 minutes, until lightly golden. Be careful not to overcook them. Remove from the heat.

3. In a small saucepan, combine the honey and lemon juice. Bring to a boil and simmer for 5 minutes, stirring constantly.

4. Stir in the sesame seeds and the pumpkin and/or sunflower seeds (if using). Continue to cook for another 2 to 3 minutes, until well mixed and heated through.

5. Spread the mixture onto the prepared baking sheet. Use a spoon or spatula brushed with olive oil to flatten the mixture.

6. Refrigerate the baking sheet for 30 minutes. Remove and cut into 20 bars. The bars will be pliable and slightly sticky, not hard. Wrap the bars in parchment paper and store in the refrigerator.

VARIATION TIP: I like pumpkin and sunflower seeds in these, but you can leave them out, or try adding chopped nuts instead.

COOKING TIP: To cut into bars, use a sharp knife or a pizza cutter.

PER SERVING (1 BAR):
CALORIES: 75; Total Fat: 5g; Saturated Fat: 1g; Protein: 2g; Total Carbohydrates: 8g; Fiber: 1g; Sugar: 7g; Cholesterol: 0mg

BAKED EGGS WITH POLENTA AND FONTINA CHEESE

Serves 4 / Prep time: 10 minutes / Cook time: 25 minutes

This creamy dish gets its fresh Mediterranean flavor from tomatoes and arugula. Polenta is low-carb, gluten-free, and cholesterol-free; eggs are a good source of protein; and arugula provides vitamin C and beta-carotene.

OVERALL WELLNESS

Extra-virgin olive oil,
for brushing

¾ cup instant polenta

1 cup baby arugula

4 tablespoons grated Fontina cheese, divided

Salt

Freshly ground black pepper

4 large eggs

1 tomato, chopped

Dried oregano, for serving

1. Preheat the oven to 400°F. Brush a small baking dish with olive oil.

2. In a saucepan, prepare the polenta according to package directions. It should take about 5 minutes.

3. Add the arugula, 2 tablespoons of grated cheese, and a pinch of salt and pepper to the cooked polenta. Stir until combined.

4. Pour the polenta mixture into the prepared baking dish. Using a spoon, make 4 wells in the polenta. Crack an egg into each well.

5. Place the baking dish on a rimmed baking sheet to catch drips. Bake for about 20 minutes, until the whites of the eggs are set, leaving the yolks a little runny.

6. Top the dish with the remaining 2 tablespoons of cheese. Let rest for 1 minute while the cheese melts.

7. Serve a portion of polenta and 1 egg per person. Top each serving with chopped tomato, a pinch of oregano, and more salt and pepper, if desired.

INGREDIENT TIP: Fontina cheese is a mild but flavorful cheese that melts easily. You can substitute cheddar if you prefer.

PER SERVING:

CALORIES: 157; Total Fat: 8g; Saturated Fat: 3g; Protein: 9g; Total Carbohydrates: 11g; Fiber: 1g; Sugar: 1g; Cholesterol: 194mg

SOUTHERN ITALIAN PEPPER AND EGG SANDWICH

Serves 2 / Prep time: 5 minutes, plus time to cool / Cook time: 25 minutes

Sweet peppers and eggs are a classic combination found in southern Italian cooking. This simple and healthy breakfast sandwich whips up in a matter of minutes.

OVERALL WELLNESS

¼ cup extra-virgin olive oil

2 large Italian sweet peppers, seeded and cut into chunks

4 large eggs

Salt

2 kaiser rolls or other sandwich rolls, lightly toasted

1. In a large skillet, heat the olive oil over low heat. Add the peppers and sprinkle with salt. Cook, stirring occasionally, for 15 to 20 minutes, until the peppers are completely soft. Allow to cool, then transfer the peppers and olive oil to a glass jar, cover, and refrigerate for up to 4 days.

2. When ready to serve, in a skillet, heat ½ cup of the prepared peppers (drained of all but about 1 tablespoon of oil) and cook for 2 minutes to reheat.

3. In a small bowl, whisk the eggs and a pinch of salt. Pour over the peppers. Cook for 3 to 5 minutes, until the eggs are set.

4. Divide the egg and pepper mixture between the rolls.

MAKE-AHEAD TIP: The sweet peppers are best when prepared in advance, as their flavor improves over time.

PER SERVING:

CALORIES: 616; Total Fat: 45g; Saturated Fat: 3g; Protein: 19g; Total Carbohydrates: 33g; Fiber: 5g; Sugar: 11g; Cholesterol: 372mg

MOROCCAN POTATOES WITH CHICKPEAS

Serves 4 / Prep time: 10 minutes / Cook time: 30 minutes

This dish makes a hearty breakfast on its own, or it can substitute for traditional home fries or hash browns alongside poached eggs. The Moroccan spices add a warm, earthy quality to the potatoes.

HEART HEALTH

2 large russet potatoes, peeled and cut into 1-inch cubes

2 cups chopped leafy greens, such as spinach, Swiss chard, or kale

1 onion, diced

1 tablespoon minced fresh ginger

1 teaspoon ground coriander

1 teaspoon ground cumin

½ teaspoon ground turmeric

½ teaspoon salt

¼ teaspoon paprika

¼ cup extra-virgin olive oil

1 (15-ounce) can chickpeas, rinsed and drained

1. Put the potatoes in a saucepan, cover with water, and bring to a boil over medium-high heat. Cook for about 10 minutes, until the potatoes begin to soften. Drain and rinse under cold running water.

2. Transfer the potatoes to a large bowl and add the greens, onion, ginger, coriander, cumin, turmeric, salt, and paprika. Toss to combine.

3. In a large skillet, heat the olive oil over medium heat. Add the potato mixture and cook, stirring occasionally, for about 10 minutes, until the potatoes start to brown.

4. Add the chickpeas. Stir everything together and cook for another 10 minutes, until everything is warmed through and the potatoes are crispy around the edges. Serve warm.

PER SERVING:

CALORIES: 363; Total Fat: 15g; Saturated Fat: 2g; Protein: 9g; Total Carbohydrates: 50g; Fiber: 7g; Sugar: 4g; Cholesterol: 0mg

MEDITERRANEAN BREAKFAST WRAP WITH ROASTED VEGETABLES

Serves 4 / Prep time: 10 minutes / Cook time: 25 minutes

Roasted vegetables provide a healthy dose of protein and vitamins to get your day started off right. I like to use a combination of eggplant, red bell peppers, onions, and carrots, but you can use your choice of vegetables.

HEART HEALTH

1 cup chopped vegetables (such as eggplant, bell peppers, onions, and carrots)

1 tablespoon extra-virgin olive oil

4 large eggs

2 cups chopped spinach

Pinch salt

Pinch freshly ground black pepper

Nonstick cooking spray

4 wraps or tortillas

4 tablespoons Classic Hummus (page 153) or store-bought hummus

2 tablespoons crumbled feta cheese

1. Preheat the oven to 400°F.

2. On a lined baking sheet, toss the chopped vegetables with the olive oil. Roast for about 20 minutes, until softened.

3. In a medium bowl, whisk together the eggs, spinach, salt, and pepper.

4. Coat a skillet with cooking spray and heat over low heat. Add the egg mixture and cook for 3 to 4 minutes, stirring occasionally, until set.

5. Lay out the wraps on a clean work surface and spread 1 tablespoon of hummus down the center of each.

6. Add one-quarter of the egg mixture to each wrap and one-quarter of the roasted vegetables on top. Sprinkle with the feta.

7. Fold the sides of the wrap in, then roll it up.

MAKE-AHEAD TIP: To save time in the morning, roast the vegetables up to 3 days before you plan to use them. Let them cool, then store in an airtight container in the refrigerator. You can reheat the vegetables before assembling your wraps, but I usually just add them cold.

PER SERVING:

CALORIES: 286; Total Fat: 13g; Saturated Fat: 4g; Protein: 12g; Total Carbohydrates: 29g; Fiber: 3g; Sugar: 3g; Cholesterol: 190mg

OATMEAL WITH SEASONAL FRUIT

Serves 4 / Prep time: 5 minutes / Cook time: 30 minutes

Oatmeal is a gluten-free whole grain that is both tasty and filling. Eating oats can assist with weight loss, help lower blood sugar levels, and help reduce the risk of heart disease. Steel-cut oats are the best choice for oats because they have a lower glycemic index than rolled or instant oats.

WEIGHT LOSS

3 to 4 cups water

1 cup steel-cut oats

½ cup chopped seasonal fruit

¼ cup chopped nuts

2 tablespoons raw honey

1. In a saucepan, bring the water to a boil over medium-high heat, using 3 cups if you prefer thicker oatmeal or 4 cups for thinner oatmeal.

2. Add the oats to the pan. Return to a boil, then reduce the heat and simmer for 20 to 30 minutes, until soft.

3. Top with the fruit and nuts, then drizzle with honey.

VARIATION TIP: To make this vegan, substitute maple syrup for the raw honey. For additional flavor variations, stir in a spoonful of your favorite nut butter, or add raisins and ground cinnamon with a sprinkle of dried coconut.

PER SERVING:

CALORIES: 230; Total Fat: 6g; Saturated Fat: 1g; Protein: 8g; Total Carbohydrates: 37g; Fiber: 5g; Sugar: 10g; Cholesterol: 0mg

GREEK YOGURT PARFAIT

Serves 4 / Prep time: 10 minutes

A classic Greek yogurt parfait is a decadent yet balanced breakfast that is super easy to make. Greek yogurt is a great source of protein, calcium, and probiotics, which support good digestive health. It's thicker and creamier than regular yogurt.

WEIGHT LOSS

2 cups low-fat plain Greek yogurt

1 cup chopped berries

1 cup granola

¼ cup chopped almonds

¼ cup raw honey

Spoon ¼ cup yogurt into each of 4 wineglasses or mason jars. Arrange a layer of berries on top, then add another ¼ cup yogurt. Top with the remaining berries, the granola, and almonds. Drizzle with the honey.

VARIATION TIP: To make vanilla yogurt, stir 1 teaspoon vanilla extract into 2 cups yogurt.

MAKE-AHEAD TIP: You can prepare these parfaits up to 2 days in advance without the granola. Cover and refrigerate, then add the granola just before serving.

PER SERVING:

CALORIES: 259; Total Fat: 6g; Saturated Fat: 2g; Protein: 11g; Total Carbohydrates: 43g; Fiber: 4g; Sugar: 33g; Cholesterol: 7mg

AVOCADO TOAST

Serves 2 / Prep time: 5 minutes

Avocado is not only colorful and creamy, it's also packed with vitamins and healthy fat that is satisfying and filling. You can customize this basic avocado toast recipe with your favorite toppings.

HEART HEALTH

1 avocado, pitted, peeled, and chopped

2 teaspoons extra-virgin olive oil

Pinch salt

Pinch freshly ground black pepper

Pinch red pepper flakes (optional)

2 bread slices, toasted

In a small bowl, mash the avocado with the olive oil, salt, black pepper, and red pepper flakes (if using) and mix well. Spread onto the toast. Serve immediately.

INGREDIENT TIP: Good bread choices for avocado toast include rye, seeded multigrain, and sourdough.

VARIATION TIP: Have fun with topping the avocado toast any way you like—try smoked salmon and a poached egg, chopped tomatoes and radish slices, or canned or cooked black beans and chopped fresh cilantro.

PER SERVING:

CALORIES: 267; Total Fat: 20g; Saturated Fat: 4g; Protein: 5g; Total Carbohydrates: 22g; Fiber: 9g; Sugar: 4g; Cholesterol: 0mg

POLENTA BOWL WITH FRUIT AND HONEY

Serves 3 / Prep time: 5 minutes / Cook time: 5 minutes

This recipe uses instant polenta so you can get a hot breakfast on the table in just a few minutes. Polenta is gluten-free and similar to American grits but with a coarser texture. It can be made savory or sweet, as with this classic combination of bananas and honey.

OVERALL WELLNESS

1 cup instant polenta

1 banana, sliced

1 tablespoon raw honey

1. In a saucepan, cook the instant polenta according to package directions. It should take about 5 minutes.

2. Spoon into bowls, top with slices of banana, and drizzle with honey.

VARIATION TIP: For a savory version, add salt, pepper, and pecorino Romano cheese to taste.

PER SERVING:

CALORIES: 131; Total Fat: 0g; Saturated Fat: 0g; Protein: 2g; Total Carbohydrates: 31g; Fiber: 2g; Sugar: 11g; Cholesterol: 0mg

SHAKSHUKA

Serves 6 / Prep time: 10 minutes / Cook time: 30 minutes

Shakshuka originated in Tunisia but has become a popular breakfast dish across the Mediterranean region. Eggs are poached in a chunky, spicy tomato sauce, along with sweet peppers, onions, and garlic, for a savory dish you won't soon forget. Serve with crusty bread.

HEART HEALTH

¼ cup extra-virgin olive oil

1 onion, chopped

1 green bell pepper, seeded and chopped

1 garlic clove, minced

1 teaspoon smoked paprika

½ teaspoon ground cumin

¼ teaspoon red pepper flakes

Pinch salt

Pinch freshly ground black pepper

1 (28-ounce) can whole peeled tomatoes, undrained

6 large eggs

¼ cup chopped fresh flat-leaf parsley

1. In a large skillet, heat the olive oil over medium heat. Cook the onion, bell pepper, garlic, paprika, cumin, red pepper flakes, salt, and black pepper for about 10 minutes, stirring often, until the vegetables soften.

2. Add the tomatoes and their juices and break apart with a potato masher or spoon. Cook the mixture for 10 minutes.

3. Using a spoon, make 6 wells in the mixture. Crack an egg into each well.

4. Cover the pan, reduce the heat to low, and simmer for 8 to 10 minutes, until the eggs whites set and the yolks are still runny.

5. Garnish with chopped parsley.

VARIATION TIP: To make it even spicier, sprinkle red pepper flakes on top just before serving. You can also serve this with a dollop of plain yogurt on top.

PER SERVING:

CALORIES: 187; Total Fat: 14g; Saturated Fat: 3g; Protein: 8g; Total Carbohydrates: 8g; Fiber: 3g; Sugar: 5g; Cholesterol: 186mg

PAN CON TOMATE (SPANISH-STYLE TOAST WITH TOMATO)

Serves 4 / Prep time: 5 minutes / Cook time: 1 minute

This quick and easy breakfast recipe is traditionally made by rubbing garlic on bread and grating a tomato on a box grater to obtain its pulp. Here, you simply combine the ingredients in a food processor for a quick and easy meal.

HEART HEALTH

2 teaspoons extra-virgin olive oil, divided

1 baguette, cut crosswise into 6-inch lengths, then sliced open

2 tomatoes

2 garlic cloves, peeled

Pinch sea salt

1. Preheat the broiler on high.

2. Brush 1 teaspoon of olive oil onto the cut sides of the baguette pieces. Toast under the broiler for 1 minute.

3. In a food processor, combine the tomatoes and garlic and process to a pulp. Transfer the tomato mixture to a bowl and add the salt.

4. Spoon the tomato mixture onto the bread slices. Drizzle with the remaining 1 teaspoon of olive oil.

VARIATION TIP: Instead of the tomatoes, you can use left-over homemade salsa for a festive alternative.

PER SERVING:

CALORIES: 265; Total Fat: 4g; Saturated Fat: 1g; Protein: 10g; Total Carbohydrates: 47g; Fiber: 3g; Sugar: 6g; Cholesterol: 0mg

MORNING COUSCOUS WITH RAISINS, NUTS, AND HONEY

Serves 4 / Prep time: 5 minutes, plus 15 minutes to rest / Cook time: 5 minutes

Couscous is Northern Africa's version of pasta. These tiny balls of semolina have a unique texture. They can be used as a breakfast cereal or an accompaniment to an entrée. Here, the couscous is deliciously spiced with cinnamon and sweetened with raisins and honey.

OVERALL WELLNESS

3 cups whole milk

¼ teaspoon ground cinnamon

1 cup couscous

½ cup raisins

2 tablespoons raw honey, plus more (optional) for drizzling

¼ teaspoon salt

¼ cup chopped almonds

1. In a saucepan, combine the milk and cinnamon and heat over medium-low heat until it just begins to simmer. Do not allow it to boil. Turn off the heat.

2. Stir in the couscous, raisins, honey, and salt. Stir to combine. Cover and let stand for 15 minutes. The couscous will absorb the liquid and soften.

3. Spoon the couscous into bowls. Top with the chopped almonds. Drizzle with more honey, if desired.

PER SERVING:

CALORIES: 346; Total Fat: 10g; Saturated Fat: 4g; Protein: 13g; Total Carbohydrates: 52g; Fiber: 3g; Sugar: 18g; Cholesterol: 18mg

five

SOUPS

Zuppa di Farro (Farro Soup) 50

Creamy Carrot Soup with Rosemary 51

Avgolemono (Greek Chicken and Rice Soup) 52

White Bean Soup 53

Root Vegetable Soup 54

Cauliflower Soup with Onion and Thyme 55

Cool Cucumber, Avocado, and Radish Soup 56

Classic Tomato Soup 57

Risi e Bisi (Italian Rice and Peas) 58

Pasta e Fagioli (Pasta and Bean Soup) 59

Roasted Butternut Squash Soup 60

Mushroom Barley Soup 61

Tortellini in Brodo (Tortellini in Broth with Shrimp) 63

Roasted Butternut Squash Soup, p. 60

ZUPPA DI FARRO (FARRO SOUP)

Serves 4 / Prep time: 10 minutes / Cook time: 1 hour

Farro, considered the ancestor of all wheat species, was a part of everyday life in ancient Rome. Farro is a good source of iron, magnesium, protein, and dietary fiber, and it is easy to digest. Serve this soup with grated Parmesan cheese and a drizzle of extra-virgin olive oil.

WEIGHT LOSS

2 tablespoons extra-virgin olive oil

1 small onion, finely chopped

1 small carrot, finely chopped

1 celery stalk, finely chopped

1 garlic clove, minced

4 thin pancetta slices

4 to 5 canned whole peeled tomatoes

1 (15-ounce) can cannellini or borlotti beans, undrained

3 cups vegetable broth, divided

1 tablespoon dried thyme

½ teaspoon salt

¼ teaspoon freshly ground black pepper

1 cup farro (semi-pearled or pearled, not whole-grain)

1. In a wide soup pot or saucepan, heat the olive oil over medium heat. Add the onion, carrot, and celery and gently cook for about 5 minutes, until soft and translucent.

2. Add the garlic and cook for 1 minute, until fragrant.

3. Add the pancetta and continue cooking for 5 minutes, until the fat has melted.

4. Stir in the tomatoes, beans with their juices, 2 cups of vegetable broth, the thyme, salt, and pepper. Bring the mixture to a boil, then reduce the heat and simmer for 10 minutes. Remove from the heat.

5. Carefully transfer the mixture to a food processor or blender, in batches if necessary, and blend until smooth. (If using a blender, remove the center cap from the lid to allow steam to escape and hold a kitchen towel over the hole.)

6. Return the mixture to the pot. Add the farro and remaining 1 cup of broth and cook over low heat for 30 to 40 minutes, until the farro is al dente, stirring occasionally to make sure the soup is not sticking to the bottom of the pan.

COOKING TIP: Farro has a naturally chewy consistency. This soup should come out fairly thick, but you can add more broth or water to achieve your desired consistency.

PER SERVING:

CALORIES: 379; Total Fat: 10g; Saturated Fat: 2g; Protein: 18g; Total Carbohydrates: 60g; Fiber: 12g; Sugar: 6g; Cholesterol: 15mg

CREAMY CARROT SOUP WITH ROSEMARY

Serves 4 / Prep time: 10 minutes / Cook time: 20 minutes

The basis of a Mediterranean diet is fresh food, and this soup recipe is both easy and quick to make with ingredients you likely already have in your kitchen. The potato acts as a thickener so you don't have to use milk or cream, significantly reducing the calories in this soup.

WEIGHT LOSS

1 pound carrots, cut into 1-inch pieces

1 small onion, cut into 1-inch pieces

½ russet potato, cut into 1-inch pieces

2 to 3 rosemary sprigs

½ teaspoon salt

Freshly ground black pepper

1. In a soup pot, combine the carrots, onion, potato, rosemary sprigs, and salt and cover with water. Bring to a boil over medium-high heat and cook for about 10 minutes, until the vegetables are soft.

2. Remove the rosemary and discard. Using a slotted spoon, transfer the vegetables to a food processor or blender, leaving the liquids in the pot.

3. Puree the vegetables until smooth and return them to the pot.

4. Bring back to a simmer and stir until the vegetables and liquids heat through and combine into a soup. If it's too thick, you can add a little more water to get your desired consistency. Season with the salt and pepper to taste.

COOKING TIP: You can further flavor this soup by adding minced fresh ginger and/or whatever other herbs you like, such as thyme or marjoram.

PER SERVING:

CALORIES: 90; Total Fat: 0g; Saturated Fat: 0g; Protein: 2g; Total Carbohydrates: 21g; Fiber: 4g; Sugar: 6g; Cholesterol: 0mg

AVGOLEMONO (GREEK CHICKEN AND RICE SOUP)

Serves 4 / Prep time: 5 minutes / Cook time: 5 minutes

Each culture has its own version of chicken soup, and for good reason: Chicken soup can help reduce symptoms of cold and flu and even diminish the blues. This comforting Greek version includes lemon and rice.

OVERALL WELLNESS

6 cups chicken broth

8 ounces boneless, skinless chicken breast, cooked and shredded

1 cup cooked rice

½ teaspoon salt

¼ teaspoon freshly ground black pepper

2 large eggs

¼ cup freshly squeezed lemon juice

1. In a large soup pot, bring the chicken broth to a boil over medium-high heat. Add the shredded chicken, rice, salt, and pepper. Reduce the heat to a simmer.

2. In a medium bowl, whisk together eggs and lemon juice. Scoop out a ladleful of hot broth and slowly stream it into the eggs, whisking constantly.

3. Slowly pour the egg mixture back into the pot, still whisking constantly. It's important to keep whisking so you don't end up with scrambled eggs. Serve hot.

COOKING TIP: After you've added the eggs, don't let the soup boil again. Serve immediately.

PER SERVING:

CALORIES: 211; Total Fat: 5g; Saturated Fat: 1g; Protein: 22g; Total Carbohydrates: 19g; Fiber: 0g; Sugar: 3g; Cholesterol: 141mg

WHITE BEAN SOUP

Serves 4 / Prep time: 5 minutes / Cook time: 20 minutes

Cannellini beans have a mild but earthy flavor, which is complemented by fresh rosemary and thyme. Once pureed, they lend creaminess to this soup.

WEIGHT LOSS

For the rosemary croutons

4 stale Italian bread slices, cut into cubes

3 tablespoons extra-virgin olive oil

½ teaspoon minced fresh rosemary

For the soup

3 (19-ounce) cans cannellini beans, rinsed and drained, divided

4 garlic cloves, peeled

1 (1-inch) piece fresh red chile, seeded

2 tablespoons extra-virgin olive oil

4 cups chicken broth

½ teaspoon finely chopped fresh rosemary

½ teaspoon fresh thyme leaves

½ teaspoon salt

¼ teaspoon freshly ground black pepper

¼ teaspoon red pepper flakes

To make the rosemary croutons

1. Preheat the oven to 400°F. Line a rimmed baking sheet with parchment paper.

2. In a large bowl, toss the bread cubes with the olive oil and rosemary. Spread out on the prepared sheet.

3. Bake for about 10 minutes, until crisp. Transfer the croutons to a plate lined with paper towels.

To make the soup

4. Meanwhile, in a food processor, puree 1 can of beans with the garlic and chile until smooth.

5. In a soup pot, heat the olive oil over medium heat. Add the bean puree and cook for 1 minute, until fragrant.

6. Add the broth, the remaining 2 cans of beans, the rosemary, thyme, salt, black pepper, and red pepper flakes. Stir carefully so as not to break up the beans.

7. Bring to a boil. Reduce the heat to a simmer and cook for 15 minutes, stirring occasionally.

8. Top each serving with rosemary croutons.

INGREDIENT TIP: It's fun to play with garnishes on this basic soup. You can crumble on some feta cheese, sprinkle on fresh herbs, or add a swirl of pesto or Italian Salsa Verde (page 246).

VARIATION TIP: Use vegetable broth to make this soup vegetarian.

PER SERVING:

CALORIES: 434; Total Fat: 18g; Saturated Fat: 3g; Protein: 18g; Total Carbohydrates: 51g; Fiber: 13g; Sugar: 1g; Cholesterol: 0mg

ROOT VEGETABLE SOUP

Serves 4 / Prep time: 10 minutes / Cook time: 20 minutes

Winter is the perfect time to serve this filling yet low-calorie, heart-healthy soup. The flavor of the carrots takes center stage, but their sweetness is balanced by the other root vegetables, including a potato to thicken the soup.

WEIGHT LOSS

1 parsnip, peeled and chopped

1 turnip, peeled and chopped

1 medium onion, chopped

2 or 3 carrots, chopped

2 celery stalks, chopped

1 small potato or ½ russet potato, peeled

1 small piece of leek, chopped

2 or 3 thyme sprigs

Salt

Freshly ground black pepper

Chopped fresh flat-leaf parsley, for garnish

1. In a soup pot, combine the parsnip, turnip, onion, carrots, celery, potato, and leek and cover with water. Bring to a boil over medium-high heat and cook for about 10 minutes, until the vegetables are soft.

2. Using a slotted spoon, transfer the softened vegetables to a food processor or blender, reserve the cooking liquid in the pot. Process until smooth, then return to the pot.

3. Add the thyme sprigs and season with salt and pepper. Bring the mixture back to a boil, then reduce the heat and simmer for 10 minutes.

4. Remove the thyme and discard. Top each bowl of soup with a sprinkle of minced parsley.

INGREDIENT TIP: You can often find soup starter "kits" in the produce section of the supermarket. These kits usually contain a parsnip, a turnip, an onion, a few carrots, a piece of leek, and some herbs. Just add a potato for the thickener and you're all set.

PER SERVING:

CALORIES: 145; Total Fat: 0g; Saturated Fat: 0g; Protein: 4g; Total Carbohydrates: 34g; Fiber: 5g; Sugar: 6g; Cholesterol: 0mg

CAULIFLOWER SOUP WITH ONION AND THYME

Serves 4 / Prep time: 10 minutes / Cook time: 25 minutes

Versatile cauliflower is high in B vitamins, antioxidants, phytonutrients, and fiber, which assists in weight loss. Serve this soup for a hearty lunch or alongside a salad and some crusty bread for a healthy dinner.

WEIGHT LOSS

2 tablespoons extra-virgin olive oil

1 onion, minced

2 tablespoons dry white wine

1 head cauliflower, cut into florets

3 cups vegetable broth

1 cup water

1 teaspoon salt

¼ teaspoon freshly ground black pepper

2 or 3 thyme sprigs

1. In a soup pot, heat the olive oil over medium heat. Add the onion and sauté until golden, about 6 minutes.

2. Add the white wine and cook for 1 to 2 minutes, until the alcohol burns off. Add the cauliflower and stir to coat.

3. Add the vegetable broth, water, salt, and pepper. Bring to a boil, then reduce the heat to a simmer. Add the thyme sprigs, cover, and cook for 10 to 15 minutes, until the cauliflower is soft. Remove the thyme and discard.

4. Using a slotted spoon, transfer the cauliflower to a food processor or blender, in batches as necessary, reserving the broth in the pot. Puree the cauliflower and transfer to a clean pot.

5. Add 2 to 3 ladles of the reserved broth, stir well, and bring the soup to a simmer. Add more broth to get your desired consistency.

COOKING TIP: You can garnish this soup with a teaspoon of Italian Salsa Verde (page 246) or Red Pesto (page 257).

PER SERVING:

CALORIES: 96; Total Fat: 7g; Saturated Fat: 1g; Protein: 2g; Total Carbohydrates: 8g; Fiber: 2g; Sugar: 4g; Cholesterol: 0mg

COOL CUCUMBER, AVOCADO, AND RADISH SOUP

Serves 4 / Prep time: 10 minutes

This nutrient-packed soup is a great way to consume several portions of fruits and vegetables in one meal. The radish and red pepper flakes add a little spice, while the cucumber and avocado impart a pleasant mellowness.

HEART HEALTH

2 cucumbers, roughly chopped

1 avocado, pitted, peeled, and roughly chopped

3 to 5 radishes, roughly chopped

1 shallot, roughly chopped

½ cup water

¼ cup extra-virgin olive oil

1 tablespoon white wine vinegar

¼ teaspoon salt

Pinch freshly ground black pepper

Pinch red pepper flakes

Chopped fresh herbs, for garnish

1. In a food processor or blender, combine the cucumbers, avocado, radishes, shallot, water, olive oil, vinegar, salt, black pepper, and red pepper flakes. Blend until creamy. It may take several minutes to get the proper consistency.

2. Serve immediately, garnished with your choice of herbs.

INGREDIENT TIP: If you are using red radishes, consider peeling them to preserve the beautiful green color of this soup.

PER SERVING:

CALORIES: 236; Total Fat: 21g; Saturated Fat: 3g; Protein: 3g; Total Carbohydrates: 12g; Fiber: 5g; Sugar: 5g; Cholesterol: 0mg

CLASSIC TOMATO SOUP

Serves 8 / Prep time: 10 minutes / Cook time: 1 hour 20 minutes

Tomato soup may sound like an American classic, but tomatoes have long been a Mediterranean staple. A superfood, tomatoes are an even greater nutrient powerhouse when cooked.

HEART HEALTH

4 to 5 pounds vine-ripened tomatoes, halved

1 head garlic

8 thyme sprigs

¼ cup extra-virgin olive oil

½ teaspoon salt

¼ teaspoon freshly ground black pepper, plus more for garnish

8 cups vegetable broth

Handful fresh basil, plus more for garnish

1. Preheat the oven to 425°F.

2. Place the tomatoes, cut-side up, in a large roasting pan.

3. Cut the head of garlic in half through all the cloves and place in the roasting pan. Add the thyme sprigs. Pour the olive oil over the tomatoes and garlic and sprinkle with the salt and pepper.

4. Roast for 30 minutes, until the ingredients are softened and starting to caramelize.

5. Remove the thyme and discard. Squeeze the garlic out of its skins and discard the skins.

6. Transfer the tomatoes and garlic to a large soup pot. Add the vegetable broth and bring to a boil. Reduce to a simmer and cook for 20 minutes.

7. Add the basil. Using an immersion blender, puree until smooth. (Alternatively, transfer the soup in batches to a countertop blender. Remove the center cap of the blender lid to allow steam to escape and hold a kitchen towel over the hole while blending. Return the puree to the pot.)

8. Simmer over low heat for about 30 minutes, until thickened.

9. Garnish each serving with additional basil and pepper.

PER SERVING:

CALORIES: 118; Total Fat: 7g; Saturated Fat: 1g; Protein: 2g; Total Carbohydrates: 13g; Fiber: 3g; Sugar: 8g; Cholesterol: 0mg

RISI E BISI (ITALIAN RICE AND PEAS)

Serves 6 / Prep time: 5 minutes / Cook time: 30 minutes

This classic dish from Venice is a cross between soup and risotto. Peas are a good source of protein and vitamin K and are reminiscent of springtime in a bowl.

OVERALL WELLNESS

4 cups chicken broth

1 cup water

1 tablespoon extra-virgin olive oil

2 shallots, chopped

2 garlic cloves, minced

1 cup Arborio or Carnaroli rice

½ cup dry white wine

2 cups fresh or frozen peas

2 tablespoons grated Parmesan cheese

1. In a saucepan, bring the broth and water to a boil over medium-high heat. Reduce to a gentle simmer.

2. Meanwhile, in another saucepan, heat the olive oil over low heat. Cook the shallots for about 3 minutes, until softened. Add the garlic and cook for about 1 minute, until fragrant.

3. Add the rice and stir to coat with the oil until it gets glossy. Cook for 1 minute, stirring constantly.

4. Add a ladleful of the hot broth to the rice and stir well for a few minutes. Continue stirring in the broth by the ladleful, cooking until the rice is softened.

5. When you get to the last ladleful of broth, add the peas and cook until tender, about 3 minutes if fresh, 1 minute if frozen. If the soup is too thick, add another cup of water.

6. Serve topped with freshly grated Parmesan.

VARIATION TIP: You can use vegetable broth to make this a vegetarian soup.

PER SERVING:

CALORIES: 200; Total Fat: 3g; Saturated Fat: 1g; Protein: 5g; Total Carbohydrates: 34g; Fiber: 4g; Sugar: 3g; Cholesterol: 1mg

PASTA E FAGIOLI (PASTA AND BEAN SOUP)

Serves 4 / Prep time: 10 minutes / Cook time: 2 hours 15 minutes

This soup is classic Italian comfort food. You can use any small-shaped pasta instead of ditalini, but don't be tempted to add more than about a cup. It won't look like much as you add it, but it will expand and keep absorbing the liquid from the soup.

OVERALL WELLNESS

1 onion, roughly chopped

1 carrot, roughly chopped

2 celery stalks, roughly chopped

2 garlic cloves, peeled

2 tablespoons extra-virgin olive oil

2 cups dried pinto beans

4 cups chicken broth

1 cup water

2 tablespoons cream sherry

1 teaspoon salt

½ teaspoon dried thyme

¼ teaspoon freshly ground black pepper

¼ teaspoon red pepper flakes

1 cup ditalini

1. In a food processor, combine the onion, carrot, celery, and garlic and pulse to process the vegetables into small pieces. (Alternatively, you can use a knife to finely chop the vegetables.)

2. In a soup pot, warm the olive oil over medium heat. Add the vegetables and cook for about 4 minutes, until they start to soften.

3. Add the beans and stir to coat.

4. Add the chicken broth and water. Bring to a boil, then reduce to a simmer and cook for about 1½ hours, until the beans are soft.

5. If desired, remove a couple of spoonfuls of the bean mixture and transfer it to the food processor or a blender. Puree until smooth, then stir it back into the pot. This helps make a thick, creamy soup.

6. Add the sherry, salt, thyme, black pepper, and red pepper flakes. Simmer for another 30 minutes.

7. Add the pasta and cook until al dente.

VARIATION TIP: You can easily make this soup vegetarian by replacing the chicken broth with vegetable broth.

INGREDIENT TIP: Traditionally, this soup is made with borlotti beans, also known as cranberry beans, but pinto beans are more readily available.

PER SERVING:

CALORIES: 529; Total Fat: 8g; Saturated Fat: 1g; Protein: 25g; Total Carbohydrates: 89g; Fiber: 17g; Sugar: 7g; Cholesterol: 0mg

ROASTED BUTTERNUT SQUASH SOUP

Serves 4 / Prep time: 15 minutes / Cook time: 1 hour

This simple roasted vegetable soup is a perfect way to celebrate the autumn harvest. The butternut squash adds a slightly sweet, nutty flavor and is loaded with antioxidants and vitamins.

WEIGHT LOSS

1 butternut squash, quartered and seeded

1 small onion, halved

2 tablespoons extra-virgin olive oil

¼ teaspoon salt, plus more to taste

1 rosemary sprig

3 cups chicken broth

1 celery stalk, cut into 1-inch pieces

1 garlic clove, lightly smashed and peeled

Freshly ground black pepper

1. Preheat the oven to 400°F.

2. On a rimmed baking sheet, rub the squash and onion with the olive oil. Sprinkle with the salt. Spread everything out in a single layer and add the rosemary sprig.

3. Roast for 1 hour, until the squash is tender and starting to brown. Set aside to rest for 5 minutes. Discard the rosemary.

4. Meanwhile, when the squash is nearly done, in a small saucepan, combine the broth, celery, and garlic and heat over medium-low heat for about 15 minutes, until the celery is tender.

5. Using a spoon, scrape the squash flesh out of the skin and into a blender. Add the roasted onion, cooked celery and garlic, and a few ladles of broth. Remove the center cap from the blender lid to allow steam to escape, hold a kitchen towel over the hole, and blend until smooth. Add more broth until you get the consistency you desire. Season to taste with salt and pepper.

VARIATION TIP: To make this recipe vegetarian, use vegetable broth in place of the chicken broth.

INGREDIENT TIP: Instead of throwing the seeds away after cleaning the squash, you can roast them on a rimmed baking sheet at 300°F and use them to garnish salads or eat as a snack.

PER SERVING:

CALORIES: 147; Total Fat: 7g; Saturated Fat: 1g; Protein: 2g; Total Carbohydrates: 22g; Fiber: 4g; Sugar: 5g; Cholesterol: 0mg

MUSHROOM BARLEY SOUP

Serves 6 / Prep time: 20 minutes / Cook time: 45 minutes

Mushrooms have a rich, earthy flavor and are full of vitamins, like folate, and minerals like copper, potassium, magnesium, and zinc. Barley contains B vitamins, vitamin E, and iron. Serve this soup with seeded rye bread for a stress-reducing meal after a long day at work.

HEART HEALTH

2 tablespoons extra-virgin olive oil

1 small onion, diced

2 garlic cloves, minced

10 ounces cremini or white button mushrooms, sliced

4 cups chicken broth

2 cups water

2 teaspoons fresh thyme leaves

½ teaspoon salt

¼ teaspoon freshly ground black pepper

1 ounce dried shiitake mushrooms

1 cup quick-cooking barley

¼ cup chopped fresh flat-leaf parsley

2 tablespoons grated Parmesan cheese, for garnish

1. In a soup pot, heat the olive oil over medium heat. Add the onion and cook for about 5 minutes, until it starts to soften. Add the garlic and cook for 1 minute.

2. Add the cremini mushrooms and cook for about 5 minutes, until they start to release their liquid and turn golden.

3. Add the broth, water, thyme, salt, and pepper. Bring to a boil. Add the shiitake mushrooms and continue to cook for about 15 minutes, until all of the mushrooms are soft.

4. Add the barley. Reduce to a simmer, cover, and cook for about 15 minutes, until the barley softens.

5. Garnish each serving with parsley and grated Parmesan.

INGREDIENT TIP: The quick-cooking barley makes this soup easy to prepare. If you can't find quick-cooking barley, you can use pearl barley. The cooking time will increase by about 50 minutes, and you'll need to add another 2 cups water.

VARIATION TIP: To make this soup vegetarian, you can use vegetable broth in place of the chicken broth.

PER SERVING:
CALORIES: 196; Total Fat: 6g; Saturated Fat: 1g; Protein: 6g; Total Carbohydrates: 33g; Fiber: 7g; Sugar: 2g; Cholesterol: 1mg

TORTELLINI IN BRODO (TORTELLINI IN BROTH WITH SHRIMP)

Serves 4 / Prep time: 10 minutes / Cook time: 20 minutes

Tortellini soup is a northern Italian recipe traditionally served as a first course during holiday meals, especially at Christmas. The addition of the protein from shrimp takes this soup from starter to main course.

OVERALL WELLNESS

2 celery stalks, chopped

1 carrot, chopped

1 shallot, finely diced

2 garlic cloves, thinly sliced

1 (1-inch) piece fresh red chile, seeded and minced

1 thyme sprig

1 (2-inch) strip lemon zest (see Tip)

1 teaspoon salt

¼ teaspoon freshly ground black pepper

Pinch ground nutmeg

1 cup water

¼ cup dry white wine (optional)

8 cups chicken broth

12 ounces large shrimp, peeled and deveined

20 ounces fresh cheese tortellini

2 tablespoons grated Parmesan or Romano cheese, for garnish

1. In a soup pot, combine the celery, carrot, shallot, garlic, chile, thyme, lemon zest, salt, pepper, and nutmeg. Add the water and wine (if using), cover, and bring to boil over medium-high heat. Boil for about 5 minutes, until the vegetables are soft.

2. Add the chicken broth, cover, and return to a boil.

3. Add the shrimp and continue to boil, uncovered, for 1 minute, until the shrimp start to turn pink.

4. Add the tortellini and continue to boil for 3 to 4 minutes, or according to package directions until cooked through.

5. Remove and discard the thyme sprig and lemon peel.

6. Serve sprinkled with the Parmesan.

> **COOKING TIP:** For the lemon zest, use a paring knife or vegetable peeler to remove a 2-inch-long strip of lemon zest—just the thin colored layer of the peel. Avoid cutting into the white pith, which is bitter.

PER SERVING:

CALORIES: 542; Total Fat: 12g; Saturated Fat: 6g; Protein: 32g; Total Carbohydrates: 76g; Fiber: 3g; Sugar: 6g; Cholesterol: 169mg

six

SALADS

Spring Greek Salad 66

Panzanella 67

Tuscan Tuna Salad 68

Mediterranean Chopped Salad 69

Green Bean and Potato Salad 70

Shrimp Salad 71

Warm Potato Salad 72

Summer Rainbow Salad 73

Arugula and White Bean Salad 74

Fennel and Orange Salad 75

Classic Niçoise Salad 77

Algerian Carrot Slaw 78

Tabbouleh (Lebanese Parsley and Bulgur Salad) 79

Cucumber and Red Onion Salad 80

Mediterranean Quinoa Salad 81

Arugula and White Bean Salad, p. 74

SPRING GREEK SALAD

Serves 4 / Prep time: 10 minutes

What makes this salad stand out is the use of escarole and chicory, which are high in dietary fiber, antioxidants, and vitamins A, C, and K. Escarole is a firm, hearty lettuce usually used in soups, but it's perfectly lovely in salads. Chicory has a pleasantly bitter taste that works especially well with this dressing.

WEIGHT LOSS

1 head escarole, chopped

1 head curly chicory, chopped

¼ cup crumbled feta cheese

¼ cup pitted halved kalamata olives

¼ cup sliced seeded peperoncini

3 tablespoons extra-virgin olive oil

Juice of ½ lemon

2 garlic cloves, minced

Pinch dried dill

Salt

Freshly ground black pepper

1. In a large bowl, toss together the escarole and chicory.

2. Scatter the feta cheese, olives, and peperoncini on top.

3. In a small bowl, whisk together the olive oil, lemon juice, and garlic. Season with the dill and salt and pepper to taste.

4. Pour the dressing over the lettuce mixture and toss to combine.

VARIATION TIP: You can substitute frisée for the chicory if preferred.

PER SERVING:

CALORIES: 173; Total Fat: 14g; Saturated Fat: 3g; Protein: 5g; Total Carbohydrates: 10g; Fiber: 4g; Sugar: 3g; Cholesterol: 8mg

PANZANELLA

This Tuscan chopped salad is made with leftover bread. A classic combination of tomatoes, cucumbers, and basil, panzanella is traditionally served in late summer, when tomatoes are at their sweetest.

OVERALL WELLNESS

¼ cup extra-virgin olive oil, plus 3 tablespoons

6 stale hearty Italian bread slices, cut into cubes

6 tomatoes, cut into 1-inch pieces

1 cucumber, halved lengthwise and cut into half-moons

1 red bell pepper, seeded and finely chopped

½ onion, thinly sliced

2 tablespoons roughly chopped capers

2 tablespoons red wine vinegar

1 garlic clove, minced

1 teaspoon salt

¼ teaspoon freshly ground black pepper

1 teaspoon chopped fresh basil

1. In a large skillet, heat 3 tablespoons of olive oil over medium heat. Add the bread cubes and cook for about 10 minutes, until browned on all sides.

2. Transfer the bread cubes to a large bowl and add the tomatoes, cucumber, bell pepper, onion, and capers.

3. In a small bowl, whisk together the remaining ¼ cup of olive oil, the vinegar, garlic, salt, and pepper. Pour the dressing over the salad and toss to combine well.

4. Let the salad rest for 30 minutes. Sprinkle the basil on top and serve.

COOKING TIP: The rest time before serving allows the flavors to combine and the bread to soak up all the tasty juices.

PER SERVING:

CALORIES: 205; Total Fat: 17g; Saturated Fat: 2g; Protein: 3g; Total Carbohydrates: 13g; Fiber: 3g; Sugar: 5g; Cholesterol: 0mg

TUSCAN TUNA SALAD

Serves 4 / Prep time: 10 minutes

This isn't your typical tuna salad. Tuna is an excellent source of omega-3 fatty acids, and white beans provide extra protein and dietary fiber. Try serving this delightfully light and lemony tuna salad on a slice of bread as an open-faced sandwich.

HEART HEALTH

¼ cup extra-virgin olive oil

Juice of ½ lemon

½ teaspoon Dijon mustard

Salt

Freshly ground black pepper

2 (5-ounce) cans tuna in olive oil, drained

1 (19-ounce) can cannellini beans, rinsed and drained

12 marinated mushrooms, rinsed and halved if large

12 grape or cherry tomatoes, halved

1 or 2 celery stalks, sliced

1 teaspoon capers (optional)

1. In a small bowl, whisk together the olive oil, lemon juice, and mustard, and season with salt and pepper.

2. In a large bowl, combine the tuna, beans, mushrooms, tomatoes, celery, and capers (if using). Add the dressing and toss well. Season with additional salt and pepper, if desired.

PER SERVING:
CALORIES: 389; Total Fat: 20g; Saturated Fat: 3g; Protein: 26g; Total Carbohydrates: 29g; Fiber: 7g; Sugar: 7g; Cholesterol: 18mg

MEDITERRANEAN CHOPPED SALAD

Serves 4 / Prep time: 15 minutes, plus time to cool / Cook time: 20 minutes

This colorful salad combines a variety of fresh seasonal vegetables with healthy fats and is a great way to incorporate whole grains into your diet.

WEIGHT LOSS

1 cup whole grains, such as red or white quinoa, millet, or buckwheat

1 (15-ounce) can chickpeas, rinsed and drained

2 cups baby spinach

1 cucumber, finely chopped

½ red bell pepper, finely chopped

½ fennel bulb, trimmed and finely chopped

1 celery stalk, finely chopped

1 carrot, finely chopped

1 plum tomato, finely chopped

½ red onion, finely chopped

1 cherry pepper, seeded and finely chopped

¼ cup extra-virgin olive oil

2 tablespoons white wine vinegar

1 teaspoon chopped fresh basil

1 garlic clove, minced

Salt

Freshly ground black pepper

1. Cook the whole grains according to package directions. Allow to cool.

2. In a large bowl, toss the grains, chickpeas, spinach, cucumber, bell pepper, fennel, celery, carrot, tomato, red onion, and cherry pepper.

3. In a small bowl, whisk together the olive oil, vinegar, basil, and garlic. Season with salt and pepper. Toss with the salad and serve.

MAKE-AHEAD TIP: This salad holds up well in the refrigerator and tastes just as good the next day.

PER SERVING:

CALORIES: 401; Total Fat: 18g; Saturated Fat: 2g; Protein: 12g; Total Carbohydrates: 50g; Fiber: 10g; Sugar: 7g; Cholesterol: 0mg

GREEN BEAN AND POTATO SALAD

Serves 4 / Prep time: 10 minutes / Cook time: 15 minutes

Green beans and potatoes combine to make a hearty vegetable salad full of nutrients, and a lemony dressing gives it a bright, summery flavor. Serve this satisfying salad for lunch or as a side dish for a fish entrée.

OVERALL WELLNESS

2 russet potatoes, peeled and cut into 1-inch pieces

2 cups green beans, trimmed

¼ cup extra-virgin olive oil

Juice of ½ lemon

1 teaspoon Italian Herb Blend (page 262)

1 teaspoon salt

½ teaspoon freshly ground black pepper

1. Put the potatoes in a saucepan, cover with water, and bring to a boil over high heat. Cook for about 10 minutes, until tender. Drain and set aside to cool.

2. While the potatoes are cooling, fill the same saucepan with water and bring to a boil over high heat. Fill a large bowl with ice cubes and cold water. Add the green beans to the boiling water and blanch for about 3 minutes, then remove with tongs or a sieve and immediately plunge them into the ice bath. Once cool, drain.

3. Combine the potatoes and green beans in a large bowl. Drizzle the olive oil over the vegetables and squeeze in the lemon juice. Add the Italian herb blend, salt, and pepper and toss to combine.

MAKE-AHEAD TIP: You can blanch the green beans ahead of time if needed. They will keep in an airtight container in the refrigerator for up to 3 days.

PER SERVING:

CALORIES: 282; Total Fat: 14g; Saturated Fat: 2g; Protein: 5g; Total Carbohydrates: 37g; Fiber: 4g; Sugar: 3g; Cholesterol: 0mg

SHRIMP SALAD

Serves 4 / Prep time: 15 minutes / Cook time: 5 minutes

Shrimp make a great protein choice because they're low in calories and high in good cholesterol. This shrimp salad is tasty served on a bed of lettuce or as a sandwich filling on your favorite whole-grain bread.

HEART HEALTH

1 pound large shrimp, peeled and deveined

Juice of ½ lemon

2 celery stalks, chopped

3 scallions, chopped

1 garlic clove, minced

Salt

Freshly ground black pepper

½ cup vegan mayonnaise

1. Put the shrimp in a skillet and add a few tablespoons of water. Cook over medium heat for 2 to 3 minutes, until the shrimp turn pink. Drain and pat dry. Cut the shrimp into bite-size pieces and transfer a bowl.

2. Add the lemon juice and toss, then add the celery, scallions, and garlic. Season with salt and pepper. Toss again to combine.

3. Add the vegan mayonnaise and fold gently to combine.

COOKING TIP: You can buy precooked shrimp for this recipe to save time.

INGREDIENT TIP: I use vegan mayonnaise in this recipe because I feel egg-based mayonnaise weighs down the shrimp.

PER SERVING:

CALORIES: 185; Total Fat: 11g; Saturated Fat: 1g; Protein: 18g; Total Carbohydrates: 4g; Fiber: 1g; Sugar: 1g; Cholesterol: 143mg

WARM POTATO SALAD

Serves 4 / Prep time: 10 minutes / Cook time: 10 minutes

Serve this salad warm to intensify the flavors of the Dijon mustard and vinegar. If you keep hard-boiled eggs on hand in the fridge, this salad comes together in no time.

OVERALL WELLNESS

6 red potatoes, cut into 1-inch pieces

1 tablespoon white wine vinegar

3 large eggs, hard-boiled, peeled, and chopped

2 celery stalks, finely chopped

1 small onion, finely chopped

½ cup mayonnaise or vegan mayonnaise

1 teaspoon Dijon mustard

1 teaspoon salt

¼ teaspoon freshly ground black pepper

1. Put the potatoes in a saucepan, cover with water, and bring to a boil over high heat. Cook for about 10 minutes, until tender. Drain and transfer to a large bowl, then sprinkle with the vinegar.

2. Add the eggs, celery, and onion and toss.

3. Add the mayonnaise, mustard, salt, and pepper and toss to combine.

MAKE-AHEAD TIP: You can store this salad in an airtight container in the refrigerator for up to 3 days and serve it chilled instead.

PER SERVING:

CALORIES: 474; Total Fat: 25g; Saturated Fat: 4g; Protein: 11g; Total Carbohydrates: 53g; Fiber: 6g; Sugar: 5g; Cholesterol: 151mg

SUMMER RAINBOW SALAD

Serves 4 / Prep time: 10 minutes

This recipe takes advantage of the bounty of vegetables available in the summer months. The more colors you add, the greater variety of nutrients you're taking in. "Eating the rainbow" makes for a very pretty plate, too. Serve with a crusty Italian baguette.

WEIGHT LOSS

1 cup chopped red or green leaf lettuce

1 cup chopped iceberg lettuce

½ cup baby arugula

½ cup chopped radicchio

1 cup mixed chopped or sliced vegetables, such as red cabbage, red onion, radish, red or yellow tomato, carrot, cucumber, and/or avocado

¼ cup extra-virgin olive oil

Juice of ½ lemon

½ teaspoon salt

¼ teaspoon freshly ground black pepper

¼ teaspoon dried oregano

1. In a large salad bowl, combine the lettuces, arugula, radicchio, and mixed vegetables and gently toss.

2. In a small bowl, whisk together the olive oil, lemon juice, salt, pepper, and oregano. Pour the dressing over the salad and toss well to coat.

> **COOKING TIP:** If you serve this salad to guests, set out all the components in separate bowls and let everyone pick and choose from all the beautiful colors before adding the dressing to serve.

PER SERVING:
CALORIES: 137; Total Fat: 14g; Saturated Fat: 2g; Protein: 1g; Total Carbohydrates: 4g; Fiber: 1g; Sugar: 2g; Cholesterol: 0mg

ARUGULA AND WHITE BEAN SALAD

Serves 2 / Prep time: 10 minutes

Arugula is an excellent source of vitamins A, C, and K and has a peppery flavor that balances the mildness of the white beans in this salad, which provide folate and dietary fiber. A lemony dressing perfectly complements the flavors.

HEART HEALTH

1 (15-ounce) can cannellini beans, rinsed and drained

2 cups baby arugula

¼ cup extra-virgin olive oil

Juice of ½ lemon

½ teaspoon dried oregano

½ teaspoon salt

¼ teaspoon freshly ground black pepper

4 Italian seeded bread slices, toasted

1. In a medium bowl, combine the beans and arugula.

2. In a small bowl, whisk together the olive oil, lemon juice, oregano, salt, and pepper. Pour over the salad and toss to coat.

3. To serve, spoon heaping portions of the salad over the toast.

PER SERVING:

CALORIES: 469; Total Fat: 29g; Saturated Fat: 4g; Protein: 14g; Total Carbohydrates: 42g; Fiber: 9g; Sugar: 1g; Cholesterol: 0mg

FENNEL AND ORANGE SALAD

Serves 6 / Prep time: 10 minutes

This winter salad has a wonderful fragrance. The combination of sweet oranges and cool fennel makes for a delightful taste sensation.

WEIGHT LOSS

4 navel oranges, peeled, halved, and thinly sliced

3 fennel bulbs, trimmed and thinly sliced, fronds reserved for garnish

2 tablespoons extra-virgin olive oil

1 tablespoon white wine vinegar

Salt

Freshly ground black pepper

1. In a large bowl, combine the orange and fennel slices.

2. In a small bowl, whisk together the olive oil and vinegar. Season with salt and pepper. Pour the dressing over the orange and fennel and toss to combine.

3. Roughly chop the fennel fronds and sprinkle them on top.

COOKING TIP: Be sure to slice the fennel thinly as it is quite crunchy, and thin slices are easier to eat. A mandoline makes this step very easy.

INGREDIENT TIP: Cara Cara oranges, with their pinkish-red flesh, make an especially beautiful choice for this salad, but any seedless orange will do just fine.

PER SERVING:

CALORIES: 122; Total Fat: 5g; Saturated Fat: 1g; Protein: 2g; Total Carbohydrates: 20g; Fiber: 6g; Sugar: 12g; Cholesterol: 0mg

CLASSIC NIÇOISE SALAD

Serves 4 / Prep time: 15 minutes / Cook time: 15 minutes

This classic salad originated in the city of Nice in the South of France. Its strong flavor comes from a combination of hard-boiled eggs, tomatoes, briny olives, and tuna. Most American versions include cooked potatoes and green beans, which add even more nutrients.

HEART HEALTH

1 pound red potatoes, cut into 1-inch pieces

4 tablespoons white wine vinegar, divided

8 ounces green beans, trimmed

¼ cup extra-virgin olive oil

1 teaspoon Dijon mustard

1 teaspoon fresh thyme leaves

½ teaspoon salt

¼ teaspoon freshly ground black pepper

1 head butter lettuce, chopped

1 (5-ounce) can tuna in olive oil, drained

½ cup pitted Niçoise olives

⅓ cup chopped tomato

2 scallions, chopped

4 large eggs, hard-boiled, peeled, and sliced

1. Put the potatoes in a saucepan, cover with water, and bring to a boil over high heat. Cook for about 10 minutes, until tender. Drain and transfer to a bowl. Sprinkle with 1 tablespoon of vinegar and let sit.

2. While the potatoes are cooling, fill the same saucepan with water and bring to a boil over high heat. Fill a large bowl with ice cubes and water. Add the green beans to the boiling water and blanch for 3 minutes, then remove with tongs or a strainer and immediately plunge them into the ice bath. Once cool, drain.

3. In a small bowl, whisk together the olive oil, remaining 3 tablespoons of vinegar, mustard, thyme, salt, and pepper.

4. In a large bowl, combine the lettuce, tuna, olives, tomato, and scallions. Add half of the dressing and toss to coat.

5. Arrange the lettuce mixture on serving plates. Divide the potatoes, green beans, and eggs on top. Drizzle with the remaining dressing.

VARIATION TIP: You can substitute oil-packed anchovies for the tuna if preferred.

PER SERVING:
CALORIES: 373; Total Fat: 23g; Saturated Fat: 4g; Protein: 18g; Total Carbohydrates: 25g; Fiber: 5g; Sugar: 4g; Cholesterol: 195mg

ALGERIAN CARROT SLAW

Serves 6 / Prep time: 20 minutes, plus 30 minutes to chill

Carrots and fennel are both good for controlling blood pressure and lowering choles-terol. Here they combine with a spicy vinaigrette in a slaw that works well as a side dish or served on sandwiches.

HEART HEALTH

¼ cup extra-virgin olive oil

Juice of ½ lemon

2 tablespoons cider vinegar

½ teaspoon salt

¼ teaspoon freshly ground black pepper

Pinch smoked paprika

Pinch red pepper flakes (optional)

1 pound carrots, shredded

2 fennel bulbs, trimmed and shredded

⅓ cup chopped pitted olives

⅓ cup thinly sliced oil-packed sun-dried tomatoes

¼ cup chopped fresh flat-leaf parsley

1. In a small bowl, whisk together the olive oil, lemon juice, vinegar, salt, black pepper, paprika, and red pepper flakes (if using).

2. In a large bowl, combine the carrots, fennel, olives, and sun-dried tomatoes. Add the dressing and toss well to coat.

3. Chill for 30 minutes, then garnish with the parsley.

PER SERVING:

CALORIES: 159; Total Fat: 11g; Saturated Fat: 2g; Protein: 2g; Total Carbohydrates: 15g; Fiber: 5g; Sugar: 7g; Cholesterol: 0mg

TABBOULEH (LEBANESE PARSLEY AND BULGUR SALAD)

Serves 4 / Prep time: 10 minutes / Cook time: 20 minutes

We usually think of parsley as a garnish or an herbal flavor enhancer, but in this classic Lebanese salad, parsley takes center stage. Tabbouleh makes a tasty side dish for kebabs and works as party dip, too.

HEART HEALTH

1 cup bulgur

4 plum tomatoes, diced, juices reserved

2 cups finely chopped fresh flat-leaf parsley

4 scallions, chopped

¼ cup extra-virgin olive oil

Juice of 2 lemons

2 tablespoons finely chopped fresh mint

½ teaspoon salt

¼ teaspoon freshly ground black pepper

1. In a saucepan, prepare the bulgur according to package directions. Drain thoroughly, transfer to a large bowl, and set aside to cool.

2. Once cool, add the tomatoes with their juices, parsley, and scallions.

3. In a small bowl, whisk together the olive oil, lemon juice, mint, salt, and pepper. Pour the dressing over the bulgur mixture and toss to coat.

VARIATION TIP: To make this recipe gluten-free, you can substitute quinoa for the bulgur.

PER SERVING:

CALORIES: 271; Total Fat: 14g; Saturated Fat: 2g; Protein: 6g; Total Carbohydrates: 34g; Fiber: 7g; Sugar: 3g; Cholesterol: 0mg

CUCUMBER AND RED ONION SALAD

Serves 4 / Prep time: 10 minutes

Red onion and cucumber combined with the zing of red wine vinegar make for a refreshing and simple summer salad.

WEIGHT LOSS

¼ cup extra-virgin olive oil

1 tablespoon red wine vinegar

1 teaspoon dried oregano

Pinch salt

Freshly ground black pepper

2 cucumbers, peeled and sliced

½ red onion, thinly sliced

1. In a small bowl, whisk together the olive oil, vinegar, and oregano. Season with the salt and pepper to taste.

2. In a bowl, combine the cucumbers and red onion. Add the dressing and toss well to coat.

INGREDIENT TIP: If you like, you can halve the cucumbers lengthwise and scrape out the seeds with a spoon. Or, choose English cucumbers (which are typically seedless) instead.

PER SERVING:

CALORIES: 143; Total Fat: 14g; Saturated Fat: 2g; Protein: 1g; Total Carbohydrates: 4g; Fiber: 1g; Sugar: 3g; Cholesterol: 0mg

MEDITERRANEAN QUINOA SALAD

Serves 4 / Prep time: 15 minutes / Cook time: 15 minutes

Quinoa is a popular gluten-free superfood with a nutty flavor. It's a good source of protein, fiber, iron, magnesium, and B vitamins. This Mediterranean-inspired salad makes for a refreshing lunch on a hot summer day.

HEART HEALTH

1½ cups quinoa

2 cucumbers, seeded and diced

1 small red onion, diced

1 large tomato, diced

1 handful fresh flat-leaf parsley, chopped

½ cup extra-virgin olive oil

¼ cup red wine vinegar

Juice of 1 lemon

1½ teaspoons salt

¾ teaspoon freshly ground black pepper

4 heads endive, trimmed and separated into spears

1 avocado, pitted, peeled, and diced

1. In a saucepan, prepare the quinoa according to package directions. Rinse the quinoa under cold running water and drain very well. Transfer to a large bowl.

2. Add the cucumbers, red onion, tomato, and parsley.

3. In a small bowl, whisk together the olive oil, vinegar, lemon juice, salt, and pepper. Pour the dressing over the quinoa mixture and toss to coat.

4. Spoon the mixture onto the endive spears and top with the avocado.

MAKE-AHEAD TIP: You can cook the quinoa ahead of time and store in an airtight container in the refrigerator for up to 5 days.

PER SERVING:

CALORIES: 669; Total Fat: 40g; Saturated Fat: 6g; Protein: 17g; Total Carbohydrates: 69g; Fiber: 20g; Sugar: 9g; Cholesterol: 0mg

seven

MEZE AND SMALL PLATES

Spicy Calabrian Shrimp 84

Eggplant Roll-Ups 85

Cauliflower Bites 86

Patatas Bravas 87

Charcuterie Board with Red Onion Jam 88

Caponata 89

Stuffed Hot Peppers 90

Ricotta-Stuffed Endive with Vegetables 91

Albóndigas (Spanish Meatballs) 93

Toasted Polenta with Mushrooms 94

Moroccan Sardines on Toast 95

Tunisian Brik Pastries 96

Pancetta-Wrapped Shrimp 97

Arancini (Italian Stuffed Rice Balls) 98

Spicy Lamb Meatballs 100

Quinoa and Cheese Stuffed Mushrooms 101

Charcuterie Board with Red Onion Jam, p. 88

SPICY CALABRIAN SHRIMP

Serves 4 / Prep time: 15 minutes / Cook time: 10 minutes

This crowd-pleasing shrimp dish is my go-to party recipe. Spicy shrimp are perfect as an appetizer, an accompaniment to risotto dishes, or an addition to salads.

OVERALL WELLNESS

¼ cup shredded Romano cheese

2 tablespoons extra-virgin olive oil

1 teaspoon Calabrian chili paste

1 teaspoon dried oregano

1 pound large shrimp, peeled and deveined, tails left on

1. Preheat the oven to 425°F. Line a rimmed baking sheet with parchment paper.

2. In a bowl, combine the cheese, olive oil, chili paste, and oregano to form a paste.

3. Dip the shrimp in the cheese mixture, coating on both sides.

4. Arrange the shrimp in a single layer on the prepared baking sheet. Bake for 8 to 10 minutes, until opaque.

INGREDIENT TIP: Calabrian chili paste is extremely hot, but it adds a lot of flavor as well as heat. You can vary the amount you use in this recipe depending on your taste. It can be found in jars in the hot pepper section of the supermarket.

PER SERVING:

CALORIES: 169; Total Fat: 10g; Saturated Fat: 2g; Protein: 17g; Total Carbohydrates: 2g; Fiber: 0g; Sugar: 0g; Cholesterol: 148mg

EGGPLANT ROLL-UPS

Serves 6 / Prep time: 15 minutes / Cook time: 30 minutes

Thin slices of eggplant baked in the oven and rolled up with herbed ricotta cheese look and taste great as an appetizer or party finger food. They also work as a side dish.

OVERALL WELLNESS

1 eggplant, cut lengthwise into ½-inch-thick slices

2 tablespoons extra-virgin olive oil

½ teaspoon sea salt

15 almonds

½ cup ricotta cheese

¼ teaspoon fresh thyme leaves

1. Preheat the oven to 375°F. Line a rimmed baking sheet with parchment paper.

2. Lay the eggplant slices on the prepared baking sheet and brush both sides with the olive oil. Sprinkle with the salt. Bake the eggplant slices for 20 to 30 minutes, until softened but not starting to brown.

3. Put the almonds in a coffee grinder and process into a powder. (Alternatively, chop them as finely as you can.)

4. Transfer the ground almonds to a bowl and add the ricotta cheese and thyme. Stir to combine.

5. Lay the eggplant slices on paper towels to drain and cool slightly.

6. Spread each eggplant slice with the ricotta cheese mixture. Roll them up tightly and insert a toothpick to hold them together.

MAKE-AHEAD TIP: You can bake the eggplant slices ahead of time, then assemble the roll-ups just before serving.

PER SERVING:

CALORIES: 116; Total Fat: 9g; Saturated Fat: 2g; Protein: 4g; Total Carbohydrates: 7g; Fiber: 3g; Sugar: 3g; Cholesterol: 11mg

CAULIFLOWER BITES

Serves 6 / Prep time: 10 minutes / Cook time: 20 minutes

Toasted cauliflower bites make for a healthy Mediterranean-style side dish or a lovely appetizer, accompanied by a glass of wine.

WEIGHT LOSS

1 head cauliflower, cut into bite-size florets

¼ cup extra-virgin olive oil

½ cup seasoned bread crumbs

1. Preheat the oven to 400°F. Line a rimmed baking sheet with parchment paper.

2. In a large bowl, toss the cauliflower and olive oil with your hands to coat evenly.

3. Put the bread crumbs in a small bowl and roll each cauliflower floret lightly in the bread crumbs. You don't need to completely coat them.

4. Place the cauliflower in a single layer on the prepared baking sheet and sprinkle with any remaining bread crumbs.

5. Bake for about 20 minutes, until lightly browned and fork tender.

COOKING TIP: Stale bread and rolls make great bread crumbs. Simply cut the bread into chunks and whiz in the food processor, or grate on a box grater. You can make your own seasoned bread crumbs by adding homemade Italian Herb Blend (page 262).

PER SERVING:

CALORIES: 140; Total Fat: 10g; Saturated Fat: 1g; Protein: 3g; Total Carbohydrates: 11g; Fiber: 2g; Sugar: 2g; Cholesterol: 0mg

PATATAS BRAVAS

Serves 4 / Prep time: 10 minutes / Cook time: 20 minutes

This classic Spanish tapas dish of crispy, fried potatoes is traditionally served with a hot smoked paprika sauce. In this healthier version, the potatoes are roasted in the oven and served with a spicy tomato sauce. This dish goes nicely with a cold glass of cava (Spanish sparkling wine).

OVERALL WELLNESS

2 russet potatoes, peeled and cut lengthwise into ⅛-inch-thick slices

¼ cup extra-virgin olive oil

1 teaspoon salt

½ teaspoon freshly ground black pepper

1 cup tomato sauce

1 teaspoon Calabrian chili paste

1. Preheat the oven to 400°F. Line a rimmed baking sheet with parchment paper.

2. Lay the potato slices in a single layer on the prepared baking sheet. Pour the olive oil over them to coat. Sprinkle with the salt and pepper.

3. Bake for 20 minutes, until golden and crispy.

4. In a small saucepan, heat the tomato sauce over medium heat until simmering. Stir in the chili paste.

5. Serve the potatoes with a side of the warm tomato sauce for dipping.

> **INGREDIENT TIP:** Calabrian chili paste is seriously hot. It takes very little to spice up the sauce. You can usually find it in the supermarket next to the jarred hot peppers or beside other Italian ingredients, but if you can't, you can substitute red pepper flakes to taste.

PER SERVING:

CALORIES: 280; Total Fat: 14g; Saturated Fat: 2g; Protein: 4g; Total Carbohydrates: 37g; Fiber: 3g; Sugar: 3g; Cholesterol: 0mg

CHARCUTERIE BOARD WITH RED ONION JAM

Serves 8 / Prep time: 15 minutes / Cook time: 55 minutes

Putting together a beautiful board of vegetables, cheese, and fruits is an art. Take your time arranging these classic treats on a wooden cutting board.

OVERALL WELLNESS

2 tablespoons extra-virgin olive oil

3 red onions, chopped

½ teaspoon salt

¼ teaspoon freshly ground black pepper

½ cup red wine vinegar

¼ cup sugar

1 pound assorted thinly sliced cured meats, such as salami, prosciutto, and pepperoni

1 pound assorted cheeses, such as slices of provolone, fresh mozzarella, Swiss, or Brie, or chunks of Parmesan or Grana Padano

1 cup assorted fresh fruit, such as grapes, strawberries, blueberries, and blackberries

1 cup assorted nuts, such as almonds, hazelnuts, cashews, and walnuts

¼ cup sliced cornichons

¼ cup grape tomatoes

2 or 3 radishes, thinly sliced

½ cup pitted black and green olives

¼ cup whole-grain or Dijon mustard

Assorted crackers and bread slices

1. To make the red onion jam, in a large saucepan, heat the olive oil over low heat. Add the red onions, salt, and pepper. Cover and cook, stirring occasionally, until the red onions are very soft, about 25 minutes.

2. Add the vinegar and sugar. Reduce the heat and simmer, uncovered, stirring occasionally, until the mixture becomes thick and syrupy, about 30 minutes. Allow to cool.

3. On a wooden cutting board, arrange the meats, cheeses, fruit, nuts, cornichons, tomatoes, and radishes, grouping small amounts of each ingredient together. Add small individual bowls of the red onion jam, olives, and mustard. Arrange the crackers around the spread.

MAKE-AHEAD TIP: The red onion jam can be made ahead and stored in an airtight container in the refrigerator for up to 1 week.

PER SERVING:

CALORIES: 668; Total Fat: 48g; Saturated Fat: 17g; Protein: 32g; Total Carbohydrates: 28g; Fiber: 4g; Sugar: 13g; Cholesterol: 100mg

CAPONATA

Serves 6 / Prep time: 15 minutes / Cook time: 1 hour

This fragrant, cooked vegetable salad originated in Sicily. Serve it on its own or use it as a relish. I love to eat it on bruschetta.

WEIGHT LOSS

4 tablespoons extra-virgin olive oil, divided

1 large eggplant, cut into ½-inch-thick slices

1 small red onion, thinly sliced

3 celery stalks, cut into thick slices

2 garlic cloves, minced

1 cup canned crushed tomatoes

½ cup chopped pitted green olives

2 tablespoons capers, rinsed

2 tablespoons red wine vinegar

1 teaspoon sugar

½ teaspoon salt

¼ teaspoon red pepper flakes

Chopped fresh flat-leaf parsley, for garnish

1. Preheat the oven to 400°F. Line a rimmed baking sheet with parchment paper and brush it with 2 tablespoons of olive oil.

2. Arrange the eggplant slices in a single layer on the prepared baking sheet. Brush them with 1 tablespoon of olive oil. Roast for 20 minutes. When cool enough to handle, cut into 1-inch cubes.

3. In a large skillet, heat the remaining 1 tablespoon of olive oil over medium heat. Cook the red onion and celery for about 5 minutes, until the red onion softens and turns golden. Add the garlic and cook for 1 minute. Add the eggplant and cook for another 5 minutes.

4. Add the crushed tomatoes, olives, capers, vinegar, sugar, salt, and red pepper flakes. Stir well and bring to a simmer. Cook, stirring occasionally, for 30 minutes. Allow to cool, then garnish with parsley.

MAKE-AHEAD TIP: I like to let the caponata rest for a day so all the glorious flavors have a chance to meld. It will keep for several days in an airtight container in the refrigerator.

PER SERVING:

CALORIES: 133; Total Fat: 11g; Saturated Fat: 1g; Protein: 2g; Total Carbohydrates: 10g; Fiber: 4g; Sugar: 5g; Cholesterol: 0mg

STUFFED HOT PEPPERS

Serves 6 / Prep time: 15 minutes / Cook time: 15 minutes

Roasted peppers stuffed with cheese and ham are classic Italian finger food. Serve them as a small plate or appetizer.

8 Italian hot peppers ("long hots")

8 red or green cherry peppers

8 ounces prosciutto, finely chopped

12 ounces mild provolone cheese, shredded

¼ cup extra-virgin olive oil

2 tablespoons bread crumbs

½ teaspoon dried oregano

1. Preheat the oven to 400°F. Line a rimmed baking sheet with parchment paper.

2. Cut a slit lengthwise in the long hots, being careful not to cut all the way through. Remove the seeds. Rinse and pat dry.

3. Cut the tops off the cherry peppers and discard. Carefully remove the seeds. Rinse and pat dry.

4. Arrange the peppers on the prepared baking sheet.

5. Divide the prosciutto evenly among the peppers, stuffing it inside. Fill the rest of each pepper with the provolone. Drizzle the peppers with the olive oil. Sprinkle with the bread crumbs and oregano.

6. Roast for 10 to 15 minutes, until the cheese is melted and the peppers are tender. Long hots are usually larger than cherry peppers and may take a little more time.

INGREDIENT TIP: Cherry peppers are pleasantly hot, but long hots are unpredictable. They always have great flavor, but sometimes they are mild and sometimes they are killer hot. You can't tell until you bite into them, but that's part of the fun!

PER SERVING:

CALORIES: 374; Total Fat: 26g; Saturated Fat: 11g; Protein: 24g; Total Carbohydrates: 15g; Fiber: 2g; Sugar: 7g; Cholesterol: 55mg

RICOTTA-STUFFED ENDIVE WITH VEGETABLES

Serves 4 / Prep time: 10 minutes

Ricotta is a widely used dairy product in the Mediterranean region. Its mild flavor complements fresh vegetables well. You can whip this dish together in just a few minutes whenever guests stop by unannounced.

WEIGHT LOSS

4 ounces part-skim ricotta cheese

¼ red bell pepper, diced

¼ red onion, diced

1 small tomato, diced

¼ teaspoon salt

Pinch freshly ground black pepper

1 head endive, leaves separated

1. Put the ricotta in a small bowl. Fold in the bell pepper, red onion, tomato, salt, and black pepper.

2. Spoon the mixture into the endive leaves.

PER SERVING:
CALORIES: 70; Total Fat: 3g; Saturated Fat: 1g; Protein: 5g; Total Carbohydrates: 8g; Fiber: 5g; Sugar: 2g; Cholesterol: 9mg

ALBÓNDIGAS (SPANISH MEATBALLS)

Serves 12 / Prep time: 20 minutes / Cook time: 45 minutes

These Spanish meatballs are a classic tapas dish, here served with a spicy tomato sauce flavored with red wine and paprika.

OVERALL WELLNESS

For the meatballs

8 ounces ground beef

8 ounces ground turkey or pork

4 ounces fresh chorizo, casing removed

½ onion, finely chopped

¼ cup grated Manchego, Parmesan, or Romano cheese

¼ cup bread crumbs

1 large egg, beaten

2 tablespoons olive oil

2 tablespoons chopped fresh flat-leaf parsley

2 garlic cloves, minced

½ teaspoon salt

¼ teaspoon black pepper

For the sauce

2 tablespoons olive oil

1 onion, chopped

1 garlic clove, minced

2 cups canned crushed tomatoes

½ cup dry red wine

1 teaspoon paprika

½ teaspoon red pepper flakes

½ teaspoon salt

¼ teaspoon freshly ground black pepper

To make the meatballs

1. Preheat the oven to 375°F. Line a rimmed baking sheet with parchment paper.

2. In a large bowl, combine all the meatball ingredients and use your hands to squeeze the ingredients together.

3. Roll the mixture into 1-inch balls. Place them on the prepared baking sheet.

4. Bake for 20 minutes, turning the meatballs over halfway through. They don't need to be completely cooked, as they'll finish cooking in the sauce.

To make the sauce

5. In a large sauté pan, heat the olive oil over medium heat. Add the onion and cook for 3 minutes, until it starts to soften. Add the garlic and cook for 1 more minute.

6. Pour in the crushed tomatoes, wine, paprika, red pepper flakes, salt, and black pepper. Stir and bring to a boil, then reduce to a simmer.

7. Add the cooked meatballs to the sauce. Simmer over low heat for 20 to 30 minutes, until cooked through.

8. Serve the meatballs in the sauce, with toothpicks for easy transfer from plate to mouth.

PER SERVING:
CALORIES: 170; Total Fat: 11g; Saturated Fat: 3g; Protein: 11g; Total Carbohydrates: 6g; Fiber: 1g; Sugar: 2g; Cholesterol: 48mg

TOASTED POLENTA WITH MUSHROOMS

Serves 2 / Prep time: 10 minutes / Cook time: 15 minutes

Inspired by a savory Neapolitan dish, this hearty recipe pairs broiled firm polenta with sherried mushrooms for an unforgettable flavor and texture combination.

HEART HEALTH

6 (½-inch-thick) slices firm polenta (see Tip)

2 tablespoons extra-virgin olive oil, divided

10 ounces cremini mushrooms, sliced

Pinch salt

¼ cup cream sherry

2 garlic cloves, minced

Freshly ground black pepper

Chopped fresh flat-leaf parsley, for garnish

1 lemon, cut into wedges, for serving

1. Preheat the oven to broil. Line a rimmed baking sheet with aluminum foil.

2. Arrange the polenta in a single layer on the prepared baking sheet and brush on both sides with 1 tablespoon of olive oil. Broil for 2 to 3 minutes, just until the polenta turns golden, taking care not to let it burn.

3. Put the mushrooms in a skillet and add the salt and a few tablespoons of water. Sauté the mushrooms until they soften and release most of their liquid. Drain the mushrooms, then return them to the skillet.

4. Add the remaining 1 tablespoon of olive oil, the sherry, and garlic to the pan. Cook, stirring occasionally, for 8 to 10 minutes, until the mushrooms caramelize.

5. Arrange 3 slices of polenta on each serving plate. Top with a large spoonful of sherried mushrooms and a few grinds of pepper. Garnish with parsley and serve with a lemon wedge.

INGREDIENT TIP: You can find tubes of firm polenta in the pasta section of the supermarket.

PER SERVING:

CALORIES: 225; Total Fat: 14g; Saturated Fat: 2g; Protein: 7g; Total Carbohydrates: 25g; Fiber: 3g; Sugar: 6g; Cholesterol: 0mg

MOROCCAN SARDINES ON TOAST

Serves 2 / Prep time: 10 minutes / Cook time: 5 minutes

Sardines are an excellent source of protein and vitamin D, as well as omega-3 fatty acids, which are essential to heart health. Chermoula is a marinade and condiment used in Morocco and some other Mediterranean countries. Its fresh green flavor makes a perfect accompaniment to fish.

HEART HEALTH

For the chermoula

½ cup finely chopped fresh cilantro

½ cup finely chopped fresh flat-leaf parsley

2 garlic cloves, minced

1 teaspoon smoked paprika

½ teaspoon ground cumin

½ teaspoon salt

½ teaspoon freshly ground black pepper

¼ cup extra-virgin olive oil

For the sardines

1 tablespoon extra-virgin olive oil

1 garlic clove, minced

1 fresh red chile, seeded and minced

2 (4-ounce) cans oil-packed sardines, drained

1 tablespoon freshly squeezed lemon juice

4 multigrain bread slices, toasted

To make the chermoula

1. In a small bowl, stir together all the chermoula ingredients.

To prepare the sardines

2. In a skillet, heat the olive oil over medium heat. Add the garlic and chile and cook for about 1 minute, until fragrant. Add the sardines and lemon juice and cook just until heated through.

3. Serve the sardine mixture on the toast, with a dollop of chermoula on top.

MAKE-AHEAD TIP: You can make the chermoula ahead of time and store it in an airtight container in the refrigerator for up to 1 week.

PER SERVING:

CALORIES: 661; Total Fat: 47g; Saturated Fat: 7g; Protein: 30g; Total Carbohydrates: 31g; Fiber: 3g; Sugar: 4g; Cholesterol: 131mg

TUNISIAN BRIK PASTRIES

Serves 6 / Prep time: 15 minutes / Cook time: 10 minutes

Savory brik pastries are traditionally deep-fried, but they can also be baked for a lighter texture and flavor. The filling can range from meat, tuna, and eggs to potatoes and other vegetables. They are especially tasty served with harissa, a pepper-based hot sauce.

HEART HEALTH

3 (5-ounce) cans tuna in olive oil, drained

¼ cup finely chopped scallions

¼ cup chopped capers

¼ cup chopped fresh flat-leaf parsley

¼ cup extra-virgin olive oil

2 tablespoons Harissa (page 251), plus more for serving

¼ teaspoon freshly ground black pepper

6 sheets phyllo dough, thawed if frozen

1 large egg, beaten

1. Preheat the oven to 400°F. Line a rimmed baking sheet with parchment paper.

2. In a bowl, flake the tuna apart using a fork. Add the scallions, capers, parsley, olive oil, harissa, and black pepper. Mix well.

3. Cut the phyllo sheets lengthwise into strips about 4 inches wide.

4. Place ¼ cup of the tuna mixture on one end of a phyllo strip. Brush the opposite edge with beaten egg. Fold the dough over into a triangle, and continue folding over and over until you reach the end. Pinch the end with a bit of the egg mixture to seal. Repeat with the remaining tuna mixture and phyllo strips.

5. Arrange the pastries on the prepared baking sheet and bake for about 10 minutes, until golden.

6. Serve with additional harissa on the side for dipping.

COOKING TIP: You can use a sharp knife to cut the phyllo into strips, but a pizza cutter is even easier.

MAKE-AHEAD TIP: You can prepare the pastries several hours before baking. Cover the baking sheet with a kitchen towel and refrigerate for up to 4 hours.

PER SERVING:

CALORIES: 247; Total Fat: 15g; Saturated Fat: 2g; Protein: 16g; Total Carbohydrates: 11g; Fiber: 1g; Sugar: 0g; Cholesterol: 47mg

PANCETTA-WRAPPED SHRIMP

Serves 4 / Prep time: 10 minutes / Cook time: 15 minutes

Pancetta-wrapped shrimp are usually fried in olive oil, but they can also be baked for less mess and fewer calories. Here they are piled on a plate of sautéed onions for a sweet accompaniment.

OVERALL WELLNESS

2 tablespoons extra-virgin olive oil, plus more for brushing

2 small onions, thinly sliced

½ teaspoon salt

12 thin pancetta slices

12 large shrimp, peeled and deveined, tails left on

1. Preheat the oven to 400°F. Line a rimmed baking sheet with parchment paper.

2. In a small saucepan, heat the olive oil over medium heat. Add the onions and salt. Cover and cook, stirring occasionally, for 10 to 15 minutes, until soft and golden.

3. Meanwhile, wrap a slice of pancetta around each shrimp. Brush lightly with olive oil on both sides and place on the prepared baking sheet.

4. Bake for 10 to 12 minutes, until the shrimp are pink and opaque.

5. Scoop the onions onto each serving plate and top with the shrimp.

> **INGREDIENT TIP:** Pancetta is a type of salt-cured pork usually sold in cubes or thick slices. For this recipe, look for thinly sliced pancetta or ask your butcher to slice it.

PER SERVING:

CALORIES: 250; Total Fat: 19g; Saturated Fat: 5g; Protein: 15g; Total Carbohydrates: 4g; Fiber: 4g; Sugar: 1g; Cholesterol: 61mg

ARANCINI (ITALIAN STUFFED RICE BALLS)

Serves 4 / Prep time: 15 minutes / Cook time: 50 minutes

Arancini—stuffed rice balls coated in bread crumbs—originated in Sicily. These small balls are meant to resemble the shape of an orange ("arancia" in Italian). Traditionally, they are deep-fried, but baking can achieve a crispy exterior. I'll often make them when I have leftover risotto.

OVERALL WELLNESS

For the risotto

3 cups chicken or vegetable broth

3 cups water

2 tablespoons extra-virgin olive oil

1 shallot, finely chopped

1½ cups Arborio rice

¼ cup grated Parmesan cheese

For the arancini

Extra-virgin olive oil, for brushing

½ cup all-purpose flour

3 large eggs, beaten

½ cup bread crumbs

2 ounces Fontina cheese, cut into small cubes

To make the risotto

1. In a small saucepan, bring the broth to a gentle simmer. In another small saucepan, bring the water to a gentle simmer.

2. In a large saucepan, heat the olive oil over medium heat. Add the shallot and cook for about 3 minutes, until it starts to soften.

3. Add the rice and stir to coat with the oil. Cook for 1 minute.

4. Add 1 ladleful of hot broth and cook until it is absorbed into the rice, continuing to stir. Then add a ladleful of hot water and cook until it is absorbed. Keep alternating these liquids until the rice is cooked through and takes on a creamy consistency, about 20 minutes total.

5. Stir in the cheese, then let cool completely.

To make the arancini

6. Preheat the oven to 425°F. Line a rimmed baking sheet with parchment paper and brush lightly with olive oil.

7. Prepare three small bowls: one with the flour, one with the beaten eggs, and one with the bread crumbs.

8. Scoop up enough cooled risotto to form a 1-inch ball.

9. Press a cube of Fontina in the center and form the risotto around it.

10. Roll the ball in the flour, then dip it in the eggs to coat. Roll the ball in the bread crumbs. Place on the prepared baking sheet. Repeat with the remaining ingredients.

11. Bake for about 25 minutes, until golden.

MAKE-AHEAD TIP: You can form the arancini up to 3 days in advance, cover, and refrigerate until ready to bake.

VARIATION TIP: Serve with Roasted Tomato Sauce with Pasta (page 131), Basil Pesto with Almond Butter (page 256), or Romesco Sauce (page 249).

PER SERVING:

CALORIES: 412; Total Fat: 14g; Saturated Fat: 5g; Protein: 14g; Total Carbohydrates: 55g; Fiber: 2g; Sugar: 1g; Cholesterol: 115mg

SPICY LAMB MEATBALLS

Serves 6 / Prep time: 20 minutes / Cook time: 30 minutes

Lamb is the red meat of choice in Greece. The spiciness of these baked meatballs contrasts beautifully with the coolness of the yogurt dipping sauce, making for a light but richly flavored dish.

OVERALL WELLNESS

For the meatballs

Extra-virgin olive oil, for brushing

1 pound ground lamb

1 hot pork sausage, casing removed

¾ cup bread crumbs

½ onion, diced

1 large egg

1 tablespoon chopped fresh flat-leaf parsley

1 teaspoon dried oregano

1 teaspoon salt

½ teaspoon dried basil

½ teaspoon freshly ground black pepper

For the dipping sauce

1 cup low-fat plain Greek yogurt

¼ cup crumbled feta cheese

2 tablespoons extra-virgin olive oil

1 tablespoon freshly squeezed lemon juice

1 teaspoon chopped fresh mint

1 teaspoon chopped fresh dill

To make the meatballs

1. Preheat the oven to 375°F. Line a rimmed baking sheet with parchment paper and lightly brush with olive oil.

2. In a bowl, combine all the meatball ingredients. Use your hands to mix well.

3. Scoop out a little lamb mixture, roll it into a 1-inch ball, and place it on the prepared baking sheet. Repeat with the remaining lamb mixture.

4. Bake for 25 to 30 minutes, until cooked through.

To make the dipping sauce

5. In a small bowl, combine all the dipping sauce ingredients. Stir well, until the olive oil disappears into the yogurt.

6. Serve the meatballs with toothpicks and a bowl of the dipping sauce.

PER SERVING:

CALORIES: 329; Total Fat: 21g; Saturated Fat: 7g; Protein: 22g; Total Carbohydrates: 14g; Fiber: 1g; Sugar: 5g; Cholesterol: 90mg

QUINOA AND CHEESE STUFFED MUSHROOMS

Serves 6 / Prep time: 10 minutes / Cook time: 30 minutes

The earthiness of mushrooms pairs well with feta and the mild nutty flavor of quinoa. Quinoa is a nutrition superfood as well as a gluten-free source of protein.

HEART HEALTH

2 tablespoons extra-virgin olive oil, plus more for brushing

¼ cup quinoa

½ red bell pepper, finely chopped

1 small shallot, minced

10 ounces large cremini mushrooms, stems and caps separated

¼ cup crumbled feta cheese

1 teaspoon fresh thyme leaves

½ teaspoon ground cumin

¼ teaspoon salt

Chopped fresh mint, for garnish

1. Preheat the oven to 375°F. Line a rimmed baking sheet with parchment paper and lightly brush it with olive oil.

2. In a small saucepan, cook the quinoa according to package directions. Allow to cool.

3. Meanwhile, in a skillet, heat the olive oil over medium heat. Add the bell pepper and shallot and cook for about 15 minutes, until softened.

4. Transfer the shallot mixture to a food processor and add the mushroom stems, feta, thyme, cumin, and salt. Process until well chopped but not a paste.

5. Transfer the mixture to a medium bowl and stir in the cooked quinoa.

6. Spoon the mixture into the mushroom caps. Arrange them on the prepared baking sheet.

7. Bake for 10 to 15 minutes, until tender.

8. Garnish with mint.

VARIATION TIP: You can vary the quinoa stuffing with a variety of ingredients. Try onions, scallions, nuts, different herbs, hot peppers, sun-dried tomatoes, or spinach.

MAKE-AHEAD TIP: The mushrooms can be stuffed a day in advance. Cover and refrigerate, then pop them in the oven when you're ready to eat.

PER SERVING:

CALORIES: 97; Total Fat: 6g; Saturated Fat: 2g; Protein: 3g; Total Carbohydrates: 7g; Fiber: 1g; Sugar: 2g; Cholesterol: 6mg

eight

VEGETABLES

Herb-Roasted Potatoes with Shallots 104

Mediterranean Stuffed Peppers 105

Red Swiss Chard with White Beans 106

Roasted Beets with Oregano and Red Pepper 107

Roasted Root Vegetables 108

Ciambotta (Neapolitan Ratatouille) 109

Broccoli Rabe with Red Pepper Flakes 110

Stuffed Tomatoes 111

Eggplant Towers 112

Collard Green Wraps 113

Sautéed Bitter Greens with Fennel 114

Asparagus with Herbs 115

Mushrooms Parmigiana 116

Spicy Roasted Carrots 117

Green Beans with Prosciutto 118

Peas with Pancetta 119

Celery Root with Yogurt Sauce 120

Vegetable Cassola 121

Eggplant "Meatballs" 122

Roasted Acorn Squash with Sage and Pistachios 123

Vegetable Bulgur 125

Sweet Potato Cakes 126

Green Bean Fritters 127

Roasted Root Vegetables, p. 108

HERB-ROASTED POTATOES WITH SHALLOTS

Serves 4 / Prep time: 10 minutes / Cook time: 15 minutes

White potatoes have their place in a Mediterranean diet; they are a healthy and all-natural source of carbohydrates, vitamins, and minerals. Roasted shallots amp up the flavor of this simple dish.

OVERALL WELLNESS

¼ cup extra-virgin olive oil, plus more for brushing

2 large russet potatoes, peeled and cut into 1-inch cubes

1 teaspoon salt

½ teaspoon garlic powder

½ teaspoon smoked paprika

½ teaspoon dried oregano

¼ teaspoon dried rosemary

¼ teaspoon dried thyme

¼ teaspoon red pepper flakes (optional)

2 or 3 shallots, cut into large chunks

1. Preheat the oven to 425°F. Line a rimmed baking sheet with aluminum foil and brush with olive oil.

2. In a large bowl, toss the potatoes with the olive oil, salt, garlic powder, paprika, oregano, rosemary, thyme, and red pepper flakes (if using).

3. Pour the potatoes onto the baking sheet and spread out in a single layer. Scatter the shallots around the potatoes.

4. Bake for 15 to 20 minutes, until everything looks golden brown with crispy edges.

PER SERVING:

CALORIES: 271; Total Fat: 14g; Saturated Fat: 2g; Protein: 4g; Total Carbohydrates: 35g; Fiber: 3g; Sugar: 2g; Cholesterol: 0mg

MEDITERRANEAN STUFFED PEPPERS

Serves 4 / Prep time: 20 minutes / Cook time: 30 minutes

Most recipes for stuffed peppers include ground beef and rice. Here the meat is replaced with seasoned beans and the rice with orzo for a tasty vegetarian take. Serve the peppers with Roasted Tomato Sauce with Pasta (page 131).

WEIGHT LOSS

2 tablespoons extra-virgin olive oil, plus more for brushing

4 large bell peppers (any color)

1 cup orzo

1 (15-ounce) can cannellini beans, rinsed and drained

1 teaspoon Italian Herb Blend (page 262)

2 teaspoon seasoned bread crumbs

1. Preheat the oven to 400°F. Brush a round cake pan or other small baking pan with a light coating of olive oil.

2. Remove the stems and cut a hole in the top of each pepper. Remove all the seeds and ribs inside.

3. Bring a large pot of water to a boil over high heat and add the peppers. Boil for 10 minutes, until softened but still firm. Drain.

4. Meanwhile, cook the orzo according to package directions. Drain and set aside.

5. In a bowl, toss the beans with the Italian herb blend.

6. Stand the peppers in the prepared cake pan. Stuff each pepper with alternating layers of the orzo and bean mixture, filling them all the way up to the top.

7. Sprinkle the bread crumbs over the opening at the top of each pepper. Drizzle the olive oil over the peppers.

8. Bake for 15 to 20 minutes, until the tops start to brown.

> **INGREDIENT TIP:** When grocery shopping, try to choose peppers that have a flat bottom so they will stand up in the pan. Otherwise, you can slice off a tiny bit of the bottom as needed, taking care not to make a hole.

PER SERVING:

CALORIES: 402; Total Fat: 8g; Saturated Fat: 1g; Protein: 12g; Total Carbohydrates: 70g; Fiber: 10g; Sugar: 7g; Cholesterol: 0mg

RED SWISS CHARD WITH WHITE BEANS

Serves 2 / Prep time: 10 minutes / Cook time: 15 minutes

Red Swiss chard has a vibrant color and a mild flavor that pairs well with protein-rich white beans. Be sure to include both the red stems and tender green leaves in this energy-boosting dish.

HEART HEALTH

1 (15-ounce) can cannellini beans, undrained

1 tablespoon extra-virgin olive oil

1 bunch red Swiss chard, stems and leaves cut into 1-inch pieces and kept separate

1 small tomato, chopped

1 garlic clove, minced

Pinch salt

Pinch freshly ground black pepper

1. Pour the cannellini beans and their liquid into a small saucepan. Bring to a boil over medium heat, then reduce to a simmer.

2. Meanwhile, in a skillet, heat the olive oil over medium heat. Add a splash of water and the chard stems, cover, and cook until they start to soften, about 5 minutes.

3. Add the tomato and garlic to the chard stems and cook for 1 minute, uncovered, then add the chard leaves, salt, and pepper. Cook until the leaves wilt, about 3 minutes more.

4. Drain the beans and add them to the chard mixture. Cook for 2 minutes, until just blended.

PER SERVING:

CALORIES: 303; Total Fat: 8g; Saturated Fat: 1g; Protein: 17g; Total Carbohydrates: 44g; Fiber: 13g; Sugar: 3g; Cholesterol: 0mg

ROASTED BEETS WITH OREGANO AND RED PEPPER

Serves 4 / Prep time: 15 minutes / Cook time: 40 minutes

Roasted red beets are a sweet treat, but also high in nutrients and low in calories. Red pepper flakes wake up their flavor and elevate them to an elegant side dish.

HEART HEALTH

3 large red beets, peeled and cut into 1-inch cubes

¼ cup extra-virgin olive oil

1 teaspoon salt

1 tablespoon dried oregano

1 teaspoon red pepper flakes

1. Preheat the oven to 400°F. Line a rimmed baking sheet with parchment paper or aluminum foil.

2. In a large bowl, toss the beets with the olive oil and salt to coat.

3. Arrange the beets in a single layer on the prepared baking sheet. Sprinkle evenly with the oregano and red pepper flakes.

4. Bake for about 40 minutes, tossing once with a spatula, until the beets are soft.

INGREDIENT TIP: Beet greens are also highly nutritious. Save them for another day to add to a salad or vegetable soup.

COOKING TIP: Red beets can stain easily, so don't wear your best clothes while preparing them!

PER SERVING:

CALORIES: 173; Total Fat: 14g; Saturated Fat: 2g; Protein: 2g; Total Carbohydrates: 12g; Fiber: 4g; Sugar: 8g; Cholesterol: 0mg

ROASTED ROOT VEGETABLES

Serves 4 / Prep time: 15 minutes / Cook time: 45 minutes

Roasted root vegetables make a classic side dish that works well with chicken, fish, or meat, or you can serve them over steamed rice for a vegetarian feast. Choose from among the vegetables listed below to create the medley of your liking. The more you include, the more nutrients you get to ingest.

HEART HEALTH

10 small fingerling potatoes in various colors, cut into 1-inch pieces

3 large carrots, cut into 1-inch pieces

2 turnips, peeled and cut into 1-inch pieces

1 rutabaga, peeled and cut into 1-inch pieces

2 parsnips, cut into 1-inch pieces

1 sweet potato, cut into 1-inch pieces

½ cup frozen pearl onions

¼ cup extra-virgin olive oil

1 teaspoon salt

½ teaspoon freshly ground black pepper

Several thyme sprigs

1. Preheat the oven to 425°F. Line a rimmed baking sheet with aluminum foil.

2. In a large bowl, combine the potatoes, carrots, turnips, rutabaga, parsnips, sweet potato, and pearl onions. Add the olive oil, salt, and pepper and toss to coat. Arrange in a single layer on the prepared baking sheet. (Use two baking sheets if necessary to prevent crowding.)

3. Add the thyme sprigs, tucking them underneath the vegetables so they don't burn.

4. Bake for 40 to 45 minutes, tossing once halfway through cooking, until the vegetables are tender.

5. Discard the thyme before serving.

COOKING TIP: Store any leftovers in an airtight container in the refrigerator for up to 3 days.

PER SERVING:

CALORIES: 540; Total Fat: 14g; Saturated Fat: 2g; Protein: 10g; Total Carbohydrates: 97g; Fiber: 17g; Sugar: 17g; Cholesterol: 0mg

CIAMBOTTA (NEAPOLITAN RATATOUILLE)

Serves 4 / Prep time: 15 minutes / Cook time: 1 hour

This vegetable dish is from Naples in southern Italy. It's a rustic Italian version of French ratatouille, with which it shares many flavors. Ciambotta is best made in the summer, when the ingredients reach their peak flavor. It can be served hot or cold.

WEIGHT LOSS

¼ cup extra-virgin olive oil

2 onions, diced

2 garlic cloves, sliced

2 russet potatoes, peeled and cut into 1-inch cubes

2 bell peppers, seeded and cut into 1-inch squares

2 eggplants, cut into 1-inch cubes

3 tomatoes, chopped

2 zucchini, cut into ½-inch slices

1 teaspoon salt

Chopped fresh basil leaves, for garnish

1. In a large, deep skillet or saucepan, heat the olive oil over medium-low heat. Add the onions and cook for 5 to 10 minutes, until soft.

2. Add the garlic and cook for about 1 minute, until fragrant. Add the potatoes and cook for 10 minutes.

3. Add the bell peppers and eggplant and cook for 10 minutes more.

4. Finally, add the tomatoes and zucchini. Sprinkle with the salt and bring to a simmer.

5. Cover, reduce the heat to low, and simmer until all the vegetables are very soft, about 30 minutes. Check occasionally to make sure the vegetables aren't drying out. If necessary, add some water.

6. Garnish with fresh basil.

MAKE-AHEAD TIP: This dish can be kept for up to 3 days in an airtight container in the refrigerator, where its flavors will continue to intensify.

COOKING TIP: If possible, cut all the vegetables to about the same size so they cook at the same rate.

PER SERVING:

CALORIES: 400; Total Fat: 15g; Saturated Fat: 2g; Protein: 9g; Total Carbohydrates: 64g; Fiber: 14g; Sugar: 16g; Cholesterol: 0mg

BROCCOLI RABE WITH RED PEPPER FLAKES

Serves 2 / Prep time: 5 minutes / Cook time: 10 minutes

Broccoli rabe, also known as rapini, is a cruciferous vegetable that is similar to broccoli in flavor. Red pepper flakes complement its mild bitterness by adding a subtle amount of heat. This classic side dish hails from southern Italy.

HEART HEALTH

1 pound broccoli rabe, thick stems trimmed

2 tablespoons extra-virgin olive oil

1 garlic clove, minced

Salt

Freshly ground black pepper

¼ teaspoon red pepper flakes

1. Bring a large pot of water to a boil over high heat. Add the broccoli rabe and cook for 3 minutes. Drain. When cool enough to handle, cut the broccoli rabe into bite-size pieces.

2. In a large skillet, heat the olive oil over medium heat. Add the broccoli rabe and garlic, season with salt and black pepper, and cook for 4 to 5 minutes, until tender.

3. Sprinkle the red pepper flakes over the top of the dish just before serving.

PER SERVING:

CALORIES: 171; Total Fat: 15g; Saturated Fat: 2g; Protein: 7g; Total Carbohydrates: 7g; Fiber: 6g; Sugar: 1g; Cholesterol: 0mg

STUFFED TOMATOES

Serves 2 / Prep time: 20 minutes

This salad is big on taste and presentation. A big, juicy red tomato is filled with tuna salad, surrounded by colorful vegetables, and topped with Greek vinaigrette.

WEIGHT LOSS

For the tomatoes

2 large tomatoes

2 (5-ounce) cans tuna in olive oil, drained

1 celery stalk, diced

½ small onion, diced

2 tablespoons mayonnaise or vegan mayonnaise

1 bell pepper (any color), seeded and sliced

½ cucumber, peeled and sliced

½ red onion, sliced

2 large eggs, hard-boiled, peeled, and halved

¼ cup pitted kalamata olives

¼ cup crumbled feta cheese

For the dressing

¼ cup extra-virgin olive oil

2 tablespoons red wine vinegar

Juice of 1 lemon

½ teaspoon dried oregano

½ teaspoon salt

¼ teaspoon freshly ground black pepper

¼ teaspoon dried mint

To prepare the tomatoes

1. With a sharp knife, cut each tomato into wedges from the top without cutting all the way through to the base. It should open like a flower.

2. In a bowl, combine the tuna, celery, onion, and mayonnaise. Fill each tomato with the tuna mixture.

3. Place a stuffed tomato in the center of each plate. Arrange the bell pepper, cucumber, red onion, eggs, olives, and feta cheese around the sides.

To make the dressing

4. In a small bowl, whisk together all the dressing ingredients.

5. Drizzle the dressing on the bell pepper, cucumber, red onion, eggs, and olives, or serve it on the side for dipping.

MAKE-AHEAD TIP: You can make the dressing and the tuna salad up to 3 days in advance to reduce prep time before serving. Store in separate airtight containers in the refrigerator.

VARIATION TIP: You can also fill the tomato with chicken salad, egg salad, hummus, or cooked whole grains.

PER SERVING:

CALORIES: 716; Total Fat: 52g; Saturated Fat: 11g; Protein: 43g; Total Carbohydrates: 20g; Fiber: 5g; Sugar: 8g; Cholesterol: 223mg

EGGPLANT TOWERS

Serves 4 / Prep time: 15 minutes / Cook time: 55 minutes

Eggplant towers are fun to eat and look beautiful on a plate. Serve them as a light meal or a hearty appetizer.

HEART HEALTH

2 medium eggplants

¼ cup extra-virgin olive oil

1 teaspoon salt

1 (8-ounce) can tomato sauce

1 tablespoon dried oregano

1 cup shredded mozzarella cheese

1 cup bread crumbs

16 fresh basil leaves

¼ cup grated Parmesan cheese

1. Preheat the oven to 375°F. Line a rimmed baking sheet with parchment paper.

2. Slice the eggplants crosswise into ¼- to ½-inch-thick slices; you should get 10 to 12 slices per eggplant.

3. Brush the eggplant slices on both sides with the olive oil and arrange in a single layer on the prepared baking sheet. Sprinkle with the salt.

4. Bake for 20 minutes. Flip each slice over and bake for another 15 minutes, or until tender and starting to brown.

5. Meanwhile, in a saucepan, combine the tomato sauce and oregano and keep warm over low heat.

6. To build each eggplant tower, place an eggplant slice on the baking sheet. Top with 1 tablespoon tomato sauce, 1 tablespoon mozzarella, 1 teaspoon bread crumbs, and 1 basil leaf. Place another eggplant slice on top and repeat the layers until the stack is 5 or 6 slices high. Form 4 stacks, leaving an inch between them.

7. Top each tower with 1 tablespoon grated Parmesan.

8. Bake for 20 minutes, until the cheese has melted.

INGREDIENT TIP: Try to find eggplants that are not extremely wide at the bottom.

PER SERVING:

CALORIES: 418; Total Fat: 23g; Saturated Fat: 7g; Protein: 15g; Total Carbohydrates: 40g; Fiber: 10g; Sugar: 14g; Cholesterol: 27mg

COLLARD GREEN WRAPS

Serves 2 / Prep time: 10 minutes / Cook time: 40 minutes

Collards have sturdy leaves that can be used in place of any wrap for a healthy way to creatively use up leftovers such as rice and vegetables. In this recipe, they are stuffed with beets and beans and baked in tomato sauce.

OVERALL WELLNESS

4 large collard green leaves

1 (15-ounce) can cannellini beans, rinsed and drained

1 cup Roasted Beets with Oregano and Red Pepper (page 107)

1 teaspoon salt, divided

½ teaspoon freshly ground black pepper

1 (8-ounce) can tomato sauce

1. Preheat the oven to 350°F.

2. Bring a large pot of water to a boil over high heat. Fill a large bowl with ice cubes and water. Add the collard greens to the boiling water and blanch for 3 minutes, then remove with tongs or a strainer and immediately plunge into the ice bath. Drain and pat dry.

3. In a bowl, combine the cannellini beans and roasted beets. Toss well and season with ½ teaspoon of salt and the pepper.

4. Lay the collard greens out flat. Fill each with the beet and bean mixture and roll them up, tucking in the sides.

5. Spread the tomato sauce in the bottom of a 2-quart (11 × 7 × 1.5 inch) baking dish. Place the wraps, seam-side down, on top of the tomato sauce. Sprinkle the remaining ½ teaspoon of salt over the top.

6. Bake for 30 minutes, then serve with some tomato sauce spooned over the top.

PER SERVING:

CALORIES: 304; Total Fat: 2g; Saturated Fat: 0g; Protein: 20g; Total Carbohydrates: 57g; Fiber: 17g; Sugar: 12g; Cholesterol: 0mg

SAUTÉED BITTER GREENS WITH FENNEL

Serves 4 / Prep time: 10 minutes / Cook time: 15 minutes

Bitter leafy greens are packed with immune-boosting nutrients. Mixed with sweet, sautéed fennel, they make a healthy lunch or side dish.

HEART HEALTH

2 tablespoons extra-virgin olive oil, divided

1 fennel bulb, trimmed, cored, and sliced

4 cups chopped mustard greens

2 cups chopped dandelion greens

1 cup chopped radicchio

½ teaspoon salt

¼ teaspoon red pepper flakes

1. In a large skillet, heat 1 tablespoon of olive oil over medium heat. Add the fennel and cook for 10 minutes, until tender.

2. Add the mustard greens, dandelion greens, radicchio, and the remaining 1 tablespoon of olive oil. Stir to coat the greens in the oil. Cook for about 5 minutes, until wilted.

3. Stir in the salt and red pepper flakes.

PER SERVING:

CALORIES: 108; Total Fat: 7g; Saturated Fat: 1g; Protein: 3g; Total Carbohydrates: 10g; Fiber: 5g; Sugar: 3g; Cholesterol: 0mg

ASPARAGUS WITH HERBS

Serves 4 / Prep time: 10 minutes / Cook time: 10 minutes

Asparagus is at its peak in the springtime. Look for firm, bright-green stalks with green or purplish tips. With this simple recipe, you can have a nutritious vegetable side dish on the table in minutes. Asparagus pairs well with seafood dishes, especially shrimp and scallops.

WEIGHT LOSS

2 tablespoons extra-virgin olive oil, plus more for brushing

1 garlic clove, minced

1 teaspoon Italian Herb Blend (page 262)

½ teaspoon salt

¼ teaspoon freshly ground black pepper

1 pound asparagus, trimmed

2 tablespoons chopped fresh flat-leaf parsley

1. Preheat the oven to 425°F. Line a rimmed baking sheet with parchment paper and lightly brush with olive oil.

2. In a small bowl, whisk together the olive oil, garlic, Italian herb blend, salt, and pepper.

3. Spread out the asparagus stalks in a single layer on the prepared baking sheet. Drizzle the olive oil mixture over the asparagus and roll them around to coat.

4. Roast for about 10 minutes, until the asparagus stalks are tender and the tips are lightly browned.

5. Sprinkle with the parsley.

INGREDIENT TIP: An easy way to trim asparagus is to bend the bottom of each stalk until it snaps, then discard the woody bottoms.

PER SERVING:

CALORIES: 84; Total Fat: 7g; Saturated Fat: 1g; Protein: 3g; Total Carbohydrates: 5g; Fiber: 3g; Sugar: 2g; Cholesterol: 0mg

MUSHROOMS PARMIGIANA

Serves 4 / Prep time: 15 minutes / Cook time: 25 minutes

Mushrooms are an excellent source of vitamin D. This recipe is a clever alternative to eggplant parmigiana, and the results go well with a side of pasta.

WEIGHT LOSS

1 pound large cremini mushrooms, stemmed

1 (28-ounce) can crushed tomatoes

1 tablespoon Italian Herb Blend (page 262)

1 teaspoon salt

½ teaspoon freshly ground black pepper

1 cup shredded Fontina cheese

2 tablespoons bread crumbs

1 teaspoon dried oregano

Chopped fresh basil, for garnish

1. Preheat the oven to 375°F.

2. Put the mushrooms in a large, deep skillet and add a few tablespoons of water. Cook over low heat for about 5 minutes, until they start to soften and release their liquid. Drain.

3. In a bowl, combine the crushed tomatoes and Italian herb blend. Spread one-third of the sauce in the bottom of a 3-quart baking dish. Arrange half of the mushrooms in a single layer on top of the sauce. Sprinkle with the salt and pepper.

4. Spoon one-half of the remaining tomato sauce over the mushrooms and top with half of the Fontina. Repeat with the remaining mushrooms, tomato sauce, and cheese.

5. Sprinkle the top evenly with the bread crumbs and oregano.

6. Bake for 15 to 20 minutes, depending on the size of the mushrooms. The cheese should be browned and bubbling.

7. Garnish with fresh basil.

> **INGREDIENT TIP:** You can substitute portobello mushrooms for the large cremini mushrooms called for here. Try to choose mushrooms of a similar size so they will cook at the same rate.

PER SERVING:

CALORIES: 227; Total Fat: 11g; Saturated Fat: 6g; Protein: 15g; Total Carbohydrates: 21g; Fiber: 5g; Sugar: 11g; Cholesterol: 38mg

SPICY ROASTED CARROTS

Serves 6 / Prep time: 10 minutes / Cook time: 20 minutes

Carrots are full of nutrients yet low in calories. Roasting carrots emphasizes their natural sweetness, and the Moroccan spices add earthiness and depth.

HEART HEALTH

2 tablespoons extra-virgin olive oil, plus more for brushing

1 tablespoon light brown sugar

1 teaspoon smoked paprika

1 teaspoon ground cumin

¼ teaspoon ground cinnamon

¼ teaspoon cayenne pepper

¼ teaspoon salt

1 pound carrots, cut into 2-inch pieces

½ cup chopped fresh cilantro

1. Preheat the oven to 450°F. Line a rimmed baking sheet with aluminum foil and brush with olive oil.

2. In a bowl, whisk together the olive oil, brown sugar, smoked paprika, cumin, cinnamon, cayenne, and salt. Add the carrots and toss to coat.

3. Spread out the carrots in a single layer on the prepared baking sheet. Cover with a second sheet of foil.

4. Roast the carrots for 10 minutes. Remove the top layer of foil, stir the carrots, and roast for another 10 minutes, uncovered, or until fork-tender and browned.

5. Transfer the carrots to a serving dish and sprinkle with the cilantro.

PER SERVING:

CALORIES: 80; Total Fat: 5g; Saturated Fat: 1g; Protein: 1g; Total Carbohydrates: 9g; Fiber: 2g; Sugar: 5g; Cholesterol: 0mg

GREEN BEANS WITH PROSCIUTTO

Serves 4 / Prep time: 10 minutes / Cook time: 10 minutes

This classic Italian vegetable dish uses meat as a flavoring instead of as the star of the meal. The shallot adds depth of flavor while the red pepper flakes bring a little heat.

OVERALL WELLNESS

1 pound green beans, trimmed

¼ cup water

2 tablespoons extra-virgin olive oil

4 prosciutto slices, torn into small pieces

1 small shallot, chopped

½ teaspoon salt

¼ teaspoon red pepper flakes

1. In a large skillet, combine the beans and water. Cover and cook over medium heat for 5 minutes, until the beans begin to soften. Drain the beans in a colander.

2. In the same skillet, heat the olive oil over medium heat. Add the prosciutto and cook for about 2 minutes, until crispy. Transfer the prosciutto to a paper towel, leaving the excess oil in the pan.

3. Add the shallot to the skillet and cook until soft. You may need to add a little more olive oil if there is not enough fat left over from the prosciutto.

4. Add the steamed green beans, salt, and red pepper flakes and toss to combine. Cook for 2 minutes to blend the flavors together.

5. Served the green beans topped with the crispy prosciutto.

MAKE-AHEAD TIP: You can steam the green beans in advance. They'll keep in an airtight container in the refrigerator for up to 2 days.

PER SERVING:

CALORIES: 120; Total Fat: 8g; Saturated Fat: 1g; Protein: 6g; Total Carbohydrates: 8g; Fiber: 3g; Sugar: 4g; Cholesterol: 9mg

PEAS WITH PANCETTA

Serves 4 / Prep time: 5 minutes / Cook time: 15 minutes

The delicate flavor of shallots perfectly complements the sweetness of the peas in this classic Italian side dish. This recipe is great for busy nights because it is ready in a matter of minutes.

OVERALL WELLNESS

1 tablespoon extra-virgin olive oil

2 ounces pancetta, cut into ¼-inch cubes

1 shallot, thinly sliced

12 ounces frozen peas

1 teaspoon salt

½ teaspoon freshly ground black pepper

¼ teaspoon red pepper flakes (optional)

1. In a large skillet, heat the olive oil over medium heat. Add the pancetta and cook for about 3 minutes, until it starts to brown and release its fat.

2. Add the shallot and cook for about 5 minutes, until the pancetta is heated through and the shallot is tender.

3. Add the peas, salt, black pepper, and red pepper flakes (if using) and continue to cook for about 5 minutes, until the peas are fully warmed through.

PER SERVING:

CALORIES: 207; Total Fat: 15g; Saturated Fat: 5g; Protein: 5g; Total Carbohydrates: 13g; Fiber: 4g; Sugar: 5g; Cholesterol: 4mg

CELERY ROOT WITH YOGURT SAUCE

Serves 6 / Prep time: 10 minutes / Cook time: 40 minutes

Celery root, also known as celeriac, is a tasty vegetable commonly used in Mediterranean cooking. It can be mashed, used in soups and stews, or roasted, as here.

WEIGHT LOSS

2 celery roots, peeled and cut into ½-inch-thick slices

¼ cup extra-virgin olive oil

1 teaspoon salt

½ teaspoon freshly ground black pepper

1 cup low-fat plain Greek yogurt

½ teaspoon grated lemon zest

2 teaspoons freshly squeezed lemon juice

½ teaspoon fresh thyme leaves

Pinch cayenne pepper

Chopped fresh cilantro, for garnish

1. Preheat the oven to 425°F. Line a rimmed baking sheet with aluminum foil.

2. In a large bowl, toss the celery root with the olive oil, salt, and black pepper.

3. Spread out the celery root in a single layer on the prepared baking sheet and roast for 20 minutes. Flip the slices and continue to roast for another 15 to 20 minutes, until tender and golden.

4. In a small bowl, combine the yogurt, lemon zest, lemon juice, thyme, and cayenne. Garnish with cilantro and serve as a dipping sauce for the celery root.

PER SERVING:

CALORIES: 108; Total Fat: 10g; Saturated Fat: 2g; Protein: 2g; Total Carbohydrates: 3g; Fiber: 4g; Sugar: 3g; Cholesterol: 2mg

VEGETABLE CASSOLA

Serves 4 / Prep time: 15 minutes / Cook time: 1 hour 15 minutes

This stew is from Sardinia, an Italian island in the Mediterranean Sea, known for its pristine beaches and rugged mountains. In its beach communities, you'll find cassola made with seafood. In the mountains, however, it's prepared with vegetables and makes for a hearty meal.

WEIGHT LOSS

¼ cup extra-virgin olive oil

1 red bell pepper, seeded and chopped

1 yellow bell pepper, seeded and chopped

1 large onion, chopped

2 carrots, thinly sliced

1 eggplant, cut into ½-inch cubes

1 zucchini, cut into ½-inch cubes

6 oil-packed sun-dried tomatoes, drained and chopped

¼ cup dry white wine

1 teaspoon dried oregano

3 thyme sprigs

2 bay leaves

2 tablespoons chopped fresh flat-leaf parsley

1 teaspoon chopped fresh mint

1. Preheat the oven to 350°F.

2. In a large ovenproof skillet, heat the olive oil over medium heat. Add the bell peppers and onion and cook for 10 to 15 minutes, until softened.

3. Add the carrots, eggplant, zucchini, sun-dried tomatoes, white wine, and oregano and toss to combine. Add the thyme sprigs and bay leaves.

4. Cover the skillet, transfer to the oven, and bake for 1 hour. Check periodically to make sure it isn't drying out; you can add water if necessary.

5. Discard the thyme sprigs and bay leaves. Garnish with the parsley and mint.

PER SERVING:
CALORIES: 233; Total Fat: 15g; Saturated Fat: 2g; Protein: 4g; Total Carbohydrates: 22g; Fiber: 7g; Sugar: 10g; Cholesterol: 0mg

EGGPLANT "MEATBALLS"

Serves 4 / Prep time: 15 minutes, plus 30 minutes to chill / Cook time: 1 hour

These eggplant "meatballs" are especially tasty with tomato sauce and are a nutritious and light addition to pasta. Try them with your next spaghetti meal.

WEIGHT LOSS

2 tablespoons extra-virgin olive oil, plus more for brushing

1 large eggplant, cut into 1-inch pieces

1 teaspoon salt

½ teaspoon freshly ground black pepper

1 medium onion, chopped

1 garlic clove, minced

1 cup canned or cooked cannellini beans

1 cup bread crumbs

¼ cup chopped fresh flat-leaf parsley

1 large egg

Pinch red pepper flakes (optional)

1. In a large skillet, heat the olive oil over low heat. Add the eggplant, salt, and black pepper and toss to coat in the oil. Cover and cook for 20 minutes, until the eggplant softens.

2. Add the onion and garlic and cook, uncovered, for about 5 minutes, until softened. Remove the pan from the heat and set aside to cool slightly.

3. Once cool, transfer the eggplant mixture to a food processor. Add the beans and pulse just until roughly mixed. Be careful not to puree.

4. Transfer the mixture to a bowl and stir in the bread crumbs, parsley, egg, and red pepper flakes (if using). Mix by hand or with a spatula, adding more bread crumbs if needed to absorb moisture. Cover and refrigerate for 30 minutes.

5. Preheat the oven to 375°F. Brush a rimmed baking sheet with olive oil.

6. Roll the eggplant mixture into 1-inch balls.

7. Place the eggplant meatballs on the prepared baking sheet with a little space between them. Bake for 30 to 40 minutes, until firm and cooked through.

PER SERVING:

CALORIES: 288; Total Fat: 10g; Saturated Fat: 2g; Protein: 11g; Total Carbohydrates: 41g; Fiber: 9g; Sugar: 8g; Cholesterol: 47mg

ROASTED ACORN SQUASH WITH SAGE AND PISTACHIOS

Serves 6 / Prep time: 10 minutes / Cook time: 40 minutes

Acorn squash has a slightly sweet flavor that mixes well in this recipe with cinnamon and sage, plus a bit of heat from the cayenne and the crunch of pistachios. Squash is low in calories and an excellent source of B vitamins as well as vitamins A and C.

WEIGHT LOSS

2 large acorn squash

¼ cup extra-virgin olive oil

1 teaspoon salt

¼ teaspoon cayenne pepper

¼ teaspoon ground cinnamon

12 fresh sage leaves

¼ cup chopped pistachios

1. Preheat the oven to 450°F. Line a rimmed baking sheet with aluminum foil.

2. Cut each squash in half lengthwise. Scoop out the seeds and discard them. Cut each half into 5 wedges, keeping the skin on.

3. In a large bowl, toss the squash wedges with the olive oil, salt, cayenne, and cinnamon.

4. Arrange the squash wedges in a single layer on the prepared baking sheet. Scatter the whole sage leaves across the top.

5. Roast for 35 to 40 minutes, until the squash is tender and cooked through.

6. Sprinkle the pistachios on top.

PER SERVING:

CALORIES: 166; Total Fat: 11g; Saturated Fat: 1g; Protein: 2g; Total Carbohydrates: 16g; Fiber: 3g; Sugar: 0g; Cholesterol: 0mg

VEGETABLE BULGUR

Serves 6 / Prep time: 35 minutes, plus 1 hour to chill / Cook time: 15 minutes

This colorful salad becomes a hearty meal with the addition of bulgur. A combination of sautéed and fresh vegetables offers varying textures, all brought together with a light Greek dressing.

HEART HEALTH

2½ cups water

2 cups bulgur

2 tablespoons extra-virgin olive oil

1 small red onion, finely chopped

1 cup halved cherry tomatoes

1 yellow bell pepper, seeded and chopped

1 cucumber, chopped

½ cup loosely packed finely chopped fresh mint

½ cup loosely packed finely chopped fresh flat-leaf parsley

Grated zest and juice of 1 lemon

½ teaspoon salt

¼ teaspoon freshly ground black pepper

1. In a saucepan, bring the water to a boil over high heat, then remove it from the heat. Stir in the bulgur, cover, and let it sit until the liquid is absorbed, about 30 minutes.

2. In a large skillet, heat the olive oil over medium heat. Add the red onion and cook for about 3 minutes, until beginning to soften.

3. Add the tomatoes and bell pepper and cook, stirring occasionally, for 10 to 12 minutes, until tender.

4. Stir the vegetables into the bulgur. Add the cucumber, mint, parsley, lemon zest and juice, salt, and black pepper. Stir to combine well.

5. Transfer the mixture to a container with a tight-fitting lid. Refrigerate for 1 hour before serving.

PER SERVING:
CALORIES: 224; Total Fat: 5g; Saturated Fat: 1g; Protein: 7g; Total Carbohydrates: 41g; Fiber: 7g; Sugar: 2g; Cholesterol: 0mg

SWEET POTATO CAKES

Serves 4 / Prep time: 30 minutes / Cook time: 35 minutes

Sweet potatoes, like most orange foods, are loaded with beta-carotene, which is an important antioxidant. These sweet potato cakes with yogurt dipping sauce make a tasty and healthy snack or a great dinner party appetizer.

OVERALL WELLNESS

For the sweet potato cakes

Extra-virgin olive oil, for brushing

2 pounds sweet potatoes, peeled and cut into ½-inch cubes

½ small onion, roughly chopped

1 (1-inch) piece fresh red chile, seeded

1 garlic clove, peeled

½ cup all-purpose flour

1 teaspoon salt

¼ teaspoon freshly ground black pepper

For the dipping sauce

½ cup low-fat plain Greek yogurt

1 tablespoon extra-virgin olive oil

1 tablespoon minced fresh cilantro

1 teaspoon freshly squeezed lemon juice

To make the sweet potato cakes

1. Preheat the oven to 375°F. Line a rimmed baking sheet with parchment paper and brush with olive oil.

2. Pour a couple of inches of water into a pot and insert a steaming basket. Bring the water to a boil over high heat. Add the sweet potatoes, cover, and steam for about 7 minutes, until tender.

3. Transfer the steamed sweet potatoes to a food processor. Add the onion, chile, and garlic and process until smooth.

4. Transfer the sweet potato mixture to a bowl. Fold in the flour, salt, and pepper and mix until combined. If the mixture is too wet, add more flour until you can form patties without the mixture sticking to your hands.

5. Using a large spoon, scoop out about 2 tablespoons of the mixture to form each small patty. Place the patties on the prepared baking sheet and brush the tops with a bit of olive oil.

6. Bake for 15 minutes, flip, and bake for another 10 to 15 minutes, until lightly browned and firm.

To make the dipping sauce

7. In a small bowl, combine the yogurt, olive oil, cilantro, and lemon juice and mix well.

8. Serve the sweet potato cakes with the yogurt dipping sauce.

PER SERVING:

CALORIES: 289; Total Fat: 4g; Saturated Fat: 1g; Protein: 8g; Total Carbohydrates: 56g; Fiber: 6g; Sugar: 5g; Cholesterol: 2mg

GREEN BEAN FRITTERS

Serves 4 / Prep time: 15 minutes / Cook time: 40 minutes

Fritters are a fun way to get several servings of vegetables into one meal—in this case nutrient-rich green beans and radishes. Traditionally, fritters are fried, but here they're baked and served with a spicy garlic dipping sauce.

OVERALL WELLNESS

For the green bean fritters

Extra-virgin olive oil, for brushing

1 pound green beans, trimmed

4 radishes, roughly chopped

1 scallion, roughly chopped

¼ cup all-purpose flour

1 large egg

¼ teaspoon salt

⅛ teaspoon baking powder

Pinch cayenne pepper

For the spicy garlic mayo

2 tablespoons vegan mayonnaise

1 garlic clove, minced

⅛ teaspoon cayenne pepper

To make the green bean fritters

1. Preheat the oven to 375°F. Line a rimmed baking sheet with parchment paper and brush with olive oil.

2. In a food processor, combine the green beans, radishes, and scallion and process until smooth.

3. Transfer the green bean mixture to a bowl. Add the flour, egg, salt, baking powder, and cayenne and mix well.

4. Using a spoon, drop about 2 tablespoons of the mixture for each fritter onto the prepared baking sheet. The batter will still be a little wet. Pat the patties down flat.

5. Bake for 20 minutes, flip, and bake for another 15 to 20 minutes, until browned and crisp.

To make the spicy garlic mayo

6. In a small bowl, mix together the mayonnaise, garlic, and cayenne.

7. Serve 2 to 3 fritters per person, topped with a dollop of dipping sauce.

> **VARIATION TIP:** You can substitute almost any kind of fresh vegetable to make these fritters—try leeks, zucchini, spinach, or mushrooms. You may need to vary the amount of dry ingredients to get the proper consistency.

PER SERVING:

CALORIES: 119; Total Fat: 5g; Saturated Fat: 1g; Protein: 5g; Total Carbohydrates: 15g; Fiber: 4g; Sugar: 4g; Cholesterol: 47mg

nine

PASTA, RICE, AND GRAINS

Spaghetti with Garlic, Olive Oil, and Red Pepper 130

Roasted Tomato Sauce with Pasta 131

Pasta Primavera 132

Lemon Linguine 133

Fusilli Arrabbiata 134

Spaghetti with Anchovy Sauce 135

White Bean Alfredo Pasta 136

Easy Rice Pilaf 137

Seafood Risotto 139

Vegetable Rice Bake 140

Baked Chicken Paella 141

Baked Rice with Swordfish and Mussels 143

Farro with Porcini Mushrooms 144

Polenta with Wild Greens 145

Shrimp and Polenta 146

Barley Risotto with Vegetables 147

Sicilian Eggplant with Israeli Couscous 148

Algerian Vegetable Couscous 149

Pasta Primavera, p. 132

SPAGHETTI WITH GARLIC, OLIVE OIL, AND RED PEPPER

Serves 2 / Prep time: 5 minutes / Cook time: 10 minutes

This elegantly simple Italian pasta dish is easy to make. The sauce cooks up in only as much time as it takes to boil the pasta, so you've got a full meal ready to go in less than 15 minutes.

OVERALL WELLNESS

Salt

8 ounces spaghetti

¼ cup extra-virgin olive oil

4 garlic cloves, 3 lightly smashed and 1 minced

½ teaspoon red pepper flakes

¼ cup grated Parmesan cheese

1 tablespoon chopped fresh flat-leaf parsley

1. Bring a large pot of water to a boil over high heat. Once boiling, salt the water to your liking, stir, and return to a boil. Add the spaghetti and cook according to package directions until al dente. Drain, reserving about ½ cup of the cooking water.

2. In a large skillet, heat the olive oil over low heat. Add the smashed garlic cloves and cook until golden brown. Remove the garlic from the pan and discard.

3. Add the red pepper flakes to the garlic-infused oil and warm for 1 minute before turning off the heat.

4. Once the spaghetti is cooked, add it to the pan.

5. Add the minced garlic and toss the spaghetti in the oil to coat. Add the reserved pasta water, a little at a time, as needed to help everything combine.

6. Sprinkle with the Parmesan and parsley.

> **COOKING TIP:** When making pasta, it is important to generously salt the water for a flavorful dish. I generally use about 2 tablespoons of salt per pound of pasta. Add the salt after the water boils, stir to dissolve, and wait for the water to return to a boil, then add the pasta.

PER SERVING:

CALORIES: 722; Total Fat: 32g; Saturated Fat: 6g; Protein: 19g; Total Carbohydrates: 89g; Fiber: 4g; Sugar: 3g; Cholesterol: 11mg

ROASTED TOMATO SAUCE WITH PASTA

Serves 2 / Prep time: 5 minutes / Cook time: 35 minutes

Roasting tomatoes with garlic and basil creates a rich sauce that shines when paired with pasta. The smooth, light sauce is a fresh alternative to jarred tomato sauce.

OVERALL WELLNESS

4 large tomatoes, quartered

4 garlic cloves, unpeeled

3 basil sprigs, plus more for garnish

3 tablespoons extra-virgin olive oil

1 teaspoon salt, plus more for the pasta water

½ teaspoon freshly ground black pepper

8 ounces whole wheat pasta

¼ cup grated Parmesan or Romano cheese

1. Preheat the oven to 450°F.

2. Put the tomatoes, garlic cloves, and basil sprigs in a small baking dish. Add the olive oil, salt, and pepper and toss to coat. Push the basil to the bottom so that it doesn't dry out.

3. Roast for 30 minutes.

4. Meanwhile, bring a large pot of water to boil over high heat. Once boiling, salt the water to your liking, stir, and return to a boil. Add the pasta and cook for 1 to 2 minutes less than the package directions for al dente, as it will continue to cook later with the sauce. Drain, reserving about ½ cup of the cooking water.

5. Remove the tomatoes from the oven. Discard the basil. Squeeze the roasted garlic from their skins and discard the skins.

6. Using a potato masher or large spoon, mash the tomato mixture. Be careful, as it will be hot and the juices can squirt out at you. Pull out any tomato skins; they should slip right off after being roasted.

7. Transfer the tomato mixture to a large skillet, set over medium-low heat, and add the cooked pasta. Toss, adding the reserved cooking water as needed to achieve the desired consistency.

8. Add the Parmesan. Continue to cook for 2 to 3 minutes, until everything is blended.

9. Garnish with fresh basil.

PER SERVING:

CALORIES: 727; Total Fat: 26g; Saturated Fat: 5g; Protein: 22g; Total Carbohydrates: 102g; Fiber: 8g; Sugar: 13g; Cholesterol: 11mg

PASTA PRIMAVERA

Serves 4 / Prep time: 15 minutes / Cook time: 15 minutes

The full vegetable bounty of the Mediterranean region can be found in this traditional summer pasta dish. The dish works best with rotini or fusilli.

WEIGHT LOSS

1 teaspoon salt, plus more for the pasta water

1 pound rotini

1 bell pepper (any color), seeded and cut into thin strips

½ cup broccoli florets

1 pint cherry or grape tomatoes, halved

2 carrots, shredded

½ cup fresh or frozen peas

1 scallion, thinly sliced

4 garlic cloves, thinly sliced

¼ cup extra-virgin olive oil

¼ teaspoon freshly ground black pepper

½ cup grated Parmesan or Romano cheese

½ cup chopped fresh flat-leaf parsley

½ teaspoon red pepper flakes

1. Bring a large pot of water to a boil over high heat. Once boiling, salt the water to your liking, stir, and return to a boil. Add the rotini and cook according to package directions until al dente. Drain, reserving about ½ cup of the cooking water.

2. Meanwhile, in a large skillet, combine the bell pepper and broccoli. Add a few tablespoons of water, cover, and cook for about 5 minutes, until they start to soften. Drain any remaining water from the pan.

3. Add the tomatoes, carrots, peas, scallion, garlic, olive oil, salt, and black pepper. Stir to coat all the vegetables and cook for 3 minutes.

4. Add the cooked pasta, Parmesan, parsley, and red pepper flakes. Toss to combine, adding the reserved cooking water a little at a time as needed to thin out the sauce.

PER SERVING:

CALORIES: 651; Total Fat: 19g; Saturated Fat: 4g; Protein: 21g; Total Carbohydrates: 99g; Fiber: 7g; Sugar: 7g; Cholesterol: 11mg

LEMON LINGUINE

Serves 2 / Prep time: 5 minutes / Cook time: 10 minutes

This bright and summery pasta sauce is made with lemon juice, Parmesan or Romano cheese, and olive oil. When combined with some of the pasta cooking water, it becomes silky and tastes wonderful with linguine.

OVERALL WELLNESS

Salt

8 ounces linguine

⅓ cup grated Parmesan or Romano cheese

⅓ cup extra-virgin olive oil

¼ cup freshly squeezed lemon juice

Chopped fresh basil, for garnish

1. Bring a large pot of water to a boil over high heat. Once boiling, salt the water to your liking, stir, and return to a boil. Add the linguine and cook according to package directions until al dente. Drain, reserving about ½ cup of the cooking water.

2. In a large bowl, whisk together the Parmesan, olive oil, and lemon juice.

3. Add the cooked pasta to the bowl and toss to combine. Add a little of the reserved cooking water as needed to help meld the flavors.

4. Garnish with fresh basil.

COOKING TIP: This pasta makes a perfect side dish for Greek Sheet Pan Chicken (page 187).

PER SERVING:

CALORIES: 812; Total Fat: 42g; Saturated Fat: 8g; Protein: 20g; Total Carbohydrates: 89g; Fiber: 4g; Sugar: 4g; Cholesterol: 14mg

FUSILLI ARRABBIATA

Serves 4 / Prep time: 5 minutes / Cook time: 20 minutes

Arrabbiata means "angry"—or, in other words, hot and spicy. You definitely won't be angry when you eat this traditional sauce from Italy.

OVERALL WELLNESS

3 tablespoons extra-virgin olive oil

1 small onion, finely chopped

Splash dry red wine (optional)

½ serrano pepper, seeded and minced

2 garlic cloves, minced

1 (28-ounce) can crushed tomatoes

1 (6-ounce) can tomato paste

¾ cup water

½ to 1 teaspoon red pepper flakes

1 tablespoon dried oregano

1 teaspoon dried basil

1 teaspoon salt, plus more for the pasta water

½ teaspoon freshly ground black pepper

1 pound fusilli or rotini

¼ cup grated Parmesan or Romano cheese

1. In a large, deep skillet, heat the olive oil over medium heat. Add the onion and cook for about 3 minutes, until just starting to soften.

2. Add a little red wine (if using) and cook for about 3 minutes, until the alcohol is burned off.

3. Add the serrano pepper and garlic and cook for about 1 minute, until fragrant.

4. Pour in the crushed tomatoes and stir everything together. Add the tomato paste and water and stir until the paste is blended in.

5. Add the red pepper flakes. You may want to do this a little at a time until you get your desired level of heat. You can always add more, but you can't take it out.

6. Season with the oregano, basil, salt, and black pepper.

7. Bring the sauce to a boil, then reduce the heat to a simmer.

8. Bring a large pot of water to a boil over high heat. Once boiling, salt the water to your liking, stir, and return to a boil. Add the fusilli and cook according to package directions until al dente. Drain.

9. Ladle the sauce over the pasta and top with the Parmesan cheese.

PER SERVING:
CALORIES: 619; Total Fat: 14g; Saturated Fat: 3g; Protein: 21g; Total Carbohydrates: 104g; Fiber: 10g; Sugar: 15g; Cholesterol: 5mg

SPAGHETTI WITH ANCHOVY SAUCE

Serves 4 / Prep time: 5 minutes / Cook time: 10 minutes

This super quick pasta dish is big on umami flavor, thanks to anchovies. Anchovies are an excellent source of calcium, iron, and zinc as well as omega-3 fatty acids. The bread crumbs provide crunch.

OVERALL WELLNESS

Salt

1 pound spaghetti

¼ cup extra-virgin olive oil

1 (2-ounce) can oil-packed anchovy fillets, undrained

3 garlic cloves, minced

¼ cup chopped fresh flat-leaf parsley

1 teaspoon red pepper flakes

¼ teaspoon freshly ground black pepper

1 tablespoon bread crumbs

1. Bring a large pot of water to a boil over high heat. Once boiling, salt the water to your liking, stir, and return to a boil. Add the spaghetti and cook according to package directions until al dente. Drain, reserving about ½ cup of the cooking water.

2. Meanwhile, in a large skillet, heat the olive oil over low heat. Add the anchovy fillets with their oil and the garlic. Cook for 7 to 10 minutes, until the pasta is ready, stirring until the anchovies melt away and form a sauce.

3. Add the spaghetti, parsley, red pepper flakes, black pepper, and a little of the reserved cooking water, as needed, and toss to combine all the ingredients.

4. Sprinkle with the bread crumbs.

PER SERVING:

CALORIES: 581; Total Fat: 17g; Saturated Fat: 3g; Protein: 19g; Total Carbohydrates: 87g; Fiber: 4g; Sugar: 3g; Cholesterol: 12mg

WHITE BEAN ALFREDO PASTA

Serves 4 / Prep time: 10 minutes / Cook time: 15 minutes

This low-fat mock Alfredo sauce is made thick and creamy with a mixture of white beans and nut milk. It's a wonderful and much lighter substitute you'll want to make again and again.

HEART HEALTH

1 teaspoon salt, plus more for the pasta water

1 pound fettuccine

2 tablespoons extra-virgin olive oil

2 garlic cloves, minced

¼ teaspoon red pepper flakes

2 (15-ounce) cans cannellini beans, rinsed and drained

2 cups vegetable broth

½ cup almond milk

¼ cup low-fat Pecorino cheese

¼ teaspoon ground nutmeg

Chopped fresh flat-leaf parsley, for garnish

1. Bring a large pot of water to boil over high heat. Once boiling, salt the water to your liking, stir, and return to a boil. Add the fettuccine and cook according to package directions until al dente. Drain, reserving about ½ cup of the cooking water.

2. Meanwhile, in a large skillet, heat the olive oil over medium heat. Add the garlic and red pepper flakes and cook for about 1 minute, until fragrant.

3. Add the beans, broth, and almond milk to the pan and bring to a boil. Remove the pan from the heat.

4. Using a slotted spoon, transfer the beans to a food processor or blender and process until smooth.

5. Return the pureed beans to the skillet. Add the Romano, salt, and nutmeg and bring to a simmer.

6. Add the cooked pasta to the bean mixture and stir to coat, adding the reserved cooking water, a little at a time, as needed. Cook for about 2 minutes.

7. Garnish with the parsley.

VARIATION TIP: Try adding steamed broccoli florets or chopped sun-dried tomatoes for an extra burst of flavor, color, and nutrients.

PER SERVING:

CALORIES: 697; Total Fat: 12g; Saturated Fat: 3g; Protein: 30g; Total Carbohydrates: 118g; Fiber: 12g; Sugar: 5g; Cholesterol: 5mg

EASY RICE PILAF

Serves 4 / Prep time: 5 minutes / Cook time: 20 minutes

This basic rice pilaf is a versatile side dish that complements many main courses, particularly those with a Greek flair.

OVERALL WELLNESS

2 tablespoons extra-virgin olive oil

1 small onion, diced

1½ cups long-grain white rice, such as jasmine

2 cups chicken broth

1 teaspoon dried oregano

½ teaspoon salt

¼ teaspoon freshly ground black pepper

1. In a large saucepan, heat the olive oil over medium heat. Add the onion and cook for about 3 minutes, until it starts to soften.

2. Add the rice and toss to coat it in the oil.

3. Add the chicken broth, oregano, salt, and pepper and bring to a boil. Reduce the heat to low, cover, and simmer for about 15 minutes, until the liquid is fully absorbed into the rice.

4. Fluff with a fork before serving.

VARIATION TIP: To spruce up this dish, you can add diced bell pepper and carrot when you cook the onion. Stir in some frozen peas at the end and cook for an additional 2 minutes.

PER SERVING:

CALORIES: 324; Total Fat: 9g; Saturated Fat: 1g; Protein: 6g; Total Carbohydrates: 55g; Fiber: 3g; Sugar: 1g; Cholesterol: 0mg

SEAFOOD RISOTTO

Serves 4 / Prep time: 15 minutes / Cook time: 30 minutes

Italians don't normally mix cheese and seafood, but this creamy risotto is an exception. The addition of mascarpone cheese complements the shrimp and makes this risotto velvety.

OVERALL WELLNESS

3 cups seafood or vegetable broth

3 cups water

4 tablespoons extra-virgin olive oil, divided

1 shallot, finely chopped

1½ cups Arborio rice

¼ cup dry white wine

1 pound mussels, scrubbed and debearded

1 pound small clams, scrubbed

1 pound large shrimp, peeled and deveined

2 garlic cloves, minced

½ teaspoon salt

½ teaspoon freshly ground black pepper

1 cup baby arugula

¼ cup mascarpone cheese

1. In a small saucepan, bring the broth to a simmer. In another small saucepan, bring the water to a simmer.

2. In a large saucepan, heat 2 tablespoons of olive oil over medium heat. Add the shallot and cook for 3 minutes, until it starts to soften.

3. Add the rice and cook for 1 minute. Add the wine and cook until it evaporates, stirring constantly.

4. Add a ladleful of hot broth and cook until it is absorbed into the rice, continuing to stir. Then add a ladleful of hot water and cook until it is absorbed. Alternate these liquids until the rice takes on a creamy consistency, about 20 minutes total.

5. Meanwhile, put the mussels and clams in a large, deep skillet. Pour in ½ inch of water. Cover and cook over high heat for 3 to 5 minutes, until all the clams and mussels have opened. Discard any that do not open.

6. In a medium skillet, heat the remaining 2 tablespoons of olive oil over low heat. Add the shrimp, garlic, salt, and pepper and cook for about 5 minutes, turning once, until the shrimp turn pink.

7. Once the rice is fully cooked, stir in the arugula and mascarpone cheese. Fold in the shrimp and all the pan drippings.

8. Divide the risotto among serving bowls. Place a few mussels and clams in each bowl, hinged-ends down.

PER SERVING:

CALORIES: 545; Total Fat: 18g; Saturated Fat: 3g; Protein: 28g; Total Carbohydrates: 63g; Fiber: 2g; Sugar: 2g; Cholesterol: 161mg

VEGETABLE RICE BAKE

Serves 4 / Prep time: 15 minutes / Cook time: 50 minutes

The wonderful thing about this dish is that the vegetables you choose can vary with the seasons. In the summer, use fresh corn, and in the winter, use various squashes. Serve this rice bake with your favorite hot sauce.

WEIGHT LOSS

1½ teaspoons paprika

1½ teaspoons dried thyme

1 teaspoon Italian Herb Blend (page 262)

1 teaspoon salt

1 teaspoon freshly ground black pepper

2 carrots, chopped

1 turnip, peeled and chopped

2 garlic cloves, minced

1½ cups long-grain white rice

1½ cups chicken broth

1½ cups water

1 head broccoli, cut into florets

2 ears corn, husks and silks removed, cut into thirds

1 red onion, cut into large chunks

1 red bell pepper, seeded and cut into chunks

¼ cup extra-virgin olive oil

1. Preheat the oven to 400°F.

2. In a small bowl, combine the paprika, thyme, Italian herb blend, salt, and pepper.

3. In a 9-by-13-inch baking pan, combine the carrots, turnip, garlic, rice, broth, and water. Stir in 1 teaspoon of the spice mix. Cover with aluminum foil and bake for 20 minutes.

4. In a large bowl, combine the broccoli, corn pieces, red onion, and bell pepper. Add the olive oil and the remaining 5 teaspoons of spice mix and toss to coat.

5. Remove the baking pan from the oven and remove the foil. Increase the oven temperature to 425°F.

6. Scatter the broccoli and corn mixture over the surface of the rice mixture. Be sure to cover the top fully so that the rice stays hidden underneath.

7. Return the dish to the oven, uncovered, and bake for 30 minutes.

PER SERVING:

CALORIES: 653; Total Fat: 23g; Saturated Fat: 4g; Protein: 30g; Total Carbohydrates: 86g; Fiber: 8g; Sugar: 6g; Cholesterol: 38mg

BAKED CHICKEN PAELLA

Serves 4 / Prep time: 15 minutes / Cook time: 1 hour 15 minutes

Paella is cooked in a large, shallow pan, traditionally over an open fire outdoors. This baked dish allows you to make Spanish paella right in your own kitchen with no open flame required.

OVERALL WELLNESS

2 tablespoons extra-virgin olive oil

2 boneless, skinless chicken breasts, cut into bite-size pieces

1 teaspoon salt

1 teaspoon freshly ground black pepper

1 hot Italian pork sausage, sliced

1 medium onion, sliced

1 red or green bell pepper, seeded and sliced

3 garlic cloves, chopped

¼ cup dry white wine

1 cup Arborio rice

3 cups chicken broth, divided

1 cup canned or cooked chickpeas

1 cup baby spinach

2 large eggs, beaten

1. Preheat the oven to 350°F.

2. In a large ovenproof skillet or braising pan, heat the olive oil over medium heat. Add the chicken and season with the salt and pepper. Brown the chicken on both sides, about 5 minutes total, then transfer to a plate.

3. Add the sausage, onion, bell pepper, and garlic to the skillet and cook for about 10 minutes, until the sausage is browned and the vegetables are softened. Transfer to the plate with the chicken.

4. Pour in the wine and deglaze the skillet, stirring to scrape up any browned bits on the bottom. Add the rice and mix with the wine until coated.

5. Add 1 cup of chicken broth, stir, and cook for 5 minutes.

6. Add the chickpeas and another 1 cup of broth and stir again. Return the browned chicken to the skillet on top of the rice and chickpeas.

7. Add the sausage, onion, and bell pepper mixture on top of the chicken. Push the chicken, sausage, and vegetables down into the rice and chickpea mixture, but do not stir. Add the remaining 1 cup of chicken broth and bring to a boil.

▶

8. Cover the skillet, transfer to the oven, and bake for 40 minutes.

9. Uncover the skillet and take a peek at the dish. If it looks dry, add ⅓ cup water to the skillet. Add the spinach and push it down into the mixture slightly. Pour the beaten eggs on top.

10. Return to the oven and bake for another 10 minutes, uncovered, until the egg is completely cooked.

11. Let rest for 5 minutes before serving.

PER SERVING:

CALORIES: 539; Total Fat: 21g; Saturated Fat: 5g; Protein: 30g; Total Carbohydrates: 52g; Fiber: 5g; Sugar: 3g; Cholesterol: 166mg

BAKED RICE WITH SWORDFISH AND MUSSELS

Serves 4 / Prep time: 10 minutes / Cook time: 1 hour

Garlic, pork sausage, bell pepper, onion, and seafood create an exceptional one-pan meal.

2 tablespoons extra-virgin olive oil

2 swordfish steaks, cut into bite-size pieces

1 teaspoon salt

1 teaspoon freshly ground black pepper

1 hot Italian pork sausage, sliced

1 medium onion, sliced

1 yellow or orange bell pepper, seeded and sliced

3 garlic cloves, chopped

¼ cup dry white wine

1 cup Arborio rice

3 cups seafood or vegetable broth, divided

1 pound mussels, scrubbed and debearded

2 large eggs, beaten

1. Preheat the oven to 325°F.

2. In a large, deep ovenproof skillet, heat the olive oil over medium heat. Add the swordfish and season with the salt and pepper. Brown the fish for about 1 minute on each side, then transfer to a plate.

3. Add the sausage, onion, bell pepper, and garlic to the skillet and cook for about 10 minutes, until the sausage is browned and the vegetables are softened. Transfer to the plate with the swordfish.

4. Pour in the wine and deglaze the skillet, stirring to scrape up any browned bits on the bottom. Add the rice and mix with the wine until coated.

5. Add 2 cups of broth and cook for 5 minutes without stirring.

6. Add the swordfish, sausage, onion, and bell pepper mixture on top of the rice. Pour in the remaining 1 cup of seafood broth and bring to a boil. Do not stir.

7. Cover, transfer to the oven, and bake for 30 minutes.

8. Uncover the skillet and take a peek at the dish. If it looks dry, add ⅓ cup water. Add the mussels, pushing the hinged-ends down into the rice. Pour the beaten eggs over the top of the dish.

9. Cook for another 10 minutes, uncovered, or until the mussels open and the egg is completely cooked. Discard any mussels that do not open.

PER SERVING:

CALORIES: 508; Total Fat: 23g; Saturated Fat: 6g; Protein: 25g; Total Carbohydrates: 46g; Fiber: 2g; Sugar: 2g; Cholesterol: 160mg

FARRO WITH PORCINI MUSHROOMS

Serves 4 / Prep time: 15 minutes / Cook time: 40 minutes

This variation of mushroom risotto uses the ancient grain farro instead of rice. Farro is the ancestor of wheat and has been eaten in Italy since the Etruscan era. It has a barley-like texture and is extremely nutritious.

HEART HEALTH

4 cups vegetable broth

2 tablespoons extra-virgin olive oil

1 shallot, finely chopped

1 cup pearled farro

½ cup dry white wine

¼ teaspoon red pepper flakes

1 pound porcini mushrooms, sliced

¼ cup water

½ teaspoon salt

2 garlic cloves, minced

1 tablespoon cream sherry (optional)

¼ cup grated Parmesan or Romano cheese

Chopped fresh flat-leaf parsley, for garnish

1. In a small saucepan, bring the vegetable broth to a gentle simmer.

2. In a large skillet, heat the olive oil over medium heat and cook the shallot for about 2 minutes, until softened.

3. Add the farro and stir until coated with oil. Cook for 1 minute.

4. Add the wine and cook until it is absorbed, stirring constantly. Add the red pepper flakes.

5. Mix in the hot broth, a ladleful at a time, and cook until absorbed, stirring frequently. Each ladleful will probably take about 5 minutes to absorb.

6. Meanwhile, in another skillet, combine the mushrooms, water, and salt. Cover and cook for about 5 minutes, until the mushrooms have softened. Add the garlic and sherry (if using) and continue to cook, uncovered.

7. When you have about 1 ladleful of broth left, add the mushroom mixture to the farro and fold it in. Add the rest of the broth and continue to cook and stir until the liquid is absorbed.

8. Add the Parmesan and stir to combine. Garnish with parsley.

INGREDIENT TIP: You can substitute cremini or white button mushrooms if porcini are not available.

PER SERVING:

CALORIES: 340; Total Fat: 9g; Saturated Fat: 2g; Protein: 10g; Total Carbohydrates: 52g; Fiber: 11g; Sugar: 5g; Cholesterol: 5mg

POLENTA WITH WILD GREENS

Serves 2 / Prep time: 10 minutes / Cook time: 25 minutes

Creamy polenta prepared with revitalizing wild greens is southern Italian comfort food at its finest. Serve it as a side dish, or enjoy it on its own.

HEART HEALTH

1 pound red or green Swiss chard, trimmed

1 pound dandelion greens, trimmed

¼ cup extra-virgin olive oil

2 celery stalks, chopped

1 small onion, finely chopped

3 garlic cloves, minced

1 teaspoon red pepper flakes

1 teaspoon Italian Herb Blend (page 262)

½ (18-ounce) tube firm polenta, cut into 1-inch-thick slices

Sea salt

1. Bring a large pot of water to a boil over high heat. Add the chard and dandelion greens and cook for 3 to 5 minutes, until the stems are soft. Drain and set aside to cool.

2. In a large skillet, heat the olive oil over low heat. Add the celery, onion, garlic, red pepper flakes, and Italian herb blend. Cook for 3 minutes, stirring, until the vegetables soften.

3. Add the polenta to the pan and stir to combine. Cook for 5 minutes. Turn the polenta over and cook for another 5 minutes.

4. Roughly chop the cooled greens and add them to the skillet. Season with salt.

5. Stir everything together—some of the polenta will break up into smaller pieces at this point. Cover and cook for about 10 minutes, until the greens are tender.

VARIATION TIP: This recipe can easily vary with the seasons. Use whatever greens are available at the time you make it.

PER SERVING:
CALORIES: 507; Total Fat: 29g; Saturated Fat: 4g; Protein: 14g; Total Carbohydrates: 52g; Fiber: 15g; Sugar: 8g; Cholesterol: 0mg

SHRIMP AND POLENTA

Serves 4 / Prep time: 15 minutes / Cook time: 30 minutes

This recipe is an Italian take on shrimp and grits. Polenta is very much like grits but with a slightly coarser texture. Here, olive oil is substituted for butter and Parmesan for cheddar cheese.

OVERALL WELLNESS

4 cups water

1 cup instant polenta

1 teaspoon salt

½ cup grated Parmesan cheese

2 tablespoons extra-virgin olive oil

4 ounces pancetta, cut into ¼-inch dice

1 pound large shrimp, peeled and deveined

1 cup sliced scallions

2 tablespoons chopped fresh flat-leaf parsley

1 tablespoon freshly squeezed lemon juice

2 garlic cloves, minced

1. In a saucepan, bring the water to a boil over high heat, then reduce the heat to low. Add the polenta and salt and cook for 15 minutes, or according to package directions.

2. Remove the polenta from the heat and stir in the Parmesan and olive oil. Cover and set aside.

3. In a large skillet, fry the pancetta for about 5 minutes, until it starts to brown. Add the shrimp and cook for about 3 minutes, until they turn pink. Add a little olive oil if the pan becomes too dry.

4. Add the scallions, parsley, lemon juice, and garlic to the pan. Cook for about 3 minutes, until fragrant.

5. Spoon the polenta into serving bowls and top with the shrimp mixture.

PER SERVING:
CALORIES: 473; Total Fat: 34g; Saturated Fat: 11g; Protein: 22g; Total Carbohydrates: 18g; Fiber: 1g; Sugar: 1g; Cholesterol: 178mg

BARLEY RISOTTO WITH VEGETABLES

Serves 4 / Prep time: 10 minutes / Cook time: 30 minutes

Zucchini and tomatoes add a fresh, summery flavor to this "risotto" made with barley. Barley is a heart-healthy whole grain with a slightly nutty flavor. The addition of beans turns this dish into a hearty and substantial meal.

WEIGHT LOSS

1½ cups pearled barley

2 tablespoons extra-virgin olive oil

1 small onion, chopped

2 zucchini, cut into small cubes

1 (15-ounce) can cannellini beans, rinsed and drained

3 cups vegetable broth, divided

12 cherry tomatoes, chopped

¼ cup grated Parmesan or Romano cheese

Chopped fresh basil, for garnish

1. In a saucepan, prepare the barley according to package directions until al dente. Drain and set aside.

2. In a large skillet, heat the olive oil over medium heat. Add the onion and cook for 3 to 5 minutes, until softened.

3. Add the zucchini, beans, and a splash of the broth and cook for 10 minutes, stirring frequently.

4. Add the barley and 1 cup of broth. Cook until the liquid absorbs, stirring constantly. Keep stirring in the broth, a ladleful at a time, allowing it to absorb before adding more, until you use it all up.

5. Fold in the tomatoes and Parmesan and stir gently until combined. Garnish with basil.

PER SERVING:

CALORIES: 469; Total Fat: 10g; Saturated Fat: 5g; Protein: 16g; Total Carbohydrates: 82g; Fiber: 18g; Sugar: 6g; Cholesterol: 2mg

SICILIAN EGGPLANT WITH ISRAELI COUSCOUS

Serves 2 / Prep time: 10 minutes / Cook time: 45 minutes

Beautiful tricolor Israeli couscous, also known as pearl couscous, is a pasta made from semolina. The grains are much larger than those of North African couscous.

WEIGHT LOSS

¼ cup extra-virgin olive oil

¼ red onion, chopped

1 small Sicilian eggplant, cut into cubes

1 garlic clove, minced

½ teaspoon salt

1 cup canned crushed tomatoes

½ teaspoon dried oregano

1½ cups water

1 cup tricolor Israeli couscous

4 fresh basil leaves, chopped

¼ teaspoon smoked paprika

Pinch cayenne pepper

1. In a large skillet, heat the olive oil over medium heat. Add the red onion and cook for 3 to 5 minutes, until it starts to soften.

2. Add the eggplant, garlic, and salt and cook for about 10 minutes, until the eggplant starts to soften and break down.

3. Add the tomatoes and oregano. Cover and cook until fully soft, about 20 minutes.

4. Meanwhile, in a saucepan, bring the water to a boil over high heat. Reduce the heat to a simmer and add the couscous. Cover and simmer for 10 minutes. Fluff it up using a fork, then remove from the heat and let stand, covered, for 3 minutes.

5. Add the couscous to the eggplant mixture. Stir in the basil, smoked paprika, and cayenne. Stir to combine and simmer for 10 minutes to meld all the flavors.

INGREDIENT TIP: Sicilian eggplants are round and practically seedless, unlike the more common globe eggplant. If you can't find one, you can use a globe eggplant for this dish, but you may want to scoop out the seeds. You could also use 2 or 3 small Japanese eggplants.

PER SERVING:

CALORIES: 680; Total Fat: 28g; Saturated Fat: 4g; Protein: 16g; Total Carbohydrates: 94g; Fiber: 15g; Sugar: 16g; Cholesterol: 0mg

ALGERIAN VEGETABLE COUSCOUS

Serves 4 / Prep time: 15 minutes / Cook time: 15 minutes

Couscous is one of the most popular foods in Algeria. Flavored with the region's fragrant spices, this vegetarian dish is a quick and light meal you can make in half an hour.

OVERALL WELLNESS

2 tablespoons extra-virgin olive oil

1 cup sliced cremini or white button mushrooms

1 small onion, chopped

1 carrot, grated

2 garlic cloves, minced

1¼ cups vegetable broth

1 cup couscous

¼ cup raisins

Grated zest and juice of 1 lemon

½ teaspoon ground cumin

½ teaspoon ground coriander

½ teaspoon salt

1. In a large skillet, heat the olive oil over medium heat. Add the mushrooms, onion, and carrot and cook for about 5 minutes, until they start to soften. Add the garlic and cook for 1 minute.

2. Stir in the broth, couscous, raisins, lemon zest and juice, cumin, coriander, and salt. Bring to a boil, then cover and remove the pan from heat. Let stand for 5 minutes before serving.

PER SERVING:

CALORIES: 248; Total Fat: 7g; Saturated Fat: 1g; Protein: 7g; Total Carbohydrates: 39g; Fiber: 3g; Sugar: 3g; Cholesterol: 0mg

ten

BEANS AND LEGUMES

White Bean Dip 152

Classic Hummus 153

Three-Bean Salad 154

Gigante Beans in Tomato Sauce 155

Mashed Fava Beans 156

Spicy Borlotti Beans 157

Black Beans with Cherry Tomatoes 158

Warm Lentil Salad 159

Moroccan Lentil Soup 160

Vegetarian Chili 161

Black-Eyed Peas with Mint 163

Chickpea and Avocado Salad 164

Peas and Tubetti with Pancetta 165

Classic Hummus, p. 153

WHITE BEAN DIP

Makes about 2 cups / Prep time: 5 minutes / Cook time: 2 minutes

Cannellini beans, also known as white kidney beans, have a delicate flavor and are packed with nutrients. This white bean dip is a crowd-pleaser without all the fat of many other dips. Serve it with crudités or flatbread.

OVERALL WELLNESS

¼ cup extra-virgin olive oil, plus more for drizzling

2 garlic cloves, chopped

3 fresh sage leaves

½ teaspoon dried oregano

2 (19-ounce) cans cannellini beans, rinsed and drained

1 teaspoon salt

¼ teaspoon freshly ground black pepper

¼ teaspoon red pepper flakes (optional)

1 to 2 tablespoons water

1. In a small saucepan, heat the olive oil over low heat. Add the garlic, sage, and oregano and cook for 1 minute, until fragrant.

2. Turn off the heat. Add the beans to the pan and toss to coat with the seasonings.

3. Transfer the mixture to a food processor. Add the salt, black pepper, and red pepper flakes (if using). Process until smooth, adding water as needed to get the consistency you want.

4. Transfer the dip to a serving bowl and drizzle with a little more olive oil.

PER SERVING (4 TABLESPOONS):
CALORIES: 191; Total Fat: 9g; Saturated Fat: 1g; Protein: 9g; Total Carbohydrates: 20g; Fiber: 8g; Sugar: 0g; Cholesterol: 0mg

CLASSIC HUMMUS

Makes about 1 cup / Prep time: 10 minutes

Hummus is a beloved and healthy dip or spread that originated in the eastern Mediterranean and is still widely enjoyed throughout the region. The base is made with chickpeas and a tahini sauce, which combine for a naturally nutty, garlicky flavor.

HEART HEALTH

½ cup toasted sesame seeds

2 tablespoons extra-virgin olive oil

1 garlic clove, peeled

1 teaspoon freshly squeezed lemon juice

1 (19-ounce) can chickpeas, rinsed and drained

¼ cup extra-virgin olive oil

1 teaspoon salt

2 tablespoons water

1. In a food processor, combine the sesame seeds, olive oil, garlic, and lemon juice and process until the mixture becomes a paste. If needed, scrape down the sides of the bowl and repeat a few times. Don't worry if the paste is not completely smooth yet.

2. Add the chickpeas, olive oil, and salt to the tahini sauce in the food processor and blend until smooth. Add the water and blend again until soft and fluffy.

VARIATION TIP: Hummus lends itself to a variety of added flavors, as shown in these variations:

FAVA BEAN HUMMUS: When you remove fava beans from their padded pods, they are still enclosed in a thick skin that should be peeled off. Put 12 unpeeled fava beans in a pot of boiling water and boil for 3 minutes. Drain and cool, then pop the beans out of their skins. In a food processor or blender, combine about ½ cup hummus and the fava beans and blend until smooth.

LEMON HUMMUS: Lay 4 lemon slices on a rimmed baking sheet lined with parchment paper. Remove and discard any seeds. Brush the lemons with olive oil on both sides and roast at 350°F for 20 minutes. In a food processor or blender, combine about ½ cup hummus and the roasted lemon slices and blend until smooth.

MAKE-AHEAD TIP: Store the hummus in an airtight container in the refrigerator for up to 5 days or in the freezer for up to 6 months.

PER SERVING (¼ CUP):
CALORIES: 379; Total Fat: 29g; Saturated Fat: 4g; Protein: 9g; Total Carbohydrates: 22g; Fiber: 8g; Sugar: 3g; Cholesterol: 0mg

THREE-BEAN SALAD

Serves 6 / Prep time: 15 minutes, plus 1 hour to chill

Beans are an excellent source of protein, an essential nutrient for building and repairing the body. Create your own protein powerhouse with this three-bean salad tossed in a light red wine vinaigrette.

WEIGHT LOSS

1 (19-ounce) can chickpeas, rinsed and drained

1 (19-ounce) can cannellini beans, rinsed and drained

1 (19-ounce) can red kidney beans, rinsed and drained

½ red onion, finely chopped

¼ cup extra-virgin olive oil

3 tablespoons red wine vinegar

½ teaspoon salt

½ teaspoon dried oregano

¼ teaspoon freshly ground black pepper

1. In a large bowl, combine the chickpeas, cannellini beans, kidney beans, and red onion.

2. In a small bowl, whisk together the olive oil, vinegar, salt, oregano, and pepper. Pour the dressing over the bean mixture and toss to combine.

3. Cover and refrigerate for 1 hour before serving.

MAKE-AHEAD TIP: This salad is best when prepared in advance. It will keep in the refrigerator for up to 3 days.

VARIATION TIP: You can substitute black beans for the cannellini beans and swap out the oregano for cilantro for a slightly different flavor profile.

PER SERVING:

CALORIES: 284; Total Fat: 10g; Saturated Fat: 1g; Protein: 14g; Total Carbohydrates: 36g; Fiber: 13g; Sugar: 3g; Cholesterol: 0mg

GIGANTE BEANS IN TOMATO SAUCE

Serves 2 / Prep time: 5 minutes / Cook time: 5 minutes

The Greek word *gigante*, which means "giant," accurately describes the size of these creamy white beans. This simple appetizer is just as good cold as warm.

HEART HEALTH

1 (12-ounce) jar gigante beans, undrained

1 (6-ounce) can tomato paste

¾ cup water

½ teaspoon dried oregano

1. Pour the beans and their liquid into a small saucepan and bring to a boil over medium-high heat. Remove the pan from the heat and drain the liquid.

2. In another small saucepan, combine the tomato paste and water and bring to a simmer to heat through.

3. Arrange the beans on a serving dish. Spoon over the tomato sauce and sprinkle with the dried oregano.

INGREDIENT TIP: If you can't find gigante beans, good substitutes are corona beans or large butter beans.

PER SERVING:
CALORIES: 238; Total Fat: 1g; Saturated Fat: 0g; Protein: 15g; Total Carbohydrates: 46g; Fiber: 12g; Sugar: 11g; Cholesterol: 0mg

MASHED FAVA BEANS

Serves 4 / Prep time: 15 minutes / Cook time: 10 minutes

Fava beans, also known as broad beans, are an immune system–boosting superfood. Fava beans come in large pods, each bean in its own thick skin. Serve these mashed fava beans as a side dish or as a spread on toast.

WEIGHT LOSS

3 pounds fava beans, removed from the pods but unpeeled

¼ cup water

½ teaspoon salt

¼ cup extra-virgin olive oil

3 garlic cloves, chopped

1 tablespoon finely chopped fresh rosemary

¼ teaspoon freshly ground black pepper

1. Bring a large pot of water to a boil over high heat and cook the beans for 3 minutes. Drain the beans and rinse under cold running water to cool.

2. Peel the outer skin off the beans. The inner bean should pop out easily. You are going to be mashing the beans, so you can be messy during this step.

3. Put the beans in a food processor, add the water and salt, and puree.

4. In a skillet, heat the olive oil over low heat. Add the fava bean puree, garlic, rosemary, and pepper. Stir to combine and cook for about 5 minutes, until most of the water evaporates.

PER SERVING:

CALORIES: 423; Total Fat: 16g; Saturated Fat: 2g; Protein: 27g; Total Carbohydrates: 61g; Fiber: 26g; Sugar: 31g; Cholesterol: 0mg

SPICY BORLOTTI BEANS

Serves 8 / Prep time: 10 minutes, plus overnight to soak / Cook time: 1 hour 30 minutes

Borlotti beans, also known as cranberry beans, are a variety of kidney bean with a speckled appearance. Here, they are spiced up with chile and red pepper flakes.

HEART HEALTH

1 pound dried borlotti beans, soaked overnight, drained, and rinsed

1 teaspoon salt, divided

2 tablespoons extra-virgin olive oil

1 large onion, chopped

½ green bell pepper, seeded and chopped

1 (14.5-ounce) can diced tomatoes, undrained

3 garlic cloves, minced

1 (1-inch) piece fresh red chile, seeded and minced

¼ teaspoon freshly ground black pepper

¼ teaspoon red pepper flakes

1. Put the beans in a large soup pot, cover with water, and add ½ teaspoon of salt. Bring to a boil over medium-high heat, then reduce the heat to low and simmer for 1 to 1½ hours, until the beans soften. Drain.

2. In a large skillet, heat the olive oil over medium heat. Cook the onion and bell pepper for about 10 minutes, until softened.

3. Add the beans, tomatoes and their juices, garlic, chile, remaining ½ teaspoon of salt, black pepper, and red pepper flakes. Bring to a boil, then reduce the heat and simmer for 10 minutes.

PER SERVING:

CALORIES: 240; Total Fat: 4g; Saturated Fat: 1g; Protein: 13g; Total Carbohydrates: 39g; Fiber: 13g; Sugar: 3g; Cholesterol: 0mg

BLACK BEANS WITH CHERRY TOMATOES

Serves 2 / Prep time: 5 minutes / Cook time: 15 minutes

This super simple bean recipe is packed with flavor and nutrition, and you can get it on the table in just 15 minutes. This dish is wonderful on its own or as a hearty accompaniment to grilled chicken or fish.

HEART HEALTH

1 (15-ounce) can black beans, undrained

1 cup halved cherry tomatoes

1 teaspoon salt

1 tablespoon dried oregano

1 teaspoon red pepper flakes

1. Pour the black beans and their liquid into a large skillet and bring to a low boil over medium-high heat. Reduce the heat to low and simmer for 5 minutes.

2. Stir in the cherry tomatoes, salt, oregano, and red pepper flakes. Cook for 10 minutes.

PER SERVING:
CALORIES: 185; Total Fat: 1g; Saturated Fat: 0g; Protein: 12g; Total Carbohydrates: 34g; Fiber: 12g; Sugar: 2g; Cholesterol: 0mg

WARM LENTIL SALAD

Serves 4 / Prep time: 15 minutes / Cook time: 20 minutes

Lentils are low in fat and high in protein and fiber. In the South of France, they are often flavored with bay leaves, onions, and garlic, as in this salad. Serve this lentil salad warm to enjoy the flavors of the mustardy vinaigrette.

WEIGHT LOSS

For the lentils

1 cup lentils

2½ cups water

1 bay leaf

2 tablespoons extra-virgin olive oil

1 cup chopped onion

1 cup chopped carrot

1 garlic clove, minced

For the dressing

¼ cup extra-virgin olive oil

2 tablespoons white wine vinegar

1 teaspoon Dijon mustard

1 teaspoon salt

¼ teaspoon freshly ground black pepper

To make the lentils

1. In a large saucepan, combine the lentils, water, and bay leaf and bring to a boil over medium-high heat. Reduce the heat to low and simmer for 20 minutes, until tender.

2. Drain the lentils and discard the bay leaf.

3. Meanwhile, in a skillet, heat the olive oil over medium heat and add the onion and carrot. Sauté for about 5 minutes, until softened. Add the garlic and cook for 1 more minute.

To make the dressing

4. In a small bowl, whisk together the olive oil, vinegar, mustard, salt, and pepper.

5. In a bowl, combine the warm lentils with the onion-carrot-garlic mixture. Add the dressing and toss to combine.

PER SERVING:

CALORIES: 380; Total Fat: 21g; Saturated Fat: 3g; Protein: 13g; Total Carbohydrates: 37g; Fiber: 7g; Sugar: 4g; Cholesterol: 0mg

MOROCCAN LENTIL SOUP

Serves 4 / Prep time: 10 minutes / Cook time: 40 minutes

This lentil soup draws its inspiration from Morocco. It is seasoned with a collection of earthy, warm spices and topped with a little yogurt for added creaminess.

WEIGHT LOSS

1 tablespoon extra-virgin olive oil

1 cup chopped onion

1 cup chopped celery

½ cup chopped carrot

2 garlic cloves, minced

2 teaspoons ground cumin

2 teaspoons smoked paprika

1 teaspoon salt

1 teaspoon freshly ground black pepper

1 teaspoon ground turmeric

1 teaspoon ground ginger

½ teaspoon ground cinnamon

4 cups chicken broth

2 cups water

2 tablespoons tomato paste

2 cups brown lentils

¼ cup nonfat plain Greek yogurt

Chopped fresh flat-leaf parsley, for garnish

1. In a soup pot, heat the olive oil over medium heat. Add the onion, celery, and carrot and cook for 5 to 7 minutes, until they start to soften. Add the garlic and cook for 1 minute.

2. Stir in the cumin, paprika, salt, pepper, turmeric, ginger, and cinnamon. Cook for 2 minutes to wake up the spices.

3. Add the broth, water, and tomato paste and stir until the tomato paste incorporates into the liquid. Stir in the lentils.

4. Bring everything to a boil, then reduce the heat to low and simmer for about 30 minutes, until the lentils are tender.

5. Serve each bowl with a dollop of yogurt and a sprinkling of parsley.

PER SERVING:
CALORIES: 421; Total Fat: 5g; Saturated Fat: 1g; Protein: 27g; Total Carbohydrates: 71g; Fiber: 13g; Sugar: 6g; Cholesterol: 1mg

VEGETARIAN CHILI

Serves 8 / Prep time: 15 minutes / Cook time: 1 hour 10 minutes

Although you may think of chili as a Mexican dish, this vegetarian version follows the basic principles of Mediterranean cooking. Beans and legumes replace meat, and a host of spices come together to create a rich and satisfying meal. Serve this chili with a dollop of sour cream on top, if you like.

HEART HEALTH

2 tablespoons extra-virgin olive oil

2 medium onions, finely chopped

1 medium leek, finely chopped

1 fresh red chile, seeded and minced

4 garlic cloves, minced

2 tablespoons ground cumin

2 tablespoons ground coriander

2 tablespoons smoked paprika

2 tablespoons dried oregano

1 teaspoon ground cinnamon

¼ teaspoon ground nutmeg

2 tablespoons tomato paste

2 tablespoons water

6 cups vegetable broth

1 cup green lentils

1 cup red lentils

2 (15-ounce) cans red kidney beans, rinsed and drained

2 (15-ounce) cans black beans, rinsed and drained

2 (14.5-ounce) cans chopped tomatoes, undrained

1 teaspoon salt

1. In a large soup pot, heat the olive oil over medium heat. Add the onions and cook for about 4 minutes, until they start to soften. Add the leek, chile, and garlic and cook for about 1 minute, until fragrant.

2. Add the cumin, coriander, paprika, oregano, cinnamon, and nutmeg and cook for another minute, stirring to wake up the spices.

3. Stir in the tomato paste and water. Cook for about 2 minutes, until warmed through.

4. Add the broth, lentils, kidney beans, black beans, tomatoes and their juices, and salt. Bring the pot to a boil, then reduce to a simmer and cook for 1 hour, stirring every 15 minutes or so.

INGREDIENT TIP: If you crave more heat in your chili, you can leave the seeds in the chile.

PER SERVING:

CALORIES: 430; Total Fat: 6g; Saturated Fat: 1g; Protein: 25g; Total Carbohydrates: 74g; Fiber: 20g; Sugar: 7g; Cholesterol: 0mg

BLACK-EYED PEAS WITH MINT

Serves 8 / Prep time: 10 minutes / Cook time: 10 minutes

This recipe comes from the Greek island of Ikaria, where many inhabitants live long past the age of 90. Black-eyed peas are packed with nutrition, and the addition of mint in this recipe accents their flavor.

OVERALL WELLNESS

4 (15-ounce) cans black-eyed peas, undrained

1 cup baby spinach

1 cup chopped fresh mint

½ red onion, finely chopped

1 carrot, grated

3 scallions, thinly sliced

½ cup extra-virgin olive oil

3 tablespoons white wine vinegar

1 teaspoon salt

½ teaspoon freshly ground black pepper

1. In a large saucepan, bring the black-eyed peas and their liquid to a boil over medium heat. Cook for about 5 minutes, until heated through. Drain.

2. Return the beans to the saucepan and stir in the spinach, mint, red onion, carrot, and scallions. Heat until warmed through.

3. In a small bowl, whisk together the olive oil, vinegar, salt, and pepper. Pour the mixture over the beans and stir to combine.

MAKE-AHEAD TIP: This dish can also be eaten cold and will keep in an airtight container in the refrigerator for up to 3 days.

PER SERVING:

CALORIES: 304; Total Fat: 14g; Saturated Fat: 2g; Protein: 12g; Total Carbohydrates: 33g; Fiber: 13g; Sugar: 1g; Cholesterol: 0mg

CHICKPEA AND AVOCADO SALAD

Serves 4 / Prep time: 10 minutes

This fresh salad combines the nutty flavor of chickpeas with the creaminess of avocado, both brightened up with lime and cilantro. It's a powerhouse of healthy fat and protein that makes for a wonderfully light lunch.

HEART HEALTH

1 (15-ounce) can chickpeas, rinsed and drained

2 avocados, pitted, peeled, and chopped

¼ cup chopped fresh cilantro

1 scallion, thinly sliced

2 tablespoons extra-virgin olive oil

Juice of 1 lime

½ teaspoon salt

¼ teaspoon freshly ground black pepper

¼ teaspoon red pepper flakes

¼ cup crumbled feta cheese

1. In a large bowl, combine the chickpeas, avocado, cilantro, and scallion.

2. In a small bowl, whisk together the olive oil, lime juice, salt, black pepper, and red pepper flakes.

3. Pour the dressing over the chickpea-avocado mixture and toss to combine.

4. Sprinkle the feta cheese over the top.

VARIATION TIP: You can use onion or shallot instead of the scallion if preferred.

PER SERVING:

CALORIES: 372; Total Fat: 26g; Saturated Fat: 5g; Protein: 10g; Total Carbohydrates: 30g; Fiber: 13g; Sugar: 7g; Cholesterol: 8mg

PEAS AND TUBETTI WITH PANCETTA

Serves 4 / Prep time: 5 minutes / Cook time: 10 minutes

Tubetti are tiny tubes of pasta that have been cut into short pieces. They are about the same size as the peas, so they're great to mix together. This dish can be served hot or cold.

OVERALL WELLNESS

Salt

1 pound tubetti

3 tablespoons extra-virgin olive oil

½ cup diced pancetta

2 scallions, thinly sliced

12 ounces frozen peas

¼ cup water

¼ cup finely grated Parmesan cheese

1. Bring a large pot of water to a boil over high heat. Once boiling, salt the water to your liking, stir, and return to a boil. Add the tubetti and cook according to package directions until al dente. Drain, reserving about ¼ cup of the cooking water.

2. In a large skillet, heat the olive oil over medium heat. Cook the pancetta for 2 minutes, then add the scallions and cook for another 2 minutes, until the pancetta is completely cooked.

3. Add the peas and water. Cover and cook for 5 minutes, stirring occasionally.

4. Add the cooked pasta and toss to combine. Add the reserved pasta water a little at a time as needed.

5. Sprinkle with the Parmesan cheese.

INGREDIENT TIP: If you can't find tubetti, you can substitute ditalini, orzo, or any other tiny pasta shape.

PER SERVING:

CALORIES: 661; Total Fat: 20g; Saturated Fat: 5g; Protein: 22g; Total Carbohydrates: 98g; Fiber: 8g; Sugar: 8g; Cholesterol: 11mg

eleven

FISH AND SHELLFISH

Herbed Salmon with Mashed Potatoes 168

Whole Branzino with Garlic and Herbs 169

Mediterranean Snapper with Olives and Feta 170

Spanish Salmon with Smoked Paprika 171

Tuna Puttanesca 172

Moroccan Cod 173

Baked Flounder with Parmesan and Herbs 174

Fish en Papillote 175

Baked Fish Fingers 176

Shrimp Scampi 177

Shrimp Margarita 178

Shrimp Fra Diavolo 179

Mussels and Clams in White Wine 181

Mussels in Tomato Sauce with Pastina 182

Sardine Pâté 183

167

Whole Branzino with Garlic and Herbs, p. 169

HERBED SALMON WITH MASHED POTATOES

Serves 4 / Prep time: 15 minutes / Cook time: 30 minutes

Salmon is a popular fish all over the Mediterranean region because of its rich flavor and numerous health benefits. In this meal, it's paired with creamy mashed potatoes and an herbed mustard sauce.

OVERALL WELLNESS

For the salmon

2 tablespoons extra-virgin olive oil, plus more for brushing

1 salmon fillet (16 to 20 ounces)

Salt

Freshly ground black pepper

2 thyme sprigs

2 marjoram sprigs

For the potatoes

2 russet potatoes, peeled and diced

3 to 4 tablespoons whole milk

1 tablespoon unsalted butter

1 teaspoon salt

For the sauce

½ cup Dijon mustard

2 tablespoons freshly squeezed lemon juice

1 teaspoon extra-virgin olive oil

3 tablespoons chopped fresh dill

2 tablespoons chopped fresh basil

To cook the salmon

1. Preheat the oven to 400°F. Line a rimmed baking sheet with parchment paper and brush it with olive oil.

2. Place the salmon, skin-side down, on the prepared baking sheet. Rub it with the olive oil and season it lightly with salt and pepper. Top with the herb sprigs.

3. Bake for 20 to 30 minutes, until the salmon flakes easily with a fork. Remove the herbs sprigs and discard.

To cook the potatoes

4. When the salmon is nearly done, bring a large pot of water to a boil over high heat. Add the potatoes and boil for 5 to 10 minutes, until soft. Drain and transfer to a bowl.

5. Using a hand mixer on low, beat the potatoes with 2 tablespoons of milk, the butter, and salt. Add the remaining 1 or 2 tablespoons of milk, a little at a time, until you reach the desired consistency.

To make the sauce

6. In a small bowl, whisk together the mustard, lemon juice, olive oil, dill, and basil.

7. Spoon the sauce over the salmon and serve with the mashed potatoes.

PER SERVING:

CALORIES: 432; Total Fat: 20g; Saturated Fat: 4g; Protein: 28g; Total Carbohydrates: 36g; Fiber: 4g; Sugar: 2g; Cholesterol: 72mg

WHOLE BRANZINO WITH GARLIC AND HERBS

Serves 2 / Prep time: 5 minutes / Cook time: 25 minutes

Branzino is Italian sea bass from the Mediterranean Sea. It has a delicate white flesh and mild flavor, and it is often served whole at the table. It is rich in omega-3 fatty acids, which are essential to heart health.

HEART HEALTH

2 whole branzino, scaled and gutted

4 thyme sprigs

4 marjoram sprigs

¼ cup extra-virgin olive oil

2 garlic cloves, minced

1 teaspoon Italian Herb Blend (page 262)

¼ teaspoon salt

1. Preheat the oven to 325°F. Line a rimmed baking sheet with parchment paper.

2. Place the fish on the prepared baking sheet. Place the thyme and marjoram sprigs inside each fish.

3. In a small bowl, stir together the olive oil, garlic, Italian herb blend, and salt. Spoon the mixture inside the fish and all around the outside as well.

4. Bake for 25 to 30 minutes, until the fish easily flakes with a fork.

5. Remove from the oven and discard the herbs. Using 2 spoons, gently remove the fish backbones.

6. Serve 1 fish per person, with the caution to look out for any small bones as you eat.

PER SERVING:
CALORIES: 510; Total Fat: 42g; Saturated Fat: 6g; Protein: 31g; Total Carbohydrates: 1g; Fiber: 0g; Sugar: 0g; Cholesterol: 38mg

MEDITERRANEAN SNAPPER WITH OLIVES AND FETA

Serves 4 / Prep time: 10 minutes / Cook time: 20 minutes

Snapper is a white fish with a delicate, mild flavor. It stands up well to strong, fragrant Mediterranean flavors like this recipe's tomatoes, olives, and garlic.

HEART HEALTH

3 tablespoons extra-virgin olive oil, divided, plus more for brushing

4 snapper fillets (4 to 5 ounces each)

½ teaspoon salt

¼ teaspoon freshly ground black pepper

1 onion, chopped

2 garlic cloves, minced

1 teaspoon dried oregano

1 (14.5-ounce) can diced tomatoes, undrained

½ cup chopped pitted kalamata olives

¼ cup crumbled feta cheese

2 tablespoons chopped fresh flat-leaf parsley

1. Preheat the oven to 425°F. Brush a 3-quart (13 × 9 × 2 inch) baking dish lightly with olive oil.

2. Place the snapper in the prepared baking dish. Massage it gently with 2 tablespoons of olive oil, then sprinkle with the salt and pepper.

3. In a large skillet, heat the remaining 1 tablespoon of olive oil over medium heat. Add the onion, garlic, and oregano and cook for about 3 minutes, until the onion starts to soften.

4. Add the tomatoes and their juices and the olives and cook for 5 minutes to warm through and combine the flavors.

5. Spoon the tomato mixture over the fish.

6. Bake for 10 to 15 minutes, until the fish is tender and flakes easily with a fork.

7. Serve with a sprinkling of crumbled feta cheese and chopped parsley.

PER SERVING:

CALORIES: 278; Total Fat: 16g; Saturated Fat: 3g; Protein: 26g; Total Carbohydrates: 8g; Fiber: 3g; Sugar: 4g; Cholesterol: 50mg

SPANISH SALMON WITH SMOKED PAPRIKA

Serves 4 / Prep time: 10 minutes / Cook time: 30 minutes

Salmon, a fish rich in omega-3 fatty acids, can be made in a variety of ways. In this recipe, Spanish smoked paprika turns this everyday fish into a festive meal. Use crusty bread to mop up the fresh tomato sauce.

HEART HEALTH

2 tablespoons extra-virgin olive oil, plus more for brushing and drizzling

4 salmon fillets (6 ounces each)

1 tablespoon smoked paprika

1 teaspoon salt, divided

½ teaspoon freshly ground black pepper

2 large tomatoes, quartered

2 yellow bell peppers, seeded and roughly chopped

1 red onion, roughly chopped

1 garlic clove, peeled

1 (1-inch) piece jalapeño, seeded

Chopped fresh flat-leaf parsley, for garnish

1. Preheat the oven to 400°F. Line a rimmed baking sheet with parchment paper and brush it lightly with olive oil.

2. Place the salmon fillets on the prepared baking sheet. Drizzle with the 2 tablespoons olive oil.

3. In a small bowl, mix the smoked paprika, ½ teaspoon of salt, and the pepper. Rub the spice mixture into each salmon fillet.

4. Bake for 20 to 30 minutes, until the salmon flakes easily with a fork.

5. Meanwhile, in a food processor, combine the tomatoes, bell peppers, red onion, garlic, jalapeño, and remaining ½ teaspoon of salt. Pulse a few times to get a chunky salsa-like texture.

6. Spoon some of the tomato mixture on each serving plate and drizzle with olive oil. Lay a salmon fillet on top. Sprinkle with chopped parsley.

VARIATION TIP: This spice rub also works well on chicken.

PER SERVING:

CALORIES: 360; Total Fat: 18g; Saturated Fat: 3g; Protein: 36g; Total Carbohydrates: 13g; Fiber: 3g; Sugar: 4g; Cholesterol: 94mg

TUNA PUTTANESCA

Serves 4 / Prep time: 10 minutes / Cook time: 30 minutes

Tuna steaks are high in protein and contain almost no fat. A staple of the Mediterranean region, tuna pairs well with bold flavors like those of the capers, olives, and garlic in this classic puttanesca sauce.

HEART HEALTH

1 tablespoon extra-virgin olive oil, plus more for brushing

1 (6-ounce) can tomato paste

½ cup water

3 garlic cloves, minced, divided

1 teaspoon dried oregano

½ teaspoon salt

¼ teaspoon freshly ground black pepper

2 tuna steaks (1 inch thick)

½ cup pitted kalamata olives

2 tablespoons capers

1 teaspoon red pepper flakes

8 fresh basil leaves, for garnish

1. Preheat the oven to 350°F. Line a rimmed baking sheet with parchment paper and lightly brush with olive oil.

2. In a skillet, heat the olive oil over medium heat. Add the tomato paste and water and stir to combine. Bring the mixture to a boil, then reduce the heat to a simmer.

3. Add 1 minced garlic clove, the oregano, salt, and black pepper. Simmer for 10 minutes, then remove the pan from the heat.

4. Halve the tuna steaks horizontally to create four ½-inch-thick steaks. Place the tuna steaks on the prepared baking sheet.

5. Spoon the tomato sauce over the tuna. Cover with the olives, capers, remaining 2 minced garlic cloves, and red pepper flakes.

6. Bake for 20 minutes, or until the tuna steaks are cooked to your preference. Garnish with fresh basil.

PER SERVING:

CALORIES: 212; Total Fat: 10g; Saturated Fat: 2g; Protein: 22g; Total Carbohydrates: 10g; Fiber: 3g; Sugar: 5g; Cholesterol: 32mg

MOROCCAN COD

Serves 4 / Prep time: 10 minutes / Cook time: 30 minutes

This recipe is easy to make because its ingredients cook together on one sheet pan. The warm Moroccan spices complement the mildness of the cod and potatoes.

HEART HEALTH

2 russet potatoes, peeled and cut into large chunks

6 carrots, cut into large chunks

4 tablespoons extra-virgin olive oil, divided

1½ teaspoons salt, divided

4 cod fillets (6 ounces each)

½ teaspoon ground cumin

½ teaspoon paprika

¼ teaspoon ground turmeric

1 large red onion, cut into large chunks

Chopped fresh flat-leaf parsley, for garnish

1. Preheat the oven to 425°F. Line a rimmed baking sheet with aluminum foil.

2. Toss the potatoes and carrots on the prepared baking sheet with 3 tablespoons of olive oil and 1 teaspoon of salt. Spread out in a single layer and roast for 15 minutes.

3. Meanwhile, rub the remaining 1 tablespoon of olive oil all over the cod. In a small bowl, combine the cumin, paprika, turmeric, and remaining ½ teaspoon of salt and sprinkle the mixture over the fish.

4. Remove the baking sheet from the oven and move the vegetables over to clear four spots for the fish. Add the fish and red onion and roast for 15 to 20 minutes, until the fish is fully cooked and flakes easily with a fork. Garnish with parsley.

PER SERVING:

CALORIES: 444; Total Fat: 15g; Saturated Fat: 2g; Protein: 31g; Total Carbohydrates: 47g; Fiber: 6g; Sugar: 8g; Cholesterol: 80mg

BAKED FLOUNDER WITH PARMESAN AND HERBS

Serves 4 / Prep time: 5 minutes / Cook time: 15 minutes

Flounder is a flatfish that contains omega-3 fatty acids. Here it is served with a crispy cheese topping that makes for an indulgent pairing.

WEIGHT LOSS

Nonstick cooking spray

4 flounder fillets
(4 ounces each)

2 tablespoons extra-virgin
olive oil

1 tablespoon dried oregano

¼ teaspoon salt

¼ teaspoon freshly ground
black pepper

½ cup chopped fresh
flat-leaf parsley

½ cup grated
Parmesan cheese

½ cup bread crumbs

1. Preheat the oven to 325°F. Line a rimmed baking sheet with parchment paper and coat with cooking spray.

2. Brush the flounder fillets with the olive oil and sprinkle with the oregano, salt, and pepper. Bake for 10 minutes.

3. In a small bowl, combine the parsley, Parmesan, and bread crumbs.

4. Sprinkle the mixture on the flounder fillets and return the baking sheet to the oven for about 5 minutes, until the topping browns and gets a bit crunchy and the fish flakes easily with a fork.

PER SERVING:

CALORIES: 248; Total Fat: 13g; Saturated Fat: 4g; Protein: 20g; Total Carbohydrates: 12g; Fiber: 1g; Sugar: 1g; Cholesterol: 62mg

FISH EN PAPILLOTE

Serves 4 / Prep time: 10 minutes / Cook time: 30 minutes

Fish baked *en papillote* ("in parchment") stays moist, tender, and flavorful. If you don't have parchment paper handy, you can create a packet using aluminum foil.

HEART HEALTH

3 tablespoons extra-virgin olive oil, divided

½ green bell pepper, seeded and chopped

½ cup chopped radicchio

1 scallion, thinly sliced

2 garlic cloves, minced

1 salmon fillet (20 ounces)

½ teaspoon salt

¼ teaspoon freshly ground black pepper

3 thyme sprigs, leaves picked

3 plum tomatoes, chopped

3 cups chopped beet greens

1. Preheat the oven to 400°F.

2. In a skillet, heat 2 tablespoons of olive oil over medium heat. Cook the bell pepper, radicchio, scallion, and garlic for about 3 minutes, until the radicchio has just wilted. Remove from the heat.

3. Place the salmon on half of a large sheet of parchment paper. Brush it with the remaining 1 tablespoon of olive oil and sprinkle with the salt and pepper. Top with the fresh thyme leaves. Spoon the sautéed vegetables over the top of the fish. Add the tomatoes on top.

4. Fold the other half of the parchment paper over the fish to enclose it. To seal, start at one end and firmly fold the paper along the edges in small pleats to create a half-moon-shaped packet.

5. Place the packet on a rimmed baking sheet and bake for 25 minutes.

6. Meanwhile, in a skillet, heat ¼ inch water over medium-high heat. Add the beet greens and cook for about 10 minutes, until wilted and tender. Drain.

7. Remove the baking sheet from the oven. Be careful when opening the parchment packet because hot steam will be released. Serve the fish on a bed of beet greens, topped with the vegetables from the packet.

PER SERVING:

CALORIES: 313; Total Fat: 19g; Saturated Fat: 3g; Protein: 29g; Total Carbohydrates: 5g; Fiber: 2g; Sugar: 2g; Cholesterol: 78mg

BAKED FISH FINGERS

Serves 4 / Prep time: 20 minutes / Cook time: 10 minutes

Kids love fish fingers, and I find that adults do as well—especially when they are baked instead of fried. Serve these fish fingers with a creamy Greek dipping sauce for a healthy snack or supper.

OVERALL WELLNESS

For the fish fingers

Nonstick cooking spray

1 pound cod fillets

1 teaspoon salt

½ teaspoon freshly ground black pepper

1 cup all-purpose flour

1 teaspoon paprika

2 large eggs

¼ cup whole milk

1 cup bread crumbs

For the dipping sauce

1 cup low-fat plain Greek yogurt

2 tablespoons extra-virgin olive oil

2 tablespoons freshly squeezed lemon juice

1 garlic clove, minced

1 teaspoon minced fresh dill

½ teaspoon salt

¼ teaspoon freshly ground black pepper

To make the fish fingers

1. Preheat the oven to 450°F. Line a rimmed baking sheet with parchment paper and coat with nonstick cooking spray.

2. Slice the cod into 1-inch-wide strips. You should get about 20 fish fingers. Season the fingers with the salt and pepper.

3. Set up an assembly line with three shallow bowls. Mix the flour and paprika together in the first bowl, beat together the eggs and milk in the second bowl, and put the bread crumbs in the third bowl.

4. Dredge a fish stick in the flour, then dip it in the egg mixture, then roll it in the bread crumbs to completely coat. Place on the prepared baking sheet and repeat with the remaining fish fingers.

5. Bake for about 10 minutes, until the fish is cooked through.

To make the dipping sauce

6. In a small bowl, stir together the yogurt, olive oil, lemon juice, garlic, dill, salt, and pepper. Serve with the fish fingers.

PER SERVING:

CALORIES: 463; Total Fat: 13g; Saturated Fat: 3g; Protein: 34g; Total Carbohydrates: 50g; Fiber: 2g; Sugar: 7g; Cholesterol: 147mg

SHRIMP SCAMPI

Serves 4 / Prep time: 10 minutes / Cook time: 10 minutes

Shrimp scampi is an easy-to-make and versatile seafood dish that has become a classic in many kitchens. Italians traditionally serve it over linguine, but you can serve it over rice or salad.

OVERALL WELLNESS

3 tablespoons extra-virgin olive oil, divided

4 garlic cloves, minced, divided

1 teaspoon salt

½ teaspoon freshly ground black pepper

1 pound large shrimp, peeled and deveined

1 shallot, chopped

¼ cup dry white wine

1 tablespoon freshly squeezed lemon juice

¼ teaspoon red pepper flakes

4 tablespoons unsalted butter

¼ cup chopped arugula

1. In a large bowl, whisk together 1 tablespoon of olive oil, half the garlic, the salt, and black pepper. Add the shrimp and toss to coat.

2. In a large skillet, heat the remaining 2 tablespoons of olive oil over medium heat. Add the shrimp and cook for 2 minutes.

3. Add the shallot, wine, lemon juice, remaining garlic, and red pepper flakes. Toss to coat the shrimp and cook until heated through and the liquid reduces by half.

4. Add the butter and arugula to the pan. Cook, stirring, until the butter melts and the arugula is wilted.

PER SERVING:

CALORIES: 292; Total Fat: 22g; Saturated Fat: 9g; Protein: 16g; Total Carbohydrates: 3g; Fiber: 0g; Sugar: 0g; Cholesterol: 173mg

SHRIMP MARGARITA

Serves 4 / Prep time: 10 minutes / Cook time: 5 minutes

This colorful and spicy shrimp dish draws its inspiration from flavors that originate in Spain. It is served warm and is topped with cool salad ingredients. I like to serve it alongside rice pilaf, but it is also tasty on its own.

WEIGHT LOSS

4 tablespoons extra-virgin olive oil, divided

2 tablespoons freshly squeezed lime juice

1 tablespoon tequila (optional)

2 garlic cloves, minced

¼ teaspoon salt

¼ teaspoon cayenne pepper

1 pound large shrimp, peeled and deveined

Easy Rice Pilaf (page 137)

1 tomato, chopped

1 avocado, pitted, peeled, and sliced

2 tablespoons diced red onion

2 tablespoons chopped fresh cilantro

1. In a bowl, whisk together 2 tablespoons of olive oil, the lime juice, tequila (if using), garlic, salt, and cayenne. Add the shrimp and toss to coat.

2. In a large skillet, heat the remaining 2 tablespoons of olive oil over medium heat. Add the shrimp and cook for about 5 minutes, until the shrimp are pink and cooked through.

3. Divide the rice pilaf into individual serving bowls. Divide the shrimp evenly among the bowls. Scatter the tomato, avocado, and red onion on top and garnish with the cilantro.

PER SERVING:

CALORIES: 627; Total Fat: 31g; Saturated Fat: 5g; Protein: 24g; Total Carbohydrates: 65g; Fiber: 8g; Sugar: 4g; Cholesterol: 143mg

SHRIMP FRA DIAVOLO

Serves 4 / Prep time: 15 minutes / Cook time: 15 minutes

Fra Diavolo ("Brother Devil") hints at the level of heat in this classic dish. This spicy tomato-based sauce works especially well with shrimp. You can control the amount of heat by adjusting the amount of red pepper flakes.

OVERALL WELLNESS

2 tablespoons extra-virgin olive oil

2 cups chopped onion

2 garlic cloves, minced

1 (28-ounce) can whole peeled tomatoes, undrained

½ cup dry red wine

1 tablespoon dried oregano

½ teaspoon red pepper flakes

½ teaspoon salt, plus more for the pasta water

¼ teaspoon freshly ground black pepper

1 pound linguine

1 pound large shrimp, peeled and deveined

1. In large skillet, heat the olive oil over medium heat. Add the onion and cook for about 3 minutes, until it starts to soften. Add the garlic and cook for another minute.

2. Add the tomatoes and their juices, using a potato masher or spoon to break up the tomatoes in the pan.

3. Add the wine, oregano, red pepper flakes, salt, and black pepper. Bring to a boil, then reduce to a simmer.

4. Meanwhile, bring a large pot of water to a boil over high heat. Once boiling, salt the water to your liking, stir, and return to a boil. Add the linguine and cook according to package directions until al dente. Drain.

5. Add the shrimp to the simmering tomato sauce and cook for about 3 minutes, until opaque.

6. Serve the shrimp and sauce over the linguine.

PER SERVING:

CALORIES: 653; Total Fat: 10g; Saturated Fat: 2g; Protein: 33g; Total Carbohydrates: 101g; Fiber: 9g; Sugar: 12g; Cholesterol: 143mg

MUSSELS AND CLAMS IN WHITE WINE

Serves 4 / Prep time: 10 minutes / Cook time: 10 minutes

You can have this seafood dish on the table in less than 20 minutes. The shallot, garlic, and wine infuse the shellfish with a bright flavor that makes for a light, protein-filled meal.

OVERALL WELLNESS

2 tablespoons extra-virgin olive oil

1 shallot, minced

2 garlic cloves, minced

1 cup dry white wine

½ teaspoon red pepper flakes

1 pound clams, scrubbed

1 pound mussels, scrubbed and debearded

¼ cup chopped arugula

1. In a large, deep skillet, heat the olive oil over low heat. Cook the shallot for about 5 minutes, until it starts to soften. Add the garlic and cook for 1 minute.

2. Stir in the white wine and red pepper flakes and cook for 1 minute to allow the alcohol to evaporate.

3. Increase the heat to medium and add the clams and mussels. Cover and steam for 3 to 5 minutes, until the shellfish have opened. Discard any that do not open. If you need more liquid to steam them, add some water.

4. Remove the shellfish from the pan and top with the sauce from the pan and chopped arugula.

VARIATION TIP: You can enjoy this dish as is or serve over linguine if you like.

PER SERVING:

CALORIES: 152; Total Fat: 8g; Saturated Fat: 1g; Protein: 7g; Total Carbohydrates: 4g; Fiber: 0g; Sugar: 1g; Cholesterol: 23mg

MUSSELS IN TOMATO SAUCE WITH PASTINA

Serves 4 / Prep time: 10 minutes / Cook time: 20 minutes

This spicy tomato sauce goes great with mussels and creates a tasty broth absorbed by the pastina, a tiny pasta that comes in a variety of shapes. Serve these mussels with crusty Italian bread.

OVERALL WELLNESS

¼ cup extra-virgin olive oil

4 garlic cloves, sliced

1 cup dry white wine

1 (28-ounce) can whole peeled tomatoes, undrained

1 tablespoon dried oregano

1 teaspoon red pepper flakes

1 teaspoon salt

½ teaspoon freshly ground black pepper

2 pounds mussels, scrubbed and debearded

2 tablespoons pastina

1. In a large, deep skillet, heat the olive oil over medium heat. Add the garlic and cook for 1 minute.

2. Add the white wine and bring to a boil.

3. Add the tomatoes and their juices, using a potato masher or spoon to break up the tomatoes in the pan.

4. Add the oregano, red pepper flakes, salt, and black pepper and stir to combine.

5. When the sauce starts to boil, add the mussels and cook for about 5 minutes, until they all open. Discard any mussels that do not open.

6. Reduce the heat to low. Stir in the pastina and simmer for 7 to 8 minutes, until the pasta is cooked.

INGREDIENT TIP: Any small shaped pasta will work in this dish. Orzo is a good alternative if you can't find pastina.

PER SERVING:

CALORIES: 256; Total Fat: 15g; Saturated Fat: 2g; Protein: 10g; Total Carbohydrates: 12g; Fiber: 4g; Sugar: 6g; Cholesterol: 18mg

SARDINE PÂTÉ

Serves 4 / Prep time: 10 minutes

Sardines are packed with omega-3 fatty acids. Serve this flavorful dip with toasted baguette slices or crackers. It tastes best when chilled for an hour before serving.

OVERALL WELLNESS

2 (7-ounce) cans oil-packed sardines, drained

2 ounces cream cheese or mascarpone

1 shallot, minced

2 scallions, thinly sliced

1 tablespoon minced fresh chives

1 tablespoon freshly squeezed lemon juice

Pinch cayenne pepper

1. Put the sardines in a bowl. Remove any spines or tails. Using a fork, mash the sardines.

2. Add the cream cheese, shallot, scallions, chives, lemon juice, and cayenne and stir until well blended.

MAKE-AHEAD TIP: This mixture can be stored in an airtight container in the refrigerator for up to 2 days.

PER SERVING:

CALORIES: 243; Total Fat: 15g; Saturated Fat: 4g; Protein: 24g; Total Carbohydrates: 1g; Fiber: 0g; Sugar: 1g; Cholesterol: 146mg

twelve

POULTRY AND MEAT

Chicken Paisano 186

Greek Sheet Pan Chicken 187

Chicken Souvlaki Skewers 188

Mediterranean Stuffed Chicken 189

Chicken Stuffed with Leeks 190

Potenza-Style Chicken 191

Chicken in a Pot 192

Game Hens Stuffed with Wild Rice and Mushrooms 193

Lime Chicken and Shrimp 194

Deconstructed Chicken Cacciatore 195

Flank Steak with Italian Salsa Verde 197

Moroccan Lamb with Couscous 199

Lamb Loin Chops with Spaghetti in Tomato Sauce 201

Lamb and Vegetable Stew 202

Sicilian Pork Ribs in Tomato Sauce 203

Chicken Souvlaki Skewers, p. 188

CHICKEN PAISANO

Serves 4 / Prep time: 10 minutes / Cook time: 20 minutes

In this recipe, boneless chicken and fresh vegetables get a kick from hot cherry peppers. The flavorful sauce is simple to make—it's just the natural juices from the pan.

OVERALL WELLNESS

¼ cup extra-virgin olive oil

½ cup all-purpose flour

2 boneless, skinless chicken breasts, cut into medallions

½ medium onion, chopped

Splash dry white wine

10 ounces cremini or white button mushrooms, sliced

1 large tomato, chopped

1 teaspoon Italian Herb Blend (page 262)

½ teaspoon salt

¼ teaspoon freshly ground black pepper

2 or 3 jarred pickled cherry peppers, seeded, chopped, and rinsed

1. In a large, deep skillet, heat the olive oil over medium heat.

2. Put the flour in a bowl. Working with one piece at a time, tap both sides of each chicken piece in the flour before placing them in the skillet. The chicken doesn't need to be completely coated with flour, just dusted. Cook for about 2 minutes, until the chicken starts to turn white on the bottom, then flip over to cook on the other side for about 2 minutes.

3. Add the onion and cook for about 3 minutes, until it starts to turn translucent. Add the white wine and continue to cook the onion for 2 more minutes while the alcohol burns off.

4. Add the mushrooms and tomato, cover, and cook for a few minutes, until the mushrooms release their water and the tomatoes start to break down and form a sauce.

5. Add the Italian herb blend, salt, and pepper. Stir, add the cherry peppers, and simmer for another 5 minutes, uncovered. Add some water if more liquid is needed.

> **COOKING TIP:** Serve the chicken with a side of pasta or ravioli, using the natural juices from the chicken dish to coat the pasta.

PER SERVING:

CALORIES: 280; Total Fat: 15g; Saturated Fat: 2g; Protein: 19g; Total Carbohydrates: 18g; Fiber: 2g; Sugar: 3g; Cholesterol: 40mg

GREEK SHEET PAN CHICKEN

Serves 4 / Prep time: 15 minutes / Cook time: 30 minutes

Lemon gives this chicken dish a bright, sunny flavor, and a light sprinkle of seasoned bread crumbs offers a healthy alternative to breaded chicken. Halloumi, a cheese from Cyprus, holds up well to roasting and adds some extra flavor to this dish.

OVERALL WELLNESS

1 tablespoon extra-virgin olive oil, plus more for brushing

2 boneless, skinless chicken breasts, cut into medallions

1 teaspoon salt

½ teaspoon freshly ground black pepper

2 lemons, sliced

2 ounces Halloumi cheese, cut into ½-inch cubes

¼ cup seasoned bread crumbs

1 garlic clove, minced

½ teaspoon finely grated lemon zest

Pinch red pepper flakes

½ teaspoon dried oregano

1. Preheat the oven to 350°F. Line a rimmed baking sheet with parchment paper and brush it lightly with olive oil.

2. Arrange the chicken in a single layer on the baking sheet and season with the salt and black pepper. Add the lemon slices between the chicken pieces.

3. Place a small piece of Halloumi cheese on top of each piece of chicken.

4. In a small bowl, combine the bread crumbs, olive oil, garlic, lemon zest, and red pepper flakes. Top each piece of chicken with a spoonful of the mixture and sprinkle the whole sheet pan with the oregano.

5. Bake for 20 to 30 minutes, until the chicken is cooked through and the juices run clear.

COOKING TIP: This dish goes well with Lemon Linguine (page 133).

VARIATION TIP: If you can't find Halloumi cheese, you can substitute feta or Fontina.

PER SERVING:

CALORIES: 268; Total Fat: 19g; Saturated Fat: 6g; Protein: 18g; Total Carbohydrates: 7g; Fiber: 0g; Sugar: 1g; Cholesterol: 67mg

CHICKEN SOUVLAKI SKEWERS

Serves 4 / Prep time: 10 minutes, plus 30 minutes to marinate / Cook time: 20 minutes

Chicken souvlaki is a classic Greek dish of marinated chicken that is typically grilled. In this recipe, the chicken is baked instead and served with tzatziki, a cucumber yogurt sauce.

OVERALL WELLNESS

Nonstick cooking spray

2 tablespoons freshly squeezed lemon juice

2 tablespoons extra-virgin olive oil

1 garlic clove, minced

1 teaspoon dried oregano

½ teaspoon salt

¼ teaspoon freshly ground black pepper

1 pound boneless, skinless chicken breast, cut into 2-inch pieces

12 cherry tomatoes

1 red onion, cut into chunks

4 whole-grain pitas, warmed

Tzatziki Sauce (page 247)

1. Preheat the oven to 350°F. Line a rimmed baking sheet with parchment paper and coat with nonstick cooking spray.

2. In a bowl, whisk together the lemon juice, olive oil, garlic, oregano, salt, and pepper.

3. Add the chicken and toss to coat. Cover and refrigerate for 30 minutes.

4. Thread 4 skewers, alternating 3 pieces of chicken, 3 tomatoes, and 3 chunks of red onion on each.

5. Place the skewers on the prepared baking sheet and bake for 10 minutes. Turn each skewer over and bake for another 10 minutes, or until the chicken is cooked through.

6. Serve with warm pita bread and tzatziki.

PER SERVING:

CALORIES: 281; Total Fat: 10g; Saturated Fat: 2g; Protein: 29g; Total Carbohydrates: 21g; Fiber: 3g; Sugar: 3g; Cholesterol: 65mg

MEDITERRANEAN STUFFED CHICKEN

Serves 4 / Prep time: 15 minutes / Cook time: 40 minutes

This chicken is stuffed with bright red vegetables that are both nutritious and beautiful on the plate. A sprinkling of seasoned bread crumbs adds a garlicky crunch.

OVERALL WELLNESS

Nonstick cooking spray

4 boneless, skinless chicken breasts

1 tomato, chopped

½ red bell pepper, seeded and chopped

1 jarred red cherry pepper, chopped

4 fresh basil leaves, chopped

½ teaspoon salt

2 tablespoons bread crumbs

1 teaspoon extra-virgin olive oil

1 teaspoon freshly squeezed lemon juice

1 garlic clove, minced

1. Preheat the oven to 375°F. Coat a 2-quart (11 × 7 × 1.5 inch) baking dish with cooking spray.

2. Cut 3 long slits in the top of each breast without cutting all the way through.

3. In a bowl, toss together the tomato, bell pepper, cherry pepper, basil, and salt.

4. In another bowl, combine the bread crumbs, olive oil, lemon juice, and garlic.

5. Stuff each slit in the chicken breasts with the tomato-pepper mixture and then sprinkle the breasts with the bread crumb mixture.

6. Bake for 40 minutes, or until cooked through.

INGREDIENT TIP: Cherry peppers come in red and green. Choose red, if available, to keep the brilliant color of the stuffing.

PER SERVING:
CALORIES: 178; Total Fat: 5g; Saturated Fat: 1g; Protein: 27g; Total Carbohydrates: 6g; Fiber: 1g; Sugar: 2g; Cholesterol: 83mg

CHICKEN STUFFED WITH LEEKS

Serves 4 / Prep time: 10 minutes / Cook time: 45 minutes

Leeks are in the onion family but have a mild flavor. When added to the inside of the chicken, it infuses flavor into each bite. They were used in ancient Egyptian cuisine, and they are especially popular today in France and Turkey.

WEIGHT LOSS

2 tablespoons extra-virgin olive oil, divided, plus more for brushing

3 leeks, trimmed

1 teaspoon fresh thyme leaves

½ teaspoon finely minced fresh rosemary

½ teaspoon salt, plus more to taste

¼ teaspoon freshly ground black pepper, plus more to taste

4 boneless, skinless chicken breasts

1. Preheat the oven to 375°F. Lightly brush a 2-quart (11 × 7 × 1.5 inch) baking dish with olive oil.

2. Thinly slice the leeks, then soak them in cold water to rinse thoroughly. Drain.

3. In a skillet, heat 1 tablespoon of olive oil over low heat. Add the leeks and cook for about 5 minutes, until they start to soften.

4. Add the thyme, rosemary, salt, and pepper and cook for 1 minute. Remove from the heat.

5. Cut a horizontal slit in the thicker side of each breast to form a pocket, without cutting all the way through. Stuff each pocket with the leek mixture.

6. Rub the remaining 1 tablespoon of olive oil on the breasts and season with additional salt and pepper.

7. Cook for 35 to 40 minutes, until the chicken is cooked all the way through and the juices run clear.

INGREDIENT TIP: Leeks can harbor a great deal of dirt and sand between the layers, so it's important to rinse them thoroughly before using.

PER SERVING:

CALORIES: 237; Total Fat: 10g; Saturated Fat: 2g; Protein: 26g; Total Carbohydrates: 10g; Fiber: 1g; Sugar: 3g; Cholesterol: 83mg

POTENZA-STYLE CHICKEN

Serves 4 / Prep time: 15 minutes / Cook time: 1 hour 5 minutes

Potenza is situated high in the Apennine Mountains of southern Italy. This chicken dish is traditionally served during the festival of San Gerardo, the patron saint of Potenza. It is usually made with a whole chicken cut into parts, but this lighter version uses boneless chicken breasts that are just as flavorful. Serve them over pasta or rice.

WEIGHT LOSS

2 tablespoons extra-virgin olive oil

2 boneless, skinless chicken breasts, cut into medallions

1 teaspoon salt

½ teaspoon freshly ground black pepper

1 large red onion, finely chopped

1 fresh cherry pepper or jalapeño, finely chopped

2 garlic cloves, minced

½ cup dry white wine

1 (28-ounce) can whole peeled tomatoes, undrained

1 teaspoon red pepper flakes

6 fresh basil leaves

1. In a skillet, heat the olive oil over medium heat. Add the chicken and cook for about 5 minutes, until browned. Season with the salt and black pepper and transfer to a plate.

2. Add the red onion, cherry pepper, and garlic to the skillet, reduce the heat to a low, and cook for about 20 minutes, until softened.

3. Add the wine and simmer for 10 minutes. Add the tomatoes and their juices, using a potato masher or spoon to break up the tomatoes in the pan. Add the red pepper flakes, stir, and let simmer for another 20 minutes, until the sauce thickens.

4. Return the chicken to the skillet and coat with the sauce. Roughly tear the basil leaves and scatter them on top. Cover and cook for 10 more minutes.

PER SERVING:
CALORIES: 219; Total Fat: 9g; Saturated Fat: 1g; Protein: 18g; Total Carbohydrates: 12g; Fiber: 5g; Sugar: 7g; Cholesterol: 52mg

CHICKEN IN A POT

Serves 4 / Prep time: 15 minutes / Cook time: 2 hours

Serve this succulent one-pot meal with a green salad and fresh bread to mop up the juices.

2 tablespoons extra-virgin olive oil

½ teaspoon red pepper flakes

1 whole chicken (4 to 5 pounds)

2 teaspoons salt, divided

2 russet potatoes, peeled and cut into 1-inch cubes

2 carrots, cut into ½-inch pieces

2 celery stalks, sliced

1 leek, white part only, chopped

2 garlic cloves, chopped

1 tablespoon herbes de Provence

Freshly ground black pepper

¼ cup dry white wine, chicken broth, or water

1. In a Dutch oven, heat the olive oil over medium heat and add the red pepper flakes.

2. Add the chicken to the pot and brown for just a minute on each side to get it started. Turn the chicken breast-side up and sprinkle with ½ teaspoon of salt. Put another ½ teaspoon of salt inside the cavity.

3. Scatter the potatoes, carrots, celery, leek, and garlic around the chicken. Push some of the vegetables into the cavity of the chicken to save space in the pot.

4. Sprinkle the herbes de Provence and remaining 1 teaspoon of salt over the chicken and vegetables. Season with a few generous grinds of black pepper.

5. Add the wine, cover, and cook over low heat until the chicken is cooked through and the vegetables are tender, 1½ to 2 hours. Check occasionally to make sure the pot doesn't dry out. The potatoes will absorb some of the juices, so you may need to add a splash of water.

6. Transfer the chicken to a serving dish. With a slotted spoon, transfer the vegetables to a bowl or arrange them around the chicken on a platter.

7. Bring the juices in the Dutch oven to a boil and reduce to make a gravy. If necessary, skim off any fat.

INGREDIENT TIP: Herbes de Provence is a blend of dried herbs, usually thyme, savory, oregano, rosemary, and marjoram. If you don't have any, use whatever herbs you like best.

PER SERVING:

CALORIES: 532; Total Fat: 28g; Saturated Fat: 7g; Protein: 31g; Total Carbohydrates: 40g; Fiber: 4g; Sugar: 4g; Cholesterol: 104mg

GAME HENS STUFFED WITH WILD RICE AND MUSHROOMS

Serves 4 / Prep time: 15 minutes / Cook time: 1 hour 45 minutes

This meal takes a little time to make because each person gets their own little bird. Wild rice and mushrooms create the light, healthy stuffing.

6 cups chicken or vegetable broth

2 cups wild rice

1 teaspoon salt, divided

2 tablespoons extra-virgin olive oil

1 onion, chopped

4 garlic cloves, minced

10 ounces cremini or white button mushrooms, sliced

1 cup chopped celery

½ cup chopped fresh flat-leaf parsley

⅓ cup chopped toasted almonds

⅓ cup dry white wine

2 teaspoons fresh thyme leaves

1 teaspoon dried ground sage

Freshly ground black pepper

4 game hens (1½ pounds each)

1 teaspoon Italian Herb Blend (page 262)

1. In a large saucepan, bring the broth to a boil over medium-high heat. Add the wild rice and ½ teaspoon of salt. Bring the broth back to a boil, then reduce the heat and simmer for 40 minutes, or until the rice is tender. Drain.

2. Preheat the oven to 375°F.

3. In a large skillet, heat the olive oil over medium heat. Add the onion and cook for about 3 minutes, until it starts to soften. Add the garlic and cook for 1 minute.

4. Add the mushrooms and celery and cook for about 5 minutes, until they start to soften.

5. Stir in the parsley, almonds, wine, thyme, sage, and a few grinds of pepper and cook for 2 minutes. Add the wild rice and stir to combine.

6. Stuff the hens with the prepared rice, packing it in tightly.

7. Place the stuffed hens in a baking dish. Sprinkle the tops with the Italian herb blend and remaining ½ teaspoon of salt.

8. Tent the pan with aluminum foil. Poke a few small holes in the top and roast for 45 minutes.

9. Remove the foil and roast for another 15 minutes, until well browned and the juices run clear.

PER SERVING:

CALORIES: 690; Total Fat: 59g; Saturated Fat: 7g; Protein: 73g; Total Carbohydrates: 72g; Fiber: 8g; Sugar: 7g; Cholesterol: 233mg

LIME CHICKEN AND SHRIMP

Serves 4 / Prep time: 15 minutes / Cook time: 30 minutes

Lime flavors this tangy, protein-rich chicken and shrimp dish. Serve it with rice or warm bread to make the best use of the succulent sauce.

OVERALL WELLNESS

Extra-virgin olive oil, for brushing

2 pounds boneless, skinless chicken breasts, cut into medallions

Grated zest and juice of 2 limes

¼ cup all-purpose flour

1 teaspoon salt

½ teaspoon freshly ground black pepper

2 tablespoons light brown sugar

2 cups chicken broth

1 pound large shrimp, peeled and deveined

1. Preheat the oven to 400°F. Brush a 9-by-13-inch baking dish with olive oil.

2. In a bowl, toss the chicken with the lime juice.

3. In a separate bowl, combine the flour, salt, and pepper. Dip each piece of chicken in the flour mixture to coat, then place in a single layer in the prepared baking dish.

4. In a small bowl, combine the lime zest and brown sugar and sprinkle it over the chicken. Pour in the chicken broth.

5. Bake for 20 minutes, basting occasionally with the pan juices.

6. Add the shrimp to the pan and bake for another 10 minutes, until the chicken is cooked through and the shrimp are pink and opaque.

7. Spoon the pan juices over the chicken and shrimp to serve.

PER SERVING:

CALORIES: 276; Total Fat: 10g; Saturated Fat: 2g; Protein: 32g; Total Carbohydrates: 13g; Fiber: 0g; Sugar: 5g; Cholesterol: 195mg

DECONSTRUCTED CHICKEN CACCIATORE

Serves 2 / Prep time: 15 minutes, plus 2 hours to marinate / Cook time: 40 minutes

Cacciatore is a tomato-based stew traditionally made in one pot. In this deconstructed version, each ingredient is prepared separately to intensify its flavor.

HEART HEALTH

1 (28-ounce) can whole peeled tomatoes, undrained

¼ cup extra-virgin olive oil, plus 3 tablespoons, divided

6 garlic cloves, roughly chopped, divided

2 teaspoons dried oregano, divided

½ teaspoon dried basil

¾ teaspoon salt, divided, plus more for the pasta water

¼ teaspoon freshly ground black pepper

½ teaspoon red pepper flakes, divided

2 boneless, skinless chicken breasts, cut into medallions

2 cups cremini mushrooms, halved

3 small onions, cut into chunks

1 red bell pepper, seeded and cut into strips

8 ounces spaghetti

¼ teaspoon red pepper flakes

1. Pour the juices from the can of tomatoes into a food processor or blender. Add 2 of the smaller tomatoes from the can and set the rest aside for later.

2. Add ¼ cup of olive oil, one-third of the chopped garlic, 1 teaspoon of oregano, the basil, ½ teaspoon of salt, the black pepper, and ¼ teaspoon of red pepper flakes. Blend to a thick puree.

3. Put the chicken in a large bowl, pour in the puree, and toss to coat. Cover the bowl and refrigerate for 2 to 3 hours.

4. Preheat the oven to 350°F. Line a rimmed baking sheet with aluminum foil.

5. Arrange the marinated chicken on two-thirds of the baking sheet. Spoon some of the marinade over the top.

6. Arrange the mushrooms, onions, bell pepper, and remaining chopped garlic on the other third of the baking sheet. Toss the vegetables lightly with 2 tablespoons of olive oil.

7. Bake for 20 minutes. Increase the oven temperature to 400°F and bake for another 15 minutes.

8. Meanwhile, bring a large pot of water to a boil over high heat. Once boiling, salt the water to your liking, stir, and return to a boil. Add the spaghetti and cook according to package directions until al dente. Drain, reserving about ½ cup of the cooking water.

9. Put the reserved canned tomatoes in the food processor and pulse a few times, just until chunky.

10. Pour the tomatoes into a wide, deep skillet and add the remaining 1 tablespoon of olive oil, 1 teaspoon of oregano, ¼ teaspoon of salt, and ¼ teaspoon of red pepper flakes. Bring to a boil over medium-high heat, then reduce the heat to low.

11. Add the cooked spaghetti to the skillet. Toss to coat it with the tomato sauce, adding the reserved cooking water, a little at a time, as needed to achieve the right consistency.

12. Serve the chicken with a side portion of spaghetti, surrounded by the peppers, mushrooms, onions, and garlic.

PER SERVING:

CALORIES: 1,050; Total Fat: 40g; Saturated Fat: 7g; Protein: 45g; Total Carbohydrates: 116g; Fiber: 15g; Sugar: 21g; Cholesterol: 73mg

FLANK STEAK WITH ITALIAN SALSA VERDE

Serves 4 / Prep time: 10 minutes / Cook time: 25 minutes

Salsa verde ingredients vary from country to country. In Mexico, tomatillos are used, whereas in Italy, parsley is used. This recipe uses the Italian version, which has bright, bold flavors that perfectly complement beef.

OVERALL WELLNESS

2 tablespoons extra-virgin olive oil, divided

1½ pounds flank steak

½ teaspoon salt

¼ teaspoon freshly ground black pepper

1 lemon wedge

Italian Salsa Verde (page 246)

1. Preheat the oven to 450°F. Brush a 9-by-13-inch baking dish with 1 tablespoon of olive oil.

2. Pierce the steak all over with a fork, about 30 times.

3. Put the steak in the prepared baking dish, brush it with the remaining 1 tablespoon of olive oil, and season with the salt and pepper.

4. Bake for 15 minutes. Turn the steak over and bake for another 10 to 15 minutes, depending on how you want your steak cooked.

5. Let the steak rest for a couple of minutes, then squeeze lemon juice over the top. Serve with the Italian salsa verde.

PER SERVING:

CALORIES: 422; Total Fat: 29g; Saturated Fat: 6g; Protein: 37g; Total Carbohydrates: 2g; Fiber: 0g; Sugar: 0g; Cholesterol: 103mg

MOROCCAN LAMB WITH COUSCOUS

Serves 4 / Prep time: 15 minutes / Cook time: 20 minutes

Couscous is tiny semolina pasta that is popular in Morocco. It goes well with lamb and vegetable dishes and can stand up to bold spices. The pomegranate marinade adds a sweet richness.

OVERALL WELLNESS

For the lamb

1 cup fresh cilantro

2 garlic cloves, peeled

¼ cup freshly squeezed lemon juice

3 tablespoons extra-virgin olive oil, divided

1 tablespoon ground cumin

1 teaspoon salt

½ teaspoon freshly ground black pepper

¼ teaspoon cayenne pepper

8 thin lamb loin chops

For the couscous

1½ cups water

1 cup couscous

1 tablespoon extra-virgin olive oil

½ teaspoon salt

½ teaspoon finely grated lemon zest

¼ teaspoon ground cinnamon

Pinch ground nutmeg

To make the lamb

1. Preheat the oven to 375°F.

2. In a food processor or blender, combine the cilantro, garlic, lemon juice, 1 tablespoon of olive oil, the cumin, salt, black pepper, and cayenne and process to a paste.

3. Set aside 1 tablespoon of the marinade paste and brush the rest on the lamb chops. Let sit for 10 minutes, then scrape the marinade off the lamb.

4. In a large ovenproof skillet, heat the remaining 2 tablespoons of olive oil over medium heat. Add the lamb chops and brown for about 2 minutes on each side.

5. Transfer the skillet to the oven and bake for 6 to 15 minutes, depending on how thick they are and how you like them cooked.

To make the couscous

6. Meanwhile, in a small saucepan, bring the water to a boil over high heat. Add the couscous, olive oil, salt, lemon zest, cinnamon, and nutmeg. Stir to combine, then remove the pan from the heat. Cover and let stand for about 15 minutes, until the liquid is absorbed into the couscous.

To finish

⅓ cup pomegranate juice

2 tablespoons choped
fresh mint

2 tablespoons chopped
pistachios

To finish

7. Remove the chops from the oven and add the pomegranate juice and reserved 1 tablespoon of marinade
to the pan. Deglaze the pan over medium heat, stirring all the browned bits from the bottom of the pan
into the sauce, and continue cooking until the liquid
reduces to ¼ cup.

8. Transfer the couscous to a bowl and fluff with a fork.
Stir in the mint and pistachios.

9. Serve the lamb chops over the couscous and drizzle
with the pomegranate sauce.

PER SERVING:

CALORIES: 688; Total Fat: 41g; Saturated Fat: 15g; Protein: 40g;
Total Carbohydrates: 35g; Fiber: 3g; Sugar: 0g; Cholesterol: 145mg

LAMB LOIN CHOPS WITH SPAGHETTI IN TOMATO SAUCE

Serves 2 / Prep time: 5 minutes / Cook time: 45 minutes

These chops are roasted in the oven and simply served with spaghetti in an extra-thick tomato sauce.

OVERALL WELLNESS

For the lamb and spaghetti

1 tablespoon extra-virgin olive oil

4 lamb loin chops

¼ teaspoon salt, plus more for the pasta water

Pinch freshly ground black pepper

4 rosemary sprigs

8 ounces spaghetti

For the sauce

1 tablespoon extra-virgin olive oil

3 garlic cloves, minced

1 (6-ounce) can tomato paste

¾ cup water

1 teaspoon dried oregano

½ teaspoon salt

¼ teaspoon freshly ground black pepper

¼ teaspoon red pepper flakes

2 tablespoons grated Parmesan or Romano cheese

To make the lamb and spaghetti

1. Preheat the oven to 385°F. Brush a baking dish with the olive oil.

2. Place the lamb chops in the baking dish and flip to coat in the oil. Season with the salt and pepper and place the rosemary sprigs on top.

3. Bake for 20 minutes. Flip and bake for another 15 to 20 minutes for well done. Discard the rosemary.

4. Meanwhile, bring a large pot of water to a boil over high heat. Once boiling, salt the water to your liking, stir, and return to a boil. Add the spaghetti and cook according to package directions until al dente. Drain, reserving about ½ cup of the cooking water.

To make the sauce

5. In a large skillet, heat the oil over medium heat. Add the garlic and cook for 1 minute. Stir in the tomato paste, water, oregano, salt, black pepper, and red pepper flakes.

6. Add the cooked spaghetti to the sauce. Stir to completely coat the spaghetti, adding the reserved cooking water a little at a time, as needed. Cook for 1 additional minute to meld the flavors.

7. Serve 2 lamb chops per person with a side of spaghetti. Sprinkle with Parmesan to taste.

PER SERVING:

CALORIES: 1,044; Total Fat: 50g; Saturated Fat: 14g; Protein: 54g; Total Carbohydrates: 105g; Fiber: 8g; Sugar: 15g; Cholesterol: 145mg

LAMB AND VEGETABLE STEW

Serves 4 / Prep time: 10 minutes / Cook time: 3 hours

This traditional Moroccan lamb stew is made with chunky vegetables. The mix of spices and dried apricots add complexity and a hint of sweetness to the sauce.

OVERALL WELLNESS

2 tablespoons extra-virgin olive oil, divided

1 fennel bulb, cored and thinly sliced

1 red onion, finely chopped

2 garlic cloves, thinly sliced

1½ pounds boneless lamb shoulder, cut into 1-inch cubes

2 teaspoons ground cumin

2 teaspoons ground coriander

1 teaspoon ground ginger

1 teaspoon salt

¼ teaspoon cayenne pepper

2 cups chicken broth

1 russet potato, peeled and cut into chunks

2 carrots, cut into 1-inch pieces

2 celery stalks, sliced

1 cup chopped dried apricots

Chopped fresh cilantro, for garnish

1. In a Dutch oven, heat 1 tablespoon of olive oil over medium heat. Add the fennel and red onion and cook for about 3 minutes, until they start to soften. Add the garlic and cook for an additional minute. Transfer the vegetables to a plate.

2. Add the remaining 1 tablespoon of olive oil to the pan. Add the lamb and cook until the lamb is browned, about 2 minutes per side.

3. Add the cumin, coriander, ginger, salt, and cayenne and stir to combine.

4. Return the vegetables to the pot. Add the chicken broth, potato, carrots, celery, and apricots. Bring the mixture to a boil, then reduce the heat to low, cover, and simmer, stirring occasionally, until the lamb is very tender and the sauce has thickened, about 2½ hours.

5. Garnish with cilantro.

PER SERVING:

CALORIES: 524; Total Fat: 21g; Saturated Fat: 7g; Protein: 38g; Total Carbohydrates: 48g; Fiber: 7g; Sugar: 23g; Cholesterol: 95mg

SICILIAN PORK RIBS IN TOMATO SAUCE

Serves 8 / Prep time: 15 minutes / Cook time: 1 hour 30 minutes

In the traditional Sicilian style, these ribs are first boiled with several kinds of pepper, then baked in a rich tomato sauce. You can serve the ribs whole or shred the meat to use in the sauce or as a sandwich filling.

OVERALL WELLNESS

⅓ cup chili powder

⅓ cup paprika

2 tablespoons freshly ground black pepper

1 teaspoon cayenne pepper

3 bay leaves

3 pounds bone-in country-style pork ribs

¼ cup extra-virgin olive oil

1 onion, chopped

2 celery stalks, chopped

1 carrot, chopped

2 garlic cloves, chopped

1 (28-ounce) can crushed tomatoes

1 (6-ounce) can tomato paste

¾ cup water

½ cup dry red wine

1 teaspoon salt

1. Fill a soup pot halfway with water. Add the chili powder, paprika, black pepper, cayenne, and bay leaves and bring it to a boil over high heat.

2. Add the ribs to the pot and make sure there is enough water to cover them. Bring the water back to a boil, then reduce to a simmer.

3. Place a dish or small pot lid on top of the ribs to keep them submerged and simmer for 45 minutes.

4. Transfer the ribs to a plate or cooling rack and let rest for 15 minutes.

5. Preheat the oven to 400°F.

6. In a large saucepan, heat the olive oil over medium heat. Add the onion, celery, and carrot and cook for about 5 minutes, until they start to soften. Add the garlic and cook for an additional minute.

7. Add the crushed tomatoes, tomato paste, water, red wine, and salt. Bring everything to a boil, then reduce the heat and simmer for 15 minutes. Turn off the heat.

8. Spread half of the tomato sauce in a 3-quart (13 × 9 × 2 inch) baking dish. Place the ribs in the sauce and then cover with the rest of the tomato sauce.

9. Roast for about 30 minutes, until the meat is falling off the bones.

PER SERVING:
CALORIES: 469; Total Fat: 37g; Saturated Fat: 12g; Protein: 26g; Total Carbohydrates: 7g; Fiber: 3g; Sugar: 4g; Cholesterol: 102mg

thirteen

BREADS, PIZZA, AND SANDWICHES

Sardinian Flatbread 206

Focaccia (Italian Flatbread) 207

Taralli (Pugliese Bread Knots) 209

Testaroli (Etruscan Pancakes) 210

Pesto Vegetable Bread 211

Tomato Bruschetta 212

White Bean Crostini 213

Pizza Dough 214

Bruschetta Pizza 215

Pizza Bianca with Spinach 216

La Dolce Vita Wrap 217

Portobello Mushroom Sandwich 218

Fishcake Sliders 219

Falafel in Pita 221

Veggie Club Sandwich 222

Greek Veggie Burgers 223

Bruschetta Pizza, p. 215

SARDINIAN FLATBREAD

Serves 6 / Prep time: 1 hour 15 minutes / Cook time: 15 minutes

This crispy flatbread is known on the island of Sardinia as *pane carasau*. Traditionally, it is baked in a wood-burning oven, where it puffs up like a balloon and is then cut into two thin rounds. Serve the crisps with olive oil and salt or grated Romano cheese.

OVERALL WELLNESS

1½ cups all-purpose flour, plus more for dusting

1½ cups semolina flour

1½ cups warm water

1 (¼-ounce) packet active dry yeast

Pinch salt

Extra-virgin olive oil, for brushing

1. In a large bowl, combine the flours, water, yeast, and salt and mix thoroughly to form a firm dough.

2. Turn out the dough onto a work surface and divide it into quarters. Set the dough pieces on a rimmed baking sheet, cover, and let rest for 1 hour.

3. Preheat the oven to 375°F. Lightly brush another rimmed baking sheet with olive oil.

4. Lightly flour a work surface and a rolling pin. Roll out one piece of dough until it is as thin as possible, then place it on the prepared baking sheet.

5. Bake for 2 minutes. Turn the flatbread over and bake for another 2 minutes, or until crisp.

6. Repeat with the remaining dough.

PER SERVING:

CALORIES: 275; Total Fat: 2g; Saturated Fat: 0g; Protein: 9g; Total Carbohydrates: 55g; Fiber: 3g; Sugar: 0g; Cholesterol: 0mg

FOCACCIA (ITALIAN FLATBREAD)

Serves 8 / Prep time: 2 hours / Cook time: 30 minutes

Focaccia is a fluffy flatbread similar in texture to Sicilian pizza dough. It can be used for sandwiches or enjoyed on its own.

OVERALL WELLNESS

2½ cups warm water, divided

2 teaspoons active dry yeast

Pinch sugar

6 cups all-purpose flour, divided

5 tablespoons extra-virgin olive oil, divided

2 tablespoons coarse sea salt, divided

1 tablespoon chopped fresh rosemary

1. Pour ½ cup of warm water into a large bowl and sprinkle on the yeast and sugar. Stir, then let rest for 1 minute. The yeast mixture should start to look foamy.

2. Add the remaining 2 cups of warm water, 2 cups of flour, 2 tablespoons of olive oil, and 1 tablespoon of sea salt. Stir until smooth.

3. Slowly add the remaining 4 cups of flour, using your hands to combine. If the dough is too sticky, add additional flour.

4. Turn out the dough onto a work surface and knead until you get a smooth, springy dough.

5. Brush a bowl with 1 tablespoon of olive oil. Place the dough in the bowl, cover with plastic wrap, and set aside in a warm place until the dough rises to double its size, about 1½ hours.

6. Preheat the oven to 425°F. Brush an 11-by-17-inch baking pan with 1 tablespoon of olive oil.

7. Press the dough into the prepared pan in an even layer, covering the entire surface. It may take a few minutes for the dough to cooperate. Cover the dough with a damp kitchen towel and let rise until doubled in size, about 30 minutes.

8. Press the dough with your fingers to add dimples all over. Brush with the remaining 2 tablespoons of olive oil, allowing it to pool in the dimples. Sprinkle with the remaining 1 tablespoon of sea salt and the rosemary.

9. Place a baking pan filled with ice on the lowest oven shelf or on the floor of the oven to create steam. Place the baking pan on the rack above.

10. Bake for about 30 minutes, until golden.

11. Transfer the focaccia to a wire rack to cool, then cut into strips or squares.

> **VARIATION TIP:** Feel free to experiment with toppings—you can add chopped tomatoes, onions, garlic, olives, or whatever you like.

PER SERVING:

CALORIES: 419; Total Fat: 9g; Saturated Fat: 1g; Protein: 10g; Total Carbohydrates: 72g; Fiber: 3g; Sugar: 0g; Cholesterol: 0mg

TARALLI (PUGLIESE BREAD KNOTS)

Makes 30 pieces / Prep time: 45 minutes / Cook time: 25 minutes

These treats from Puglia in southern Italy are a cross between a cracker and a bread-stick. They can be sweet or savory. Here, they're seasoned with olive oil and pepper.

OVERALL WELLNESS

2 cups all-purpose flour

½ teaspoon salt

½ cup dry white wine

⅓ cup extra-virgin olive oil

½ teaspoon freshly ground black pepper

1. In a large bowl, combine the flour and salt. Add the wine and olive oil and mix together with a fork until the mixture starts to form a rough dough.

2. Turn out the dough onto a work surface and knead until smooth, sprinkling with the pepper as you work until it is all combined and the dough is smooth.

3. Cover the dough with a kitchen towel and let it rest for 15 minutes.

4. Preheat the oven to 375°F. Line a rimmed baking sheet with parchment paper. Bring a large pot of water to a boil over high heat.

5. For each bread knot, roll a tablespoon of the dough into a rope about 4 inches long and ½ inch thick. Form a circle with the rope, then crisscross the ends to form a knot shape and press the ends together to seal.

6. Drop a few knots at a time into the boiling water. When they float, after about 30 seconds, transfer them with a slotted spoon to a kitchen towel to dry.

7. Arrange the taralli on the prepared baking sheet in a single layer, making sure they do not touch.

8. Bake for 25 minutes, or until golden.

9. Transfer to a rack to cool a bit before serving.

PER SERVING (3 PIECES):

CALORIES: 164; Total Fat: 7g; Saturated Fat: 1g; Protein: 3g; Total Carbohydrates: 19g; Fiber: 1g; Sugar: 0g; Cholesterol: 0mg

TESTAROLI (ETRUSCAN PANCAKES)

Serves 2 / Prep time: 5 minutes / Cook time: 15 minutes

These ancient pancakes are the precursor to pasta and are still enjoyed in the Tuscany region of Italy. They are made simply, using just flour, water, and sea salt. Their texture is similar to that of crepes. Try them with a little pesto and Parmesan cheese.

OVERALL WELLNESS

½ cup whole wheat flour

½ cup all-purpose flour

1 cup warm water

Salt

2 tablespoons extra-virgin olive oil

1. In a bowl, whisk together the flours, water, and a pinch of salt until you get a thick batter. Let the mixture rest while you heat a cast-iron skillet over high heat. At the same time, fill a large pot with warm salted water.

2. Brush the skillet with about 1 teaspoon of olive oil, then pour about ¼ cup of the batter into the hot pan, just enough to cover the bottom. Cook for 1 to 2 minutes, until golden brown, flip, and cook the other side until golden.

3. Remove the pancake from the pan and cut the testaroli like a pizza, into 6 or 8 wedges. Transfer the wedges to the pot of warm salted water and let them sit for 1 minute, then remove from the water.

4. Repeat with the remaining batter and oil.

COOKING TIP: If you want a drier pancake, you can skip the step of dunking the testaroli in warm water. They are just as tasty fresh out of the skillet.

PER SERVING:

CALORIES: 335; Total Fat: 15g; Saturated Fat: 2g; Protein: 7g; Total Carbohydrates: 45g; Fiber: 4g; Sugar: 0g; Cholesterol: 0mg

PESTO VEGETABLE BREAD

Serves 4 / Prep time: 15 minutes / Cook time: 20 minutes

Focaccia is delicious on its own, but you can also pile a variety of vegetables on top and toast it in the oven for a perfect accompaniment to soup. Use the vegetables suggested here or create your own blend using your favorites. Be sure to choose a variety of colors to maximize your nutrients.

OVERALL WELLNESS

2 tablespoons extra-virgin olive oil, plus more for drizzling

½ eggplant, cut into cubes

½ fennel bulb, trimmed and sliced

1 red bell pepper, seeded and cut into strips

1 bunch broccoli rabe

1 loaf Focaccia (page 207)

2 tablespoons Basil Pesto with Almond Butter (page 256) or store-bought pesto

½ small onion, thinly sliced

4 radishes, sliced

1 teaspoon fresh thyme leaves

½ teaspoon salt

1 teaspoon minced garlic

1. Preheat the oven to 350°F.

2. In a large skillet, heat the olive oil over medium heat. Add the eggplant, fennel, and bell pepper and cook for about 10 minutes, until they start to soften.

3. Meanwhile, bring a large pot of water to a boil over high heat. Add the broccoli rabe and cook for 3 minutes. Drain, squeeze out any excess water, and cut into bite-size pieces.

4. Slice the focaccia in half horizontally all the way through and brush each cut side with the pesto. Arrange the eggplant, fennel, bell pepper, and broccoli rabe on the pesto. Top with the onion and radish slices and sprinkle with the thyme and salt.

5. Bake for 5 to 10 minutes, until the fresh ingredients start to warm.

6. Turn the oven to broil and toast for 1 minute.

7. Remove the bread from the oven. Sprinkle with the garlic and drizzle with a bit of olive oil. Cut into slices.

INGREDIENT TIP: Leftover roasted vegetables are ideal for this recipe.

PER SERVING:

CALORIES: 1,003; Total Fat: 30g; Saturated Fat: 4g; Protein: 24g; Total Carbohydrates: 158g; Fiber: 18g; Sugar: 6g; Cholesterol: 1mg

TOMATO BRUSCHETTA

Serves 6 / Prep time: 10 minutes / Cook time: 4 minutes

Tomatoes are one of the healthiest foods you can put on your plate. This summery treat works great as an appetizer before a meal. Be sure to toast the bread, or it will end up soggy from the tomato juice.

HEART HEALTH

1 baguette, sliced

3 large tomatoes, finely chopped

1 small onion, diced

¼ cup extra-virgin olive oil

4 garlic cloves, minced

1 teaspoon dried oregano

1 teaspoon salt

¼ teaspoon freshly ground black pepper

Chopped fresh basil, for garnish

1. Preheat the oven to 350°F.

2. Place the baguette slices on a rimmed baking sheet. Toast for 2 minutes, turn them over, and toast for another 2 minutes.

3. In a large bowl, combine the tomatoes, onion, olive oil, garlic, oregano, salt, and pepper and toss to mix thoroughly.

4. Arrange the toasted baguette slices on a serving plate and spoon the tomato mixture generously over each piece. Sprinkle with basil.

MAKE-AHEAD TIP: You can make the tomato mixture an hour ahead of time, cover, and store in the refrigerator.

PER SERVING:

CALORIES: 206; Total Fat: 10g; Saturated Fat: 1g; Protein: 5g; Total Carbohydrates: 25g; Fiber: 2g; Sugar: 5g; Cholesterol: 0mg

WHITE BEAN CROSTINI

Serves 4 / Prep time: 5 minutes

Crostini are slices of toasted bread garnished with toppings such as beans, vegetables, cheese, and herbs. This white bean crostini is a tasty blend of cannellini beans, garlic, olive oil, and spices.

WEIGHT LOSS

1 baguette, sliced

1 (19-ounce) can cannellini beans, rinsed and drained

2 tablespoons extra-virgin olive oil, plus more for drizzling

1 garlic clove, peeled

1 teaspoon salt

½ teaspoon dried oregano

¼ teaspoon red pepper flakes

¼ teaspoon freshly ground black pepper

1. Preheat the oven to 350°F.

2. Place the baguette slices on a rimmed baking sheet. Toast for 2 minutes, turn them over, and toast for another 2 minutes.

3. In a food processor or blender, combine the beans, olive oil, garlic, salt, oregano, red pepper flakes, and black pepper and puree.

4. Spoon the bean mixture onto the toasted baguette slices and drizzle with extra-virgin olive oil.

PER SERVING:

CALORIES: 481; Total Fat: 11g; Saturated Fat: 2g; Protein: 17g; Total Carbohydrates: 79g; Fiber: 9g; Sugar: 4g; Cholesterol: 0mg

PIZZA DOUGH

Serves 4 / Prep time: 15 minutes, plus 1 hour to rise

The city of Naples in southern Italy is known to have the best pizza in the world. Traditionally, these pizzas are cooked in a wood-burning oven, but this recipe re-creates the magic in your home oven.

OVERALL WELLNESS

4 cups 00 flour or bread flour, plus more for dusting

½ teaspoon salt

¼ cup water

2 tablespoons extra-virgin olive oil, plus 1 teaspoon

1¼ teaspoons active dry yeast

1 teaspoon sugar

1. Sift together the flour and salt onto a work surface. Make a well in the middle.

2. In a bowl, combine the water, 2 tablespoons of olive oil, the yeast, and sugar. Let the mixture sit for a few minutes for the yeast to activate, then pour it into the well in the flour.

3. Using a fork, bring the flour in gradually from the sides and swirl it into the liquid. Keep mixing, bringing in more and more flour, until it is all combined.

4. Knead the mixture with your hands until you get a smooth, bouncy ball of dough.

5. Oil a bowl with the remaining 1 teaspoon of olive oil and place the dough in it. Sprinkle the top with flour, cover the bowl with a damp kitchen towel, and set it aside in a warm place to double in size, about 1 hour.

6. Dust a work surface with flour and knead the dough again, releasing the air until it is back to normal size.

7. Divide the dough into 4 pieces and roll each piece into a round.

> **INGREDIENT TIP:** 00 (double zero) flour is a gluten-rich Italian flour that helps give pizza that tough pull. You can find it in the international section of supermarkets or online.

PER SERVING:

CALORIES: 533; Total Fat: 9g; Saturated Fat: 1g; Protein: 13g; Total Carbohydrates: 96g; Fiber: 4g; Sugar: 1g; Cholesterol: 0mg

BRUSCHETTA PIZZA

Serves 4 / Prep time: 10 minutes / Cook time: 10 minutes

This pizza is a fresh take on a classic tomato pie bursting with the flavors of late summer, when tomatoes are at their peak.

OVERALL WELLNESS

¼ cup extra-virgin olive oil, plus 1 tablespoon

4 garlic cloves, minced, divided

1 teaspoon Italian Herb Blend (page 262)

¼ teaspoon red pepper flakes

1 teaspoon salt, plus a pinch

2 rounds Pizza Dough (page 214) or 12-inch store-bought pizza crusts

1 cup shredded pizza cheese (such as a mozzarella-provolone blend)

4 large tomatoes, chopped

2 tablespoons diced red onion

1 tablespoon dried oregano

1. Preheat the oven to 425°F.

2. In a small bowl, combine ¼ cup of olive oil with half the garlic, the Italian herb blend, red pepper flakes, and a pinch of salt. Using a spoon, spread this mixture evenly over the pizza crusts.

3. Sprinkle the cheese on top.

4. Bake the pizzas for 8 to 10 minutes, until the dough is cooked through and the cheese is melted.

5. Meanwhile, in a bowl, toss together the tomatoes, red onion, remaining garlic, remaining 1 tablespoon of olive oil, remaining 1 teaspoon of salt, and the oregano.

6. Remove the pizza from the oven and turn the oven to broil.

7. Spoon the tomato mixture over the top of the pizzas. Broil for 1 to 2 minutes, just enough to quickly warm up the tomato mixture.

8. Cut into slices.

> **INGREDIENT TIP:** You can find prerolled pizza crusts at your local Italian deli or market or sometimes in the bakery section of the supermarket. Keep in mind that the quality of your pizza will be directly related to the quality of the dough you use. The closer to fresh, the better, so stay away from overly processed products.

PER SERVING:
CALORIES: 580; Total Fat: 29g; Saturated Fat: 7g; Protein: 20g; Total Carbohydrates: 62g; Fiber: 5g; Sugar: 11g; Cholesterol: 23mg

PIZZA BIANCA WITH SPINACH

Serves 4 / Prep time: 15 minutes / Cook time: 15 minutes

Pizza doesn't always have to start with tomato sauce. White pizza originated in Rome, where it is known as *pizza bianca*. This recipe features garlic, spinach, and a mix of cheeses.

OVERALL WELLNESS

2 rounds Pizza Dough (page 214) or 12-inch store-bought pizza crusts

2 tablespoons extra-virgin olive oil

2 garlic cloves, minced

2 cups frozen chopped spinach, thawed and drained

1 cup shredded provolone cheese

1 cup shredded mozzarella cheese

1 tablespoon dried oregano

1. Preheat the oven to 450°F.

2. Brush the pizza crusts with the olive oil and sprinkle with the garlic and spinach.

3. Cover the pizzas with the cheeses and sprinkle with the oregano.

4. Bake for 10 to 15 minutes, until the cheese is browned and bubbling.

5. Let rest for 1 minute before slicing.

PER SERVING:

CALORIES: 586; Total Fat: 38g; Saturated Fat: 18g; Protein: 25g; Total Carbohydrates: 39g; Fiber: 5g; Sugar: 8g; Cholesterol: 77mg

LA DOLCE VITA WRAP

Serves 2 / Prep time: 15 minutes / Cook time: 5 minutes

This Mediterranean take on a classic bean burrito replaces refried beans with cannellini beans and cheese with hummus. The filling is a variety of colorful salad ingredients.

WEIGHT LOSS

1 (15-ounce) can cannellini beans, undrained

1 teaspoon Italian Herb Blend (page 262)

Pinch salt

2 flour tortillas

4 tablespoons Classic Hummus (page 153)

6 grape tomatoes, halved

8 cucumber slices, cut in half

¼ cup shredded red cabbage

2 tablespoons chopped red onion

½ carrot, grated

8 small broccoli florets

2 tablespoons Lemon-Dijon Vinaigrette (page 254)

4 lettuce leaves

1. In a small saucepan, combine the beans and their liquid, the Italian herb blend, and salt over medium heat. Cook for 5 minutes, until heated through. Drain.

2. Lay the tortillas on a work surface. Spread 2 tablespoons of hummus down the center of each. Divide the beans on top of the hummus.

3. Place the tomatoes, cucumber, red cabbage, red onion, carrot, and broccoli on top of the beans.

4. Sprinkle the vinaigrette on top of the vegetables. Add the lettuce on top to hold everything together.

5. Fold in the sides of the tortilla and roll them up before serving.

PER SERVING:
CALORIES: 430; Total Fat: 7g; Saturated Fat: 1g; Protein: 19g; Total Carbohydrates: 76g; Fiber: 19g; Sugar: 7g; Cholesterol: 0mg

PORTOBELLO MUSHROOM SANDWICH

Serves 4 / Prep time: 10 minutes / Cook time: 15 minutes

With their rich flavor and texture, portobello mushrooms can be used in place of meat in many recipes. Here, they make a wonderfully healthy stand-in for a hamburger.

WEIGHT LOSS

2 tablespoons extra-virgin olive oil, plus more for brushing

4 large portobello mushroom caps, stemmed

½ teaspoon salt

¼ teaspoon freshly ground black pepper

4 slices provolone cheese

4 kaiser rolls

4 lettuce leaves

1 large tomato, sliced

½ red onion, sliced

1. Preheat the oven to 325°F. Line a rimmed baking sheet with parchment paper and lightly brush it with olive oil.

2. Place the mushrooms, stemmed-side down, on the prepared baking sheet. Brush the tops with the olive oil and sprinkle with the salt and pepper.

3. Bake for 10 minutes, then turn them over. Add the cheese on top and bake for another 5 minutes.

4. Place 1 mushroom on each roll. Dress with lettuce, tomato, and red onion.

INGREDIENT TIP: Choose the largest mushrooms you can find because they shrink during the cooking process.

PER SERVING:

CALORIES: 347; Total Fat: 17g; Saturated Fat: 6g; Protein: 15g; Total Carbohydrates: 35g; Fiber: 3g; Sugar: 4g; Cholesterol: 19mg

FISHCAKE SLIDERS

Serves 6 / Prep time: 15 minutes / Cook time: 30 minutes

Fishcake sliders make for a healthy Mediterranean alternative to burgers in the summertime. Dress them with refreshing Tzatziki Sauce (page 247) and serve them with a tomato salad and corn on the cob.

WEIGHT LOSS

Nonstick cooking spray

1 pound flounder or catfish fillets

1 shallot, roughly chopped

1 (1-inch) piece jalapeño, roughly chopped

2 garlic cloves, peeled

2 tablespoons cream sherry

½ cup seasoned bread crumbs, divided

12 slider buns

1. Preheat the oven to 385°F. Line a rimmed baking sheet with parchment paper and lightly coat it with cooking spray.

2. Put the fish fillets in a food processor and pulse a few times just to break up the fish.

3. Add the shallot, jalapeño, and garlic and process until well combined.

4. Add the sherry and ¼ cup of bread crumbs and pulse. You want the consistency to be where you can pick it up and mold it into patties, so adjust the amount of bread crumbs as necessary.

5. Put the remaining ¼ cup of bread crumbs in a small bowl.

6. Take about a tablespoon of the fish mixture and roll it around in your hands to form a ball. Flatten it out a little, dip each side into the bread crumbs, and place on the prepared baking sheet. Continue until you use up all the fish mixture. You should have about 12 fish cakes.

7. Bake for 15 minutes, then flip the cakes and bake for another 10 to 15 minutes, until golden.

8. Place a fish cake on each slider bun.

> **INGREDIENT TIP:** This recipe works well with any white fillet of fish, like catfish, tilapia, or cod.

PER SERVING (2 SLIDERS):
CALORIES: 264; Total Fat: 6g; Saturated Fat: 1g; Protein: 18g; Total Carbohydrates: 33g; Fiber: 3g; Sugar: 2g; Cholesterol: 44mg

FALAFEL IN PITA

Serves 4 / Prep time: 25 minutes / Cook time: 40 minutes

Falafel are chickpea patties that originated in Egypt and remain popular all over the Middle East. They are usually deep-fried, but they can also be baked. Dress them up with tzatziki and stuff them in a pita for a classic Mediterranean sandwich.

WEIGHT LOSS

3 tablespoons extra-virgin olive oil, divided, plus more for brushing

1 cup dried chickpeas

1 medium onion, roughly chopped

2 garlic cloves, peeled

3 tablespoons chopped fresh flat-leaf parsley

1 tablespoon all-purpose flour

1 teaspoon ground coriander

1 teaspoon ground cumin

1 teaspoon salt

⅛ teaspoon cayenne pepper

4 pita breads

½ iceberg lettuce head, chopped

1 tomato, chopped

1 red onion, chopped

¼ cup Tzatziki Sauce (page 247)

1. Preheat the oven to 350°F. Line a rimmed baking sheet with parchment paper and lightly brush with olive oil.

2. Put the chickpeas in a pot and cover with water. Bring to a boil over high heat, then reduce the heat to low and simmer for 15 minutes. Drain the chickpeas and let cool.

3. In a food processor, combine the onion, garlic, parsley, flour, 1 tablespoon of olive oil, the coriander, cumin, salt, and cayenne. Pulse a few times to combine. Add the chickpeas and process to form a thick paste.

4. Scoop out about 1 tablespoon of the falafel mixture, roll it in your hands to create a ball, then flatten into a patty about 2 inches wide. You should get 12 to 15 patties. Place the patties on the prepared baking sheet.

5. Brush the patties with the remaining 2 tablespoons of olive oil. Bake for 15 minutes. Flip and bake for 10 more minutes, or until lightly browned.

6. Place 3 falafel in each pita pocket. Top with lettuce, tomato, red onion, and a dollop of tzatziki.

PER SERVING:

CALORIES: 290; Total Fat: 12g; Saturated Fat: 2g; Protein: 9g; Total Carbohydrates: 39g; Fiber: 8g; Sugar: 8g; Cholesterol: 0mg

VEGGIE CLUB SANDWICH

Serves 2 / Prep time: 15 minutes

Club sandwiches are usually triple-decker layers of deli meat held together with frilly toothpicks. This tasty version instead features a variety of colorful vegetables and a bright homemade dressing.

WEIGHT LOSS

1 tablespoon extra-virgin olive oil

1 teaspoon freshly squeezed lemon juice

1 garlic clove, minced

⅛ teaspoon freshly ground black pepper

Pinch cayenne pepper

1 cup alfalfa sprouts

½ cup shredded carrots

6 multigrain or sourdough bread slices, toasted

½ cup baby spinach or watercress

1 large tomato, sliced

½ cucumber, peeled and sliced

1 avocado, pitted, peeled, and sliced

2 radishes, thinly sliced

½ red onion, sliced

1. In a bowl, whisk together the olive oil, lemon juice, garlic, black pepper, and cayenne. Add the sprouts and carrots and toss until coated with dressing.

2. Start building the sandwiches with 2 slices of toast. Dividing equally, top each with spinach, a slice of tomato, and the cucumber slices. Top each with another slice of toast. Dividing equally, top with the avocado slices, radish slices, red onion slices, and the sprout-carrot mixture. Close the sandwiches with the last 2 slices of toast.

3. Cut the sandwiches diagonally into quarters and secure each triangle with a toothpick.

PER SERVING:
CALORIES: 533; Total Fat: 26g; Saturated Fat: 5g; Protein: 17g; Total Carbohydrates: 63g; Fiber: 14g; Sugar: 13g; Cholesterol: 0mg

GREEK VEGGIE BURGERS

Serves 4 / Prep time: 15 minutes / Cook time: 1 hour

These veggie burgers feature spinach, mushrooms, and cheese for a refreshing change from meatless burgers made from grains and beans.

HEART HEALTH

Nonstick cooking spray

4 tablespoons extra-virgin olive oil, divided

2 shallots, chopped

8 ounces cremini mushrooms, stemmed and chopped

½ teaspoon salt, divided

½ teaspoon freshly ground black pepper, divided

1 pound spinach, stems removed

1 cup part-skim ricotta cheese

2 large eggs

½ cup all-purpose flour

½ cup bread crumbs

1. Preheat the oven to 425°F. Line a rimmed baking sheet with aluminum foil.

2. In a large skillet, heat 2 tablespoons of olive oil over medium heat. Cook the shallots for about 3 minutes, until they start to soften.

3. Add the mushrooms and cook for about 10 minutes, until they start to turn golden and the liquid evaporates. Stir in ¼ teaspoon of salt and ¼ teaspoon of pepper. Transfer the mushrooms and shallots to a plate.

4. Add the remaining 2 tablespoons of olive oil, the spinach, and the remaining ¼ teaspoon of salt and ¼ teaspoon of pepper. Cook until the spinach has wilted, about 5 minutes.

5. Transfer the spinach to a colander and let cool, then squeeze out the excess liquid and chop.

6. Transfer the spinach to a bowl and add the mushroom-shallot mixture, ricotta, and eggs. Stir well to mix. Add the flour and stir to combine. Form the veggie mixture into 4 large patties.

7. Put the bread crumbs in a shallow dish. Dip both sides of each patty in the bread crumbs, then place on the prepared baking sheet, leaving about 1 inch of space in between.

8. Bake for 20 minutes. Flip and bake for another 15 to 20 minutes, until browned and firm.

PER SERVING:

CALORIES: 394; Total Fat: 22g; Saturated Fat: 6g; Protein: 19g; Total Carbohydrates: 32g; Fiber: 4g; Sugar: 3g; Cholesterol: 112mg

fourteen

SNACKS AND SIPS

Jazzed-Up Olives 226

Olive Tapenade 227

Spicy Chickpeas 228

Layered Hummus Dip 229

Kibbeh (Lebanese Croquettes) 230

Cheese Plate with Fruit and Crackers 231

Radicchio Stuffed with Goat Cheese and Salmon 232

Rosemary–Sea Salt Crackers with Lemon-Parsley Dip 233

Spinach and Artichoke Dip 234

Stuffed Cherry Tomatoes 235

Mediterranean Antipasto Skewers 236

Spiced Baked Pita Chips 237

Roasted Red Pepper Dip 238

Deviled Eggs with Spanish Smoked Paprika 239

Aperol Spritz 241

Vin Brulé 242

Sparkling Spa Water 243

Stuffed Cherry Tomatoes, p. 235

JAZZED-UP OLIVES

Serves 8 / Prep time: 5 minutes, plus 1 hour to marinate / Cook time: 4 minutes

This quick, tasty treat is fun to serve and packed with health benefits. Olives are a good source of healthy fat and antioxidants. Try to find a selection of green and black Sicilian, Greek, and French olives.

HEART HEALTH

½ cup extra-virgin olive oil

2 garlic cloves, minced

2 teaspoons fresh thyme leaves

1 teaspoon dried oregano

½ teaspoon red pepper flakes

2 cups mixed olives

1 tablespoon freshly squeezed lemon juice

1. In a skillet, warm the olive oil over low heat. Add the garlic, thyme, oregano, and red pepper flakes and cook for about 2 minutes, until the garlic starts to turn golden.

2. Add the olives and stir for about 1 minute to coat them in the oil mixture.

3. Transfer the olive mixture, including the oil, to a bowl and toss with the lemon juice.

4. Allow to marinate at room temperature for 1 hour before serving.

MAKE-AHEAD TIP: Store the olives in an airtight container in the refrigerator for up 3 days.

PER SERVING:

CALORIES: 160; Total Fat: 17g; Saturated Fat: 2g; Protein: 0g; Total Carbohydrates: 3g; Fiber: 1g; Sugar: 0g; Cholesterol: 0mg

OLIVE TAPENADE

Serves 2 / Prep time: 10 minutes

Tapenade is a condiment from Provence in the South of France. It consists of olives, capers, garlic, and anchovies—some of the healthiest foods you can eat. Spread the tapenade on sandwiches or serve as a dip for breadsticks or crackers.

HEART HEALTH

10 to 12 meaty olives, pitted and finely chopped

2 tablespoons extra-virgin olive oil

1 teaspoon freshly squeezed lemon juice

1 garlic clove, minced

½ teaspoon chopped capers

½ teaspoon anchovy paste or 1 anchovy fillet, minced

2 or 3 fresh basil leaves, chopped

½ teaspoon red pepper flakes

Pinch freshly ground black pepper

In a bowl, combine the olives, olive oil, lemon juice, garlic, capers, anchovy paste, basil, red pepper flakes, and black pepper and stir well.

MAKE-AHEAD TIP: Store the tapenade in an airtight container in the refrigerator for up to 3 days.

PER SERVING:
CALORIES: 144; Total Fat: 16g; Saturated Fat: 2g; Protein: 1g; Total Carbohydrates: 1g; Fiber: 1g; Sugar: 0g; Cholesterol: 1mg

SPICY CHICKPEAS

Serves 6 / Prep time: 5 minutes / Cook time: 10 minutes

When you want a crunchy snack, fried chickpeas make a healthy alternative to chips. Chickpeas are rich in protein, folate, and iron.

HEART HEALTH

1 (15-ounce) can chickpeas, rinsed and drained

3 tablespoons extra-virgin olive oil

1 teaspoon paprika

½ teaspoon salt

½ teaspoon cayenne pepper

1. Pat the chickpeas dry with a paper towel. Remove as many of the soft skins as you can.

2. In a large skillet, heat the olive oil over low heat. Add the chickpeas and stir to coat. Slowly toast the chickpeas, stirring occasionally, until they get a little crunchy, about 10 minutes.

3. Using a slotted spoon, transfer the chickpeas to a bowl lined with paper towels to absorb any excess oil.

4. Transfer the chickpeas to a serving bowl, sprinkle with the paprika, salt, and cayenne, and toss to coat.

MAKE-AHEAD TIP: Store the chickpeas in an airtight container in the refrigerator for up to 1 week.

PER SERVING:

CALORIES: 114; Total Fat: 8g; Saturated Fat: 5g; Protein: 3g; Total Carbohydrates: 8g; Fiber: 3g; Sugar: 2g; Cholesterol: 0mg

LAYERED HUMMUS DIP

Serves 4 / Prep time: 5 minutes

Using hummus as a base makes for a low-calorie, healthy dip. This colorful crowd-pleaser always disappears quickly at a party. Serve it with cucumber slices, baby carrots, and red bell pepper slices.

WEIGHT LOSS

1 cup Classic Hummus (page 153)

½ cup finely chopped tomatoes

¼ cup shredded Fontina cheese

2 tablespoons chopped pitted kalamata olives

1 tablespoon Sweet Hot Cherry Pepper Relish (page 252)

1. Spread the hummus in the bottom of a small serving bowl.

2. Cover the hummus with the chopped tomatoes. Add a layer of cheese, followed by a layer of kalamata olives.

3. Spoon the cherry pepper relish in the center. (Don't put the hot peppers all over the top, so guests can decide whether they want to add them.)

PER SERVING:

CALORIES: 144; Total Fat: 8g; Saturated Fat: 2g; Protein: 5g; Total Carbohydrates: 14g; Fiber: 3g; Sugar: 1g; Cholesterol: 8mg

KIBBEH (LEBANESE CROQUETTES)

Serves 12 / Prep time: 1 hour 30 minutes / Cook time: 40 minutes

Kibbeh are like little meatballs but with a crispy exterior. They are usually deep-fried, but you can also bake them. Serve them with Tahini (page 255) or Tzatziki Sauce (page 247).

For the kibbeh dough

1½ cups fine bulgur

2 cups warm water

1½ pounds ground beef

1 onion, cut into chunks

2 teaspoons ground allspice

1 teaspoon ground coriander

1 teaspoon freshly ground black pepper

½ teaspoon ground cinnamon

Pinch salt

For the stuffing

2 tablespoons extra-virgin olive oil

1 onion, finely chopped

8 ounces ground beef or lamb

½ teaspoon ground allspice

¼ teaspoon ground cinnamon

Pinch salt

Pinch freshly ground black pepper

1. **To make the dough:** In a bowl, combine the bulgur and warm water and soak for 15 minutes. Drain. Wrap the bulgur in a kitchen towel and squeeze out the excess water.

2. In a food processor, combine the ground beef, onion, allspice, coriander, pepper, cinnamon, and salt. Process until the mixture forms a paste.

3. Transfer the mixture to a bowl and add the bulgur. Mix by hand to form a dough. Cover and refrigerate while you make the stuffing.

4. **To make the stuffing:** In a large skillet, heat the olive oil over medium heat. Add the onion and cook for about 3 minutes, until it starts to soften. Add the ground meat and cook for 5 to 7 minutes, until cooked through. Add the allspice, cinnamon, salt, and pepper and stir to combine. Remove from the heat and allow to cool.

5. Set up an assembly line with a bowl of water, the bowl of kibbeh dough, and the bowl of stuffing. Line a rimmed baking sheet with parchment paper.

6. Dampen your hands with water. Shape 2 tablespoons of dough into a flat disc. Wrap 1 tablespoon of stuffing inside the dough. Pinch to close.

7. Continue until you use all the ingredients, wetting your hands before forming each one. Place the kibbeh on the prepared baking sheet and refrigerate for 1 hour. Preheat the oven to 350°F.

8. Bake for 30 to 35 minutes, until golden brown.

PER SERVING:

CALORIES: 216; Total Fat: 9g; Saturated Fat: 3g; Protein: 18g; Total Carbohydrates: 18g; Fiber: 3g; Sugar: 3g; Cholesterol: 49mg

CHEESE PLATE WITH FRUIT AND CRACKERS

Serves 8 / Prep time: 15 minutes

A great Mediterranean cheese plate features cheeses from several countries. In keeping with Mediterranean diet principles, fruits and nuts are the focus of this platter. Enjoy it with red wine, sparkling wine, or sparkling water.

OVERALL WELLNESS

8 fresh figs, quartered

2 cups red and/or green grapes

8 ounces goat cheese

8 ounces Gorgonzola cheese

8 ounces Manchego cheese

8 ounces Parmigiano-Reggiano cheese

Rosemary and thyme sprigs

1 cup pistachios

1 cup hazelnuts

1 cup almonds

2 cups red, green, and/or black olives

1 (8-ounce) package whole wheat crackers

1 baguette, sliced

Arrange the fruits and cheeses artfully on a wooden board. Scatter the herb sprigs here and there. Put the nuts and olives in small bowls and the crackers and baguette slices on a plate or in a basket.

PER SERVING:

CALORIES: 990; Total Fat: 66g; Saturated Fat: 22g; Protein: 42g; Total Carbohydrates: 64g; Fiber: 10g; Sugar: 21g; Cholesterol: 73mg

RADICCHIO STUFFED WITH GOAT CHEESE AND SALMON

Serves 8 / Prep time: 15 minutes

These savory wraps are packed with color and flavor: mildly bitter lettuce filled with tangy, creamy goat cheese and smoky salmon.

WEIGHT LOSS

8 ounces goat cheese, at room temperature

2 tablespoons low-fat plain Greek yogurt

2 garlic cloves, peeled

1 tablespoon chopped fresh oregano

1 tablespoon chopped fresh basil

1 tablespoon chopped fresh rosemary

4 ounces smoked salmon

1 head radicchio, separated into leaves

¼ teaspoon freshly ground black pepper

1. In a food processor, combine the goat cheese, yogurt, garlic, oregano, basil, and rosemary and blend until combined.

2. Place a piece of smoked salmon on each radicchio leaf. Top with 1 tablespoon of the cheese mixture. Sprinkle with black pepper.

PER SERVING:

CALORIES: 99; Total Fat: 7g; Saturated Fat: 4g; Protein: 8g; Total Carbohydrates: 1g; Fiber: 0g; Sugar: 0g; Cholesterol: 17mg

ROSEMARY–SEA SALT CRACKERS WITH LEMON-PARSLEY DIP

Serves 4 / Prep time: 15 minutes / Cook time: 15 minutes

Rosemary is used extensively in the Mediterranean to flavor bread, crackers, and focaccia, as well as potatoes and soups. These rosemary crackers go nicely with a lemony herb dip.

OVERALL WELLNESS

For the dip

8 ounces cream cheese

½ cup low-fat plain Greek yogurt

½ cup vegan mayonnaise

3 scallions, chopped

¼ cup chopped fresh flat-leaf parsley

1 teaspoon chopped fresh thyme

Finely grated zest of 1 lemon

1 teaspoon sea salt

¼ teaspoon freshly ground black pepper

For the crackers

1½ cups all-purpose flour, plus more for dusting

1 tablespoon finely chopped fresh rosemary

1 teaspoon coarse sea salt, plus more for sprinkling

1 teaspoon sugar

½ cup water, plus more for brushing

1½ tablespoons extra-virgin olive oil

To make the dip

1. In a food processor, combine the cream cheese, yogurt, mayo, scallions, parsley, thyme, lemon zest, salt, and pepper and process until smooth. Transfer to a bowl, cover, and refrigerate for 30 minutes.

To make the crackers

2. Meanwhile, preheat the oven to 425°F. Line a rimmed baking sheet with parchment paper.

3. In a bowl, whisk together the flour, rosemary, salt, and sugar. Add the water and olive oil and stir to combine.

4. Turn out the dough onto a lightly floured work surface. Roll out the dough until very thin, about $\frac{1}{16}$ inch, adding more flour if the dough is too sticky.

5. Using a pizza cutter or nonserrated knife, cut the dough into rectangles about 2 inches by 1 inch. Place on the prepared baking sheet. Brush with water and sprinkle with salt.

6. Bake for 12 to 15 minutes, until the crackers are golden.

7. Serve the crackers with the dip.

PER SERVING:
CALORIES: 535; Total Fat: 35g; Saturated Fat: 12g; Protein: 12g; Total Carbohydrates: 43g; Fiber: 2g; Sugar: 6g; Cholesterol: 64mg

SPINACH AND ARTICHOKE DIP

Serves 8 / Prep time: 10 minutes / Cook time: 20 minutes

This classic dip is easy to make Mediterranean-diet friendly: Instead of cream cheese or mayo, this recipe uses a combination of low-fat yogurt and strongly flavored cheeses. Serve the dip with pita, crackers, chips, or lightly steamed asparagus stalks.

WEIGHT LOSS

Extra-virgin olive oil,
for brushing

1 (10-ounce) package frozen
chopped spinach, thawed and
squeezed dry

1 (12-ounce) jar marinated
artichoke hearts, drained
and chopped

1 cup low-fat plain
Greek yogurt

1 cup shredded
Fontina cheese

⅓ cup crumbled feta cheese

2 garlic cloves, minced

Pinch salt

⅓ cup grated
Parmesan cheese

1. Preheat the oven to 350°F. Brush a 1-quart baking dish lightly with olive oil.

2. In a bowl, combine the spinach, artichoke hearts, yogurt, Fontina, feta, garlic, and salt. Stir to combine thoroughly.

3. Pour into the prepared baking dish. Top with the Parmesan.

4. Bake for 20 minutes, or until golden and bubbling.

PER SERVING:

CALORIES: 141; Total Fat: 8g; Saturated Fat: 5g; Protein: 10g; Total Carbohydrates: 9g; Fiber: 4g; Sugar: 3g; Cholesterol: 27mg

STUFFED CHERRY TOMATOES

Serves 8 / Prep time: 15 minutes

These pretty little pop-in-your-mouth treats make great party appetizers. Kids love their fresh summery flavor, too.

WEIGHT LOSS

24 cherry tomatoes

⅓ cup part-skim ricotta cheese

¼ cup chopped peeled cucumber

1 tablespoon finely chopped red onion

2 teaspoons minced fresh basil

1. Slice off the top of each tomato. Carefully scrape out and discard the pulp inside.

2. In a bowl, combine the ricotta, cucumber, red onion, and basil. Stir well.

3. Spoon the ricotta cheese mixture into the tomatoes and serve cold.

MAKE-AHEAD TIP: The tomatoes can be stuffed, covered, and refrigerated for up to 1 hour before serving.

PER SERVING (3 TOMATOES):

CALORIES: 75; Total Fat: 3g; Saturated Fat: 0g; Protein: 6g; Total Carbohydrates: 9g; Fiber: 1g; Sugar: 1g; Cholesterol: 3mg

MEDITERRANEAN ANTIPASTO SKEWERS

Serves 12 / Prep time: 15 minutes

These antipasto skewers make for a fun party food and are easy to assemble. They look impressive even though all the ingredients are premade.

OVERALL WELLNESS

1 (8-ounce) pepperoni stick, cut into ¼-inch slices

1 pound mild provolone cheese, cut into ½-inch cubes

1 (7-ounce) jar marinated pitted black olives, drained

1 (12-ounce) jar marinated mushrooms, drained

1 (12-ounce) jar roasted red peppers, drained and cut into 1-inch pieces

On each of 12 skewers, alternately thread the pepperoni, cheese, olives, mushrooms, and red peppers, using 2 pieces of each.

PER SERVING:

CALORIES: 254; Total Fat: 20g; Saturated Fat: 9g; Protein: 15g; Total Carbohydrates: 4g; Fiber: 1g; Sugar: 2g; Cholesterol: 46mg

SPICED BAKED PITA CHIPS

Serves 6 / Prep time: 10 minutes / Cook time: 10 minutes

Pita bread is an essential part of daily life across most of the Mediterranean region. Serve these pita chips with any of the dips or spreads in this book or enjoy them on their own.

OVERALL WELLNESS

2 tablespoons extra-virgin olive oil

1 teaspoon dried oregano

½ teaspoon paprika

½ teaspoon salt

¼ teaspoon freshly ground black pepper

¼ teaspoon cayenne pepper

3 pita breads, each cut into 8 triangles

1. Preheat the oven to 350°F. Line a rimmed baking sheet with parchment paper.

2. In a bowl, combine the olive oil, oregano, paprika, salt, black pepper, and cayenne. Mix well.

3. Spread out the pita triangles on the prepared baking sheet. Brush with the oil mixture. Flip over and brush the other side.

4. Bake for 10 minutes, or until golden and crisp.

MAKE-AHEAD TIP: These chips will keep for up to 3 days in an airtight container at room temperature.

PER SERVING:

CALORIES: 78; Total Fat: 5g; Saturated Fat: 1g; Protein: 1g; Total Carbohydrates: 8g; Fiber: 1g; Sugar: 0g; Cholesterol: 0mg

ROASTED RED PEPPER DIP

Serves 6 / Prep time: 10 minutes, plus 1 hour to chill / Cook time: 45 minutes

Red bell peppers are packed with vitamin C and make a powerfully flavored dip. Many Mediterranean countries enjoy some type of red pepper dip as part of their cuisine. You can also use this recipe as a delectable sandwich spread.

WEIGHT LOSS

4 large red bell peppers, seeded and quartered

1 large onion, chopped

2 tablespoons extra-virgin olive oil

1 teaspoon red wine vinegar

1½ teaspoons salt

¼ teaspoon freshly ground black pepper

2 garlic cloves, peeled

1. Preheat the oven to 425°F. Line a rimmed baking sheet with aluminum foil.

2. In a large bowl, toss the peppers and onion with the olive oil, vinegar, salt, and pepper.

3. Spread out the peppers and onion in a single layer on the prepared baking sheet. Roast for 30 minutes, then add the garlic cloves and roast for another 15 minutes, until the peppers start to blacken on the edges. Remove from the oven and set aside to cool.

4. Transfer the contents of the baking sheet, including the oil, to a food processor or blender. Process until smooth.

5. Transfer to a bowl, cover, and refrigerate for 1 hour before serving.

MAKE-AHEAD TIP: This dip will keep in an airtight container in the refrigerator for up to 3 days.

PER SERVING:

CALORIES: 85; Total Fat: 5g; Saturated Fat: 1g; Protein: 1g; Total Carbohydrates: 9g; Fiber: 3g; Sugar: 5g; Cholesterol: 0mg

DEVILED EGGS WITH SPANISH SMOKED PAPRIKA

Serves 6 / Prep time: 15 minutes / Cook time: 15 minutes

Smoked paprika is a Spanish seasoning that gives these eggs an earthy Mediterranean flavor. Serve the eggs as a luncheon appetizer or pack them up for a protein-filled afternoon snack at work.

OVERALL WELLNESS

6 large eggs

1 to 2 tablespoons mayonnaise

1 teaspoon Dijon mustard

½ teaspoon mustard powder

½ teaspoon salt

¼ teaspoon freshly ground black pepper

1 teaspoon smoked paprika

1. Put the eggs in a saucepan and pour in enough water to completely submerge them. Bring the water to a boil over high heat. Turn off the heat, cover the pan, and let sit for 10 minutes.

2. Drain the hot water and fill the pot with fresh cold water. Do this several times to cool the eggs.

3. When the eggs are completely cool, peel them and halve them lengthwise. Remove the yolks and put them in a small bowl.

4. To the yolks, add 1 tablespoon of mayonnaise, the Dijon mustard, mustard powder, salt, and pepper. Stir to blend completely, then add the remaining 1 tablespoon of mayonnaise if desired to achieve a smoother consistency. Spoon ½ tablespoon of the yolk mixture into each egg white.

5. Arrange the deviled eggs on a plate. and sprinkle with the smoked paprika.

COOKING TIP: For an extra-fancy look, put the yolk mixture in a piping bag and pipe it into the egg whites.

PER SERVING:

CALORIES: 89; Total Fat: 7g; Saturated Fat: 2g; Protein: 6g; Total Carbohydrates: 1g; Fiber: 0g; Sugar: 0g; Cholesterol: 187mg

APEROL SPRITZ

Serves 1 / Prep time: 5 minutes

If you visit Italy in summer, you'll see many people sitting at outdoor cafes sipping bright-orange drinks. The Aperol spritz is the unofficial drink of summer in Italy. It uses prosecco, which is Italy's fruity sparkling wine, and Aperol, a slightly bittersweet orange aperitif.

OVERALL WELLNESS

Ice

3 ounces prosecco

2 ounces Aperol

Splash club soda

Orange wedge, for garnish

Fill a wineglass with ice. Add the prosecco and Aperol. Top with a splash of club soda. Garnish with an orange wedge.

MAKE-AHEAD TIP: If you're having a party, you can mix a pitcher of the prosecco and Aperol, then add the soda and orange as you serve each glass.

PER SERVING:

CALORIES: 125; Total Fat: 0g; Saturated Fat: 0g; Protein: 0g; Total Carbohydrates: 17g; Fiber: 0g; Sugar: 16g; Cholesterol: 0mg

VIN BRULÉ

Serves 4 / Prep time: 5 minutes / Cook time: 5 minutes

Vin brulé is a simplified version of mulled wine and a real holiday crowd pleaser: You set it aflame before serving.

OVERALL WELLNESS

1 bottle dry red wine, such as Burgundy

3 cinnamon sticks

3 tablespoons sugar

Peel of 1 orange

In a medium saucepan, combine all the ingredients, cover, and bring to a boil over high heat. As soon as it starts to boil, remove the lid, and carefully ignite with a flame. When the flame dies down, ladle into mugs.

PER SERVING:

CALORIES: 169; Total Fat: 0g; Saturated Fat: 0g; Protein: 0g; Total Carbohydrates: 13g; Fiber: 0g; Sugar: 9g; Cholesterol: 0mg

SPARKLING SPA WATER

Serves 2 / Prep time: 5 minutes

This fruit-infused mineral water is a light alternative to soda. It looks pretty served in wineglasses. Watermelon gives it a beautiful color.

WEIGHT LOSS

1 cup watermelon balls or ½-inch cubes

¼ cup fresh watermelon juice, reserved while cutting

1 lime

Italian sparkling mineral water, chilled

2 thyme sprigs

1. Divide the watermelon balls between 2 red-wine glasses.

2. Divide the watermelon juice between the glasses.

3. Cut the lime in half. Cut one half into quarters and squeeze the juice from one quarter into each glass. Slice the remaining half and set aside.

4. Top off the glasses with cold mineral water.

5. Add a sprig of fresh thyme to each glass, and garnish with a slice of lime.

INGREDIENT TIP: As you cut up the watermelon, place the pieces in a bowl as you go. By the time you are done, you should have about ¼ cup of fresh juice in the bottom of the bowl to use for this refreshing drink.

PER SERVING:

CALORIES: 29; Total Fat: 0g; Saturated Fat: 0g; Protein: 1g; Total Carbohydrates: 8g; Fiber: 0g; Sugar: 5g; Cholesterol: 0mg

fifteen

SAUCES, SPREADS, AND SEASONINGS

Italian Salsa Verde 246

Tzatziki Sauce 247

Olive Oil Dipping Sauce 248

Romesco Sauce 249

Harissa 251

Sweet Hot Cherry Pepper Relish 252

Hot Sauce 253

Lemon-Dijon Vinaigrette 254

Tahini 255

Basil Pesto with Almond Butter 256

Red Pesto 257

Kalamata Spread 258

Lemon Aioli 259

Baba Ghanoush 260

Turkish Garlic Yogurt Sauce 261

Italian Herb Blend 262

Za'atar 263

Italian Salsa Verde, p. 246

ITALIAN SALSA VERDE

Serves 6 / Prep time: 10 minutes

Italian *salsa verde* is a green sauce made with herbs, and not to be confused with Mexican salsa verde, which is made with tomatillos. Traditionally, these ingredients would be hand-chopped, but you can use a food processor for convenience. This sauce is lovely on steak, fish, and egg dishes.

OVERALL WELLNESS

1 to 2 cups loosely packed fresh flat-leaf parsley

¼ cup extra-virgin olive oil

2 garlic cloves, peeled

1 teaspoon freshly squeezed lemon juice

1 teaspoon white wine vinegar

1 teaspoon anchovy paste

½ teaspoon grated lemon zest

½ teaspoon salt

¼ teaspoon freshly ground black pepper

In a food processor, combine all the ingredients and blend until smooth.

MAKE-AHEAD TIP: The salsa verde will keep in an airtight container in the refrigerator for up to 3 days.

PER SERVING:

CALORIES: 86; Total Fat: 9g; Saturated Fat: 1g; Protein: 1g; Total Carbohydrates: 1g; Fiber: 0g; Sugar: 0g; Cholesterol: 1mg

TZATZIKI SAUCE

Makes 2½ cups / Prep time: 15 minutes, plus 1 hour to chill

Tzatziki sauce is a brilliant combination of tangy yogurt, fresh cucumbers, and zippy garlic. This Greek staple can be used as a dipping sauce, a sandwich topping, or even a salad dressing.

OVERALL WELLNESS

½ English cucumber, grated

½ to ¾ teaspoon salt, divided

2 cups low-fat plain Greek yogurt

2 tablespoons extra-virgin olive oil

1 tablespoon white wine vinegar

2 garlic cloves, minced

1 tablespoon dried dill

1. Put the grated cucumber in a colander, sprinkle with ¼ teaspoon of salt, and allow to drain.

2. Meanwhile, in a small bowl, stir together the yogurt, olive oil, vinegar, garlic, and ¼ teaspoon of salt. It may look like it won't combine, but keep stirring and the olive oil will eventually disappear into the yogurt.

3. Transfer the cucumber to several paper towels or a kitchen towel and squeeze out the excess water.

4. Add the cucumber and dill to the yogurt mixture and stir to combine. Taste to see if it needs a little more salt and add up to ¼ teaspoon more, if desired.

5. Cover and refrigerate for 1 hour before serving.

MAKE-AHEAD TIP: The tzatziki can be stored in an airtight container in the refrigerator for up to 5 days.

VARIATION TIP: Traditionally the herb used in tzatziki is dill, but you can replace that with whatever you like. Try basil, oregano, mint, or flat-leaf parsley to see which ones you like best.

PER SERVING (2 TABLESPOONS):

CALORIES: 30; Total Fat: 2g; Saturated Fat: 0g; Protein: 1g; Total Carbohydrates: 2g; Fiber: 0g; Sugar: 2g; Cholesterol: 1mg

OLIVE OIL DIPPING SAUCE

Makes ¼ cup / Prep time: 5 minutes

Italians often create a seasoned dipping sauce for their bread. It's simple to do with good olive oil, and it's healthier than eating bread with butter. Try a variety of dried herbs to bring out different flavors.

OVERALL WELLNESS

¼ cup extra-virgin olive oil

1 tablespoon Italian Herb Blend (page 262)

2 garlic cloves, minced

¼ teaspoon salt

¼ teaspoon freshly ground black pepper

In a small bowl, combine all the ingredients and stir to blend.

VARIATION TIP: Drizzle in a little balsamic vinegar for some zesty sweetness, or try adding a variety of herbs for different tastes.

PER SERVING (1 TABLESPOON):

CALORIES: 122; Total Fat: 13g; Saturated Fat: 2g; Protein: 0g; Total Carbohydrates: 1g; Fiber: 0g; Sugar: 0g; Cholesterol: 0mg

ROMESCO SAUCE

Makes 1½ cups / Prep time: 10 minutes

Romesco sauce comes from Catalonia in northeastern Spain. It is traditionally served with fish but also works well with chicken and grilled vegetables or as a sandwich spread. If you want a heartier sauce, you can add some bread crumbs to thicken it.

OVERALL WELLNESS

1 cup chopped roasted red pepper

½ cup almonds, toasted

2 tablespoons tomato paste

1 tablespoon sherry vinegar

1 garlic clove, peeled

1 teaspoon smoked paprika

½ teaspoon salt

½ teaspoon cayenne pepper

¼ teaspoon freshly ground black pepper

½ cup extra-virgin olive oil

1. In a food processor, combine the roasted pepper, almonds, tomato paste, vinegar, garlic, paprika, salt, cayenne, and black pepper and pulse until finely chopped.

2. Scrape down the sides. With the food processor running, slowly drizzle in the olive oil until smooth.

MAKE-AHEAD TIP: The sauce can be stored in an airtight container in the refrigerator for up to 4 days.

PER SERVING (2 TABLESPOONS):

CALORIES: 121; Total Fat: 12g; Saturated Fat: 1g; Protein: 2g; Total Carbohydrates: 3g; Fiber: 1g; Sugar: 1g; Cholesterol: 0mg

HARISSA

Makes 1 cup / Prep time: 10 minutes / Cook time: 10 minutes

Harissa is a spicy North African paste made with roasted red bell peppers mixed with hot peppers and lots of spices. Once you taste this, you'll want to use it on everything.

HEART HEALTH

2 tablespoons extra-virgin olive oil

1 small red onion, chopped

3 garlic cloves, chopped

3 fresh red chiles, seeded and chopped

1 (12-ounce) jar roasted red peppers, drained

2 tablespoons freshly squeezed lemon juice

1 tablespoon white wine vinegar

½ teaspoon ground coriander

½ teaspoon ground cumin

½ teaspoon ground caraway

½ teaspoon smoked paprika

½ teaspoon salt

1 tablespoon tomato paste

1. In a small skillet, heat the olive oil over medium heat. Add the red onion, garlic, and chiles and cook for about 10 minutes, until caramelized.

2. Transfer the contents of the skillet to a food processor and add the roasted peppers, lemon juice, vinegar, coriander, cumin, caraway, paprika, salt, and tomato paste. Blend until smooth.

> **MAKE-AHEAD TIP:** Harissa paste can be stored in an airtight container in the refrigerator for up to 2 weeks.

PER SERVING (2 TABLESPOONS):

CALORIES: 48; Total Fat: 4g; Saturated Fat: 0g; Protein: 1g; Total Carbohydrates: 4g; Fiber: 1g; Sugar: 2g; Cholesterol: 0mg

SWEET HOT CHERRY PEPPER RELISH

Makes 2 cups / Prep time: 15 minutes / Cook time: 1 hour

Cherry peppers, also known as pimientos, are used often in Spanish and Portuguese cuisine. Although they are typically found in the supermarket jarred in vinegar, this recipe calls for fresh peppers. You can usually find them at farmers' markets in the late summer to early autumn. Cherry peppers are high in vitamin C and antioxidants.

WEIGHT LOSS

40 to 50 hot cherry peppers, stemmed and seeded, seeds reserved

1 small onion, roughly chopped

1 garlic clove, peeled

1 tablespoon extra-virgin olive oil

½ cup white wine vinegar

⅓ cup sugar

1. In a food processor, combine the cherry peppers, onion, garlic, and your desired amount of seeds. The more seeds you add, the hotter the relish will be—start with the seeds from just 4 peppers. Pulse the mixture until finely chopped.

2. In a large skillet, heat the olive oil over medium heat. Add the pepper mixture, vinegar, and sugar. Cover and cook for 30 minutes. Check periodically to make sure it isn't drying out; add water if necessary.

3. Uncover and cook for an additional 30 minutes. The liquid should be mostly cooked away by the end of the hour.

4. Remove from the heat and allow to cool.

MAKE-AHEAD TIP: The relish will keep in an airtight container in the refrigerator for up to 1 week.

INGREDIENT TIP: Cherry peppers come in red and green. I like to use red peppers for their bright color, but the recipe works just as well with green peppers or a combination.

PER SERVING (1 TABLESPOON):
CALORIES: 25; Total Fat: 1g; Saturated Fat: 0g; Protein: 1g; Total Carbohydrates: 5g; Fiber: 0g; Sugar: 4g; Cholesterol: 0mg

HOT SAUCE

Makes 1 cup / Prep time: 10 minutes / Cook time: 30 minutes

Cherry peppers are hot, but not overly so, and they have wonderful flavor. For a milder sauce, you could try Hatch chiles. For medium heat, try jalapeños or serranos. For an even hotter sauce, go for habaneros.

OVERALL WELLNESS

1 pound hot cherry peppers, stemmed and seeded

4 garlic cloves, peeled

½ cup water

½ cup distilled white vinegar

1 teaspoon salt

1. In a food processor or blender, combine the cherry peppers, garlic, and water. Blend until smooth.

2. Transfer the pepper mixture to a skillet and add the vinegar and salt. Cook over medium heat for 30 minutes.

3. Remove from the heat and allow to cool.

MAKE-AHEAD TIP: The hot sauce will keep in an airtight container in the refrigerator for up to 1 week.

VARIATION TIP: For a sweet-hot sauce, try adding some mango or pineapple in step 1.

PER SERVING (1 TEASPOON):
CALORIES: 5; Total Fat: 0g; Saturated Fat: 0g; Protein: 0g; Total Carbohydrates: 1g; Fiber: 0g; Sugar: 1g; Cholesterol: 0mg

LEMON-DIJON VINAIGRETTE

Makes about ½ cup / Prep time: 5 minutes

This classic vinaigrette can be used to dress up vegetable dishes, as a marinade, and of course, on salads. It will give your dishes a classic French flavor. The lemon and mustard are a refreshing change from vinegar.

OVERALL WELLNESS

¼ cup extra-virgin olive oil

2 tablespoons freshly squeezed lemon juice

1 garlic clove, minced

1 teaspoon Dijon mustard

½ teaspoon salt

¼ teaspoon freshly ground black pepper

In a small bowl, whisk together all the ingredients.

MAKE-AHEAD TIP: This dressing will keep in an airtight container in the refrigerator for up to 1 week.

VARIATION TIP: Try adding a pinch of red pepper flakes for an exciting bit of heat.

PER SERVING (2 TABLESPOONS):
CALORIES: 123; Total Fat: 13g; Saturated Fat: 2g; Protein: 0g; Total Carbohydrates: 1g; Fiber: 0g; Sugar: 0g; Cholesterol: 0mg

TAHINI

Makes about ½ cup / Prep time: 5 minutes

Tahini is a paste made from toasted sesame seeds that is used all across the Mediterranean region. It's similar to nut butter but has a thinner consistency. It's well known for being one of the main ingredients in hummus, but it's also delicious on its own. Try drizzling it over steamed or roasted vegetables just before serving.

WEIGHT LOSS

1 cup toasted sesame seeds

3 tablespoons extra-virgin olive oil

Pinch salt

In a food processor, combine all the ingredients and blend, scraping down the sides once or twice, until you get a smooth paste.

INGREDIENT TIP: If you can't find toasted sesame seeds, you can easily make them yourself. Simply put the sesame seeds in a skillet over low heat for about 3 minutes, stirring constantly, until lightly toasted.

COOKING TIP: Make sure you put the stopper in the food processor's tube, because sesame seeds can easily go flying all over.

PER SERVING (2 TABLESPOONS):
CALORIES: 271; Total Fat: 25g; Saturated Fat: 4g; Protein: 5g; Total Carbohydrates: 8g; Fiber: 5g; Sugar: 0g; Cholesterol: 0mg

BASIL PESTO WITH ALMOND BUTTER

Makes 1 cup / Prep time: 5 minutes

Basil pesto sauce is traditionally made with pine nuts, but a quick and inexpensive way to make it at home is to use almond butter. The flavor is just as good, it's easier to blend, and it's full of even more heart-healthy nutrients.

HEART HEALTH

4 cups loosely packed fresh basil

¼ cup grated Parmesan cheese

1 tablespoon almond butter

2 garlic cloves, peeled

2 teaspoons freshly squeezed lemon juice

½ teaspoon salt

¼ teaspoon freshly ground black pepper

½ cup extra-virgin olive oil

1. In a food processor, combine the basil, Parmesan, almond butter, garlic, lemon juice, salt, and pepper.

2. With the food processor running, slowly drizzle in the olive oil.

3. Blend for about 3 minutes, scraping down the sides as necessary, until completely smooth.

VARIATION TIP: You can substitute any nut butter you prefer, or use pine nuts in place of the nut butter for a more traditional preparation.

PER SERVING (1 TABLESPOON):

CALORIES: 74; Total Fat: 8g; Saturated Fat: 1g; Protein: 1g; Total Carbohydrates: 1g; Fiber: 0g; Sugar: 0g; Cholesterol: 1mg

RED PESTO

Makes 2 cups / Prep time: 5 minutes

Red pesto, or *pesto rosso* in Italian, uses a mix of sun-dried tomatoes and roasted red peppers. Traditionally this would be made with a mortar and pestle, but a food processor yields a smoother texture.

OVERALL WELLNESS

1 cup dry-packed sun-dried tomatoes

1 cup chopped roasted red pepper

¼ cup grated Parmesan cheese

¼ cup extra-virgin olive oil

2 tablespoons almond butter

1 tablespoon fresh basil leaves

2 garlic cloves, peeled

½ teaspoon salt

¼ teaspoon freshly ground black pepper

In a food processor, combine all the ingredients and blend until smooth. If it looks too thick, you can add a little water to thin it out.

MAKE-AHEAD TIP: The pesto can be stored in an airtight container in the refrigerator for up to 4 days.

PER SERVING (1 TABLESPOON):

CALORIES: 30; Total Fat: 3g; Saturated Fat: 0g; Protein: 1g; Total Carbohydrates: 2g; Fiber: 0g; Sugar: 1g; Cholesterol: 1mg

KALAMATA SPREAD

Makes 1 cup / Prep time: 5 minutes

This Greek olive spread is delicious on toast, as an omelet filling, as a dip, or even as a garnish for soups. It packs a briny, flavorful punch you'll find yourself reaching for again and again.

HEART HEALTH

1 cup pitted kalamata olives

3 garlic cloves, peeled

1 tablespoon capers

1 tablespoon chopped fresh flat-leaf parsley

1 tablespoon grated Parmesan cheese

1 teaspoon anchovy paste

1 teaspoon freshly ground black pepper

¼ cup extra-virgin olive oil

1. In a food processor, combine the olives, garlic, capers, parsley, Parmesan, anchovy paste, and pepper. Pulse a few times to chop and combine.

2. With the food processor running, slowly drizzle in the olive oil until you get a smooth puree.

MAKE-AHEAD TIP: The spread will keep in an airtight container in the refrigerator for up to 3 days.

PER SERVING (2 TABLESPOONS):

CALORIES: 85; Total Fat: 9g; Saturated Fat: 1g; Protein: 1g; Total Carbohydrates: 2g; Fiber: 1g; Sugar: 0g; Cholesterol: 1mg

LEMON AIOLI

Makes about ¾ cup / Prep time: 5 minutes

This zesty sauce makes for a lovely sandwich spread or dip, but it can also be used as a complement to many other meals. It goes very well with fish dishes and roasted vegetables, such as potatoes and Brussels sprouts.

½ cup mayonnaise or vegan mayonnaise

1 teaspoon grated lemon zest

2 tablespoons freshly squeezed lemon juice

1 garlic clove, minced

1 teaspoon Dijon mustard

¼ teaspoon salt

⅛ teaspoon freshly ground black pepper

In a bowl, combine all the ingredients and stir to combine.

MAKE-AHEAD TIP: Store the aioli in an airtight container in the refrigerator for up to 3 days.

PER SERVING (1 TABLESPOON):

CALORIES: 64; Total Fat: 7g; Saturated Fat: 1g; Protein: 0g; Total Carbohydrates: 0g; Fiber: 0g; Sugar: 0g; Cholesterol: 4mg

BABA GHANOUSH

Makes about 2 cups / Prep time: 15 minutes / Cook time: 45 minutes

This eggplant-based spread is an appetizer from Lebanon that is full of flavor and anti-oxidants. It makes a tasty dip for pita or vegetables, or a spread for tomato sandwiches.

WEIGHT LOSS

2 small eggplants, halved lengthwise

¼ cup extra-virgin olive oil, plus 2 tablespoons, divided

2 tablespoons freshly squeezed lemon juice

2 garlic cloves, peeled

½ cup Tahini (page 255) or store-bought tahini

2 tablespoons chopped fresh flat-leaf parsley, divided

½ teaspoon salt

½ teaspoon ground cumin

½ teaspoon smoked paprika

1. Preheat the oven to 450°F. Line a rimmed baking sheet with aluminum foil.

2. Brush the cut sides of the eggplant with 1 tablespoon of olive oil. Place the eggplant halves, cut-side down, on the prepared baking sheet.

3. Roast for 40 to 45 minutes, until completely softened.

4. Set the eggplants aside to cool for a few minutes, then flip them over and scoop out the flesh with a large spoon, discarding the skin.

5. Transfer the eggplant flesh to a food processor. Add the lemon juice and garlic and pulse briefly to combine.

6. Add the tahini. With the food processor running, slowly drizzle in ¼ cup of olive oil. Continue blending until the mixture is smooth.

7. Add 1 tablespoon of parsley, the salt, and cumin. Blend one final time to incorporate the spices.

8. Transfer the baba ghanoush to a serving bowl and lightly drizzle the remaining 1 tablespoon of olive oil on top. Sprinkle with the smoked paprika and garnish with the remaining 1 tablespoon of parsley.

INGREDIENT TIP: Using 2 small eggplants instead of 1 large helps cut down on the number of seeds.

PER SERVING (¼ CUP):

CALORIES: 217; Total Fat: 18g; Saturated Fat: 3g; Protein: 4g; Total Carbohydrates: 12g; Fiber: 6g; Sugar: 5g; Cholesterol: 0mg

TURKISH GARLIC YOGURT SAUCE

Makes 1 cup / Prep time: 5 minutes

This recipe for a garlic-flavored yogurt sauce comes from Turkey. It is often used on lamb and chicken dishes, and is excellent on sandwiches. Greek restaurants often use it in gyros and on chicken shawarma.

OVERALL WELLNESS

1 cup low-fat plain Greek yogurt

2 teaspoons freshly squeezed lemon juice

2 garlic cloves, peeled

1 teaspoon dried dill

½ teaspoon salt

In a food processor or blender, combine all the ingredients and process until smooth.

MAKE-AHEAD TIP: Store the yogurt sauce in an airtight container in the refrigerator for up to 4 days.

PER SERVING (¼ CUP):

CALORIES: 42; Total Fat: 1g; Saturated Fat: 1g; Protein: 3g; Total Carbohydrates: 5g; Fiber: 0g; Sugar: 4g; Cholesterol: 4mg

ITALIAN HERB BLEND

Makes about ¼ cup / Prep time: 5 minutes

Having a homemade spice blend on hand saves a lot of time when cooking. Prepare it in advance and keep it in a glass jar with your spices so that you can reach for it whenever you need it.

2 tablespoons dried oregano

1 teaspoon dried basil

1 teaspoon dried marjoram

1 teaspoon dried thyme

1 teaspoon red pepper flakes

½ teaspoon dried rosemary

½ teaspoon fennel seeds

¼ teaspoon freshly ground black pepper

In a bowl, combine all the ingredients and stir to combine.

MAKE-AHEAD TIP: Store this herb blend in an airtight container in a cool, dark cabinet for up to 1 year.

PER SERVING (1 TEASPOON):

CALORIES: 2; Total Fat: 0g; Saturated Fat: 0g; Protein: 0g; Total Carbohydrates: 0g; Fiber: 0g; Sugar: 0g; Cholesterol: 0mg

ZA'ATAR

Makes about 6 tablespoons / Prep time: 5 minutes

Za'atar is a healthy, flavorful spice mix from the Middle East. It is used as an everyday seasoning for meats and vegetables. One of the simplest ways to enjoy it is to dip pita bread in olive oil and then in za'atar.

HEART HEALTH

2 tablespoons sesame seeds, toasted

2 tablespoons fresh thyme leaves

1 tablespoon dried oregano

2 teaspoons ground sumac

½ teaspoon salt

In a bowl, combine all the ingredients and stir to combine.

INGREDIENT TIP: If you can't find ground sumac, grated lemon zest is a close substitute. Add it fresh at time of use.

PER SERVING (1 TEASPOON):

CALORIES: 7; Total Fat: 1g; Saturated Fat: 0g; Protein: 0g; Total Carbohydrates: 0g; Fiber: 0g; Sugar: 0g; Cholesterol: 0mg

sixteen

FRUITS AND SWEETS

Polenta Cake 266

Banana "Ice Cream" 267

Pistachio Ricotta Cookies 268

Citrus Granita 269

Figs with Pecorino and Honey 270

Peach Galette 271

Red Wine–Poached Pears 272

Red Wine Chocolate Cake 273

Classic Italian Olive Oil Cake 275

Peach Galette, p. 271

POLENTA CAKE

Serves 6 / Prep time: 20 minutes / Cook time: 1 hour

This beautifully simple cake from Italy features polenta in the batter for a hearty texture. A layer of glazed orange slices graces the top. Enjoy it on its own or top it with fresh fruit or whipped cream.

Unsalted butter, for greasing

⅓ cup packed light brown sugar

2 teaspoons cornstarch

1 teaspoon salt, divided

2 oranges, zested and sliced

1½ cups instant polenta

1 cup whole milk

1 cup all-purpose flour

1 teaspoon baking powder

½ teaspoon baking soda

1 cup granulated sugar

3 large eggs

¼ cup extra-virgin olive oil

2 teaspoons vanilla extract

1. Preheat the oven to 350°F. Lightly butter a 9-inch round cake pan.

2. In a small bowl, combine the brown sugar, cornstarch, and ½ teaspoon of salt. Scatter this mixture over the bottom of the prepared cake pan.

3. Arrange the orange slices in a single layer in the cake pan on top of the brown sugar mixture.

4. In a medium bowl, combine the polenta, milk, and orange zest. Mix well to combine. If the mixture seems lumpy, you can add a few more tablespoons of milk to smooth it out.

5. In a large bowl, whisk together the flour, baking powder, baking soda, and remaining ½ teaspoon of salt. Add the granulated sugar and eggs and, using an electric hand mixer on low, beat to combine. Slowly add the olive oil and vanilla.

6. Add the polenta mixture and mix into a thick batter. Pour over the oranges in the cake pan.

7. Bake for 1 hour, until a toothpick inserted in the center comes out clean.

8. Allow the cake to cool before turning out of the pan with the orange slices facing up.

PER SERVING:

CALORIES: 478; Total Fat: 13g; Saturated Fat: 3g; Protein: 8g; Total Carbohydrates: 82g; Fiber: 2g; Sugar: 52g; Cholesterol: 97mg

BANANA "ICE CREAM"

Serves 2 / Prep time: 5 minutes, plus 1 hour to freeze

In Italy during the summer months, you'll see Italians and tourists alike enjoying cones of gelato, an Italian ice cream that comes in a multitude of fruit and nut flavors. This banana dessert is reminiscent of gelato, although much lighter. The texture of bananas works well to mimic that creamy texture.

WEIGHT LOSS

3 bananas, sliced and frozen

1 teaspoon vanilla extract

¼ cup blueberries

1. In a blender, combine the frozen banana slices and vanilla and process on low or "chop" at first to break down the frozen bananas. Then switch to regular speed and process until you get a soft-serve consistency.

2. Freeze for 1 hour for a scoopable ice cream consistency.

3. Top with blueberries.

VARIATION TIP: You could add a little cocoa powder to this for a chocolate treat.

PER SERVING:

CALORIES: 174; Total Fat: 1g; Saturated Fat: 0g; Protein: 2g; Total Carbohydrates: 43g; Fiber: 5g; Sugar: 24g; Cholesterol: 0mg

PISTACHIO RICOTTA COOKIES

Makes 30 cookies / Prep time: 20 minutes / Cook time: 15 minutes

These cookies, traditionally served at Easter, get their mildly sweet flavor from pistachios and ricotta cheese. Pistachios are cholesterol-free and loaded with nutrients.

OVERALL WELLNESS

6 ounces pistachios

2 cups all-purpose flour

1½ teaspoons baking powder

½ teaspoon salt

8 tablespoons (1 stick) unsalted butter

1 cup granulated sugar

18 ounces part-skim ricotta cheese

1 large egg

1 teaspoon vanilla extract

For decoration

1 cup powdered sugar

1½ teaspoons whole milk

¼ cup chopped pistachios

1. Preheat the oven to 350°F. Line a rimmed baking sheet with parchment paper.

2. In a food processor, process the pistachios until finely ground.

3. In a bowl, whisk together the flour, baking powder, and salt.

4. In a large bowl, using an electric mixer on low, cream the butter and sugar together until fluffy.

5. Add the ricotta, egg, vanilla, and ground pistachios and beat until well combined.

6. Add the flour mixture and beat until it forms a dough.

7. Drop the cookie dough by the tablespoon onto the prepared baking sheet, leaving about 2 inches between the cookies.

8. Bake for 15 minutes, until golden. Allow the cookies to cool on the baking sheet.

To decorate the cookies

9. In a small bowl, stir together the powdered sugar and milk to form a smooth icing. Spoon the icing over the cookies and sprinkle with the chopped pistachios.

PER SERVING (3 COOKIES):
CALORIES: 500; Total Fat: 25g; Saturated Fat: 11g; Protein: 13g; Total Carbohydrates: 56g; Fiber: 3g; Sugar: 32g; Cholesterol: 69mg

CITRUS GRANITA

Serves 4 / Prep time: 3 hours

Granita is a Sicilian dessert of fruit-flavored frozen ice. This recipe features the classic combination of lemon and lime, but you can experiment with your favorite fruits.

WEIGHT LOSS

2 to 3 lemons
2 to 3 limes
1½ cups cold water
½ cup sugar

1. Grate the zest from the lemons and limes until you have 1 teaspoon of each.

2. Juice the lemons and limes until the combined juices total ½ cup.

3. In a bowl, combine the zest and juices. Add the water and sugar. Stir until sugar has dissolved. This may take several minutes.

4. Pour the mixture into a 9-by-13-inch ceramic or glass baking dish. Place in the freezer for 30 minutes.

5. Stir the granita with a spoon, scraping down the edges. Return to the freezer for another 30 minutes. You'll repeat this process 5 to 6 times, for about 3 hours overall, until the mixture is frozen through and creamy.

PER SERVING:

CALORIES: 108; Total Fat: 0g; Saturated Fat: 0g; Protein: 0g; Total Carbohydrates: 29g; Fiber: 0g; Sugar: 26g; Cholesterol: 0mg

FIGS WITH PECORINO AND HONEY

Serves 4 / Prep time: 10 minutes / Cook time: 5 minutes

Figs are a favorite treat across the Mediterranean region and are a good source of calcium and iron. Their honey-like sweetness contrasts well with nutty, salty Pecorino Romano cheese.

OVERALL WELLNESS

8 fresh figs, halved lengthwise

4 ounces Pecorino Romano cheese

4 tablespoons raw honey

Freshly ground black pepper

4 heaping tablespoons mascarpone cheese

1. Preheat the oven to 450°F. Line a rimmed baking sheet with parchment paper.

2. Place the figs, cut-side up, on the prepared baking sheet. Bake for about 5 minutes, until the edges are toasted.

3. Remove the figs from the oven. While still warm, place 4 halves on each serving plate.

4. Shave the pecorino cheese onto the figs and the plate. Drizzle each with 1 tablespoon of honey and add a few grinds of pepper. Top each with 1 tablespoon of mascarpone cheese.

PER SERVING:

CALORIES: 262; Total Fat: 10g; Saturated Fat: 6g; Protein: 9g; Total Carbohydrates: 37g; Fiber: 2g; Sugar: 34g; Cholesterol: 35mg

PEACH GALETTE

Serves 8 / Prep time: 15 minutes / Cook time: 45 minutes

One of the beautiful things about the Mediterranean diet is that you don't have to give up the pleasure of dessert. The key is moderation. This rustic peach pie is a sweet treat that uses very little sugar, so go ahead and enjoy.

OVERALL WELLNESS

5 or 6 peaches, pitted and sliced

½ cup all-purpose flour

⅓ cup granulated sugar

1 teaspoon salt

1 store-bought pie crust

1 tablespoon turbinado sugar

1. Preheat the oven to 400°F.

2. In a large bowl, toss the peaches with the flour, granulated sugar, and salt.

3. Place the pie crust flat in a 9-inch pie pan but don't press it into place.

4. Pour the peach mixture into the crust in the pie pan and fold the sides of the crust over the peach filling, overlapping them with pleats but leaving the center of the pie uncovered.

5. Bake for 20 minutes, then sprinkle the turbinado sugar over the top. Return to the oven and bake for an additional 20 to 25 minutes, until the crust is golden brown.

6. Let cool before slicing.

VARIATION TIP: This recipe also works well with apples.

PER SERVING:
CALORIES: 184; Total Fat: 5g; Saturated Fat: 1g; Protein: 2g; Total Carbohydrates: 33g; Fiber: 2g; Sugar: 18g; Cholesterol: 0mg

RED WINE–POACHED PEARS

Serves 4 / Prep time: 10 minutes / Cook time: 35 minutes

This traditional recipe comes from the South of France. The pears take on some of the color from the wine and look beautiful when they are sliced. Bosc pears work especially well for this recipe, but any pear will do.

OVERALL WELLNESS

4 firm pears, peeled, with stems intact

2 cups fruity red wine, such as Beaujolais

1 small orange, sliced

1 cinnamon stick

2 whole cloves

1. Slice off the bottoms of the pears so they can sit flat on a plate.

2. In a pot, combine the wine, orange slices, cinnamon stick, and cloves and bring to a boil over medium-high heat.

3. Reduce to a simmer and lay the pears in the wine mixture. Cook for 30 minutes, turning the pears occasionally, until the wine mixture becomes a syrup. Remove the pears and stand each on a plate.

4. Increase the heat under the pot and let the wine reduce and thicken for another 5 minutes. Drizzle the wine syrup over the pears.

PER SERVING (1 PEAR):
CALORIES: 220; Total Fat: 0g; Saturated Fat: 0g; Protein: 1g; Total Carbohydrates: 36g; Fiber: 6g; Sugar: 20g; Cholesterol: 0mg

RED WINE CHOCOLATE CAKE

Serves 8 / Prep time: 20 minutes / Cook time: 45 minutes

Red wine and chocolate are a marriage made in heaven. This cake recipe combines both flavors for a sophisticated dessert. Its not-too-sweet richness pairs especially well with freshly whipped cream.

OVERALL WELLNESS

Butter and flour, for the pan

2 cups all-purpose flour

¾ cup unsweetened cocoa powder

1¼ teaspoons baking soda

½ teaspoon salt

1 cup (2 sticks) unsalted butter, at room temperature

1¾ cups sugar

2 large eggs

1 teaspoon vanilla extract

1¼ cups dry red wine

1. Preheat the oven to 350°F.

2. Lightly brush a Bundt pan with butter and dust it with flour.

3. In a medium bowl, whisk together the flour, cocoa powder, baking soda, and salt.

4. In a large bowl, using an electric mixer on low, cream together the butter and sugar until light and fluffy. Add the eggs and vanilla and beat until combined.

5. Add half of the flour mixture and beat on low until just combined. Add the red wine and fold in until combined. Add the rest of the flour mixture and beat on low until just combined.

6. Pour the batter into the prepared cake pan. Bake for 45 minutes, or until a knife inserted into the center comes out clean.

7. Allow to cool completely before removing from the pan and slicing.

PER SERVING:

CALORIES: 555; Total Fat: 25g; Saturated Fat: 15g; Protein: 7g; Total Carbohydrates: 74g; Fiber: 3g; Sugar: 44g; Cholesterol: 107mg

CLASSIC ITALIAN OLIVE OIL CAKE

Serves 6 / Prep time: 15 minutes / Cook time: 35 minutes

Olive oil helps create a lovely moist cake with a crispy coating. This recipe includes a hint of orange flavor from the liqueur. The texture and flavor of this cake improve overnight, so this dessert is an ideal one to make the day before a party. Try serving it with fresh berries.

OVERALL WELLNESS

Nonstick cooking spray

1½ cups all-purpose flour, plus more for dusting

1½ teaspoons baking powder

½ teaspoon salt

3 large eggs

⅔ cup sugar

½ cup extra-virgin olive oil

½ cup whole milk

¼ cup Grand Marnier

½ teaspoon vanilla extract

¼ teaspoon almond extract

1. Preheat the oven to 350°F.

2. Coat an 8-inch round cake pan with cooking spray and dust with flour. Line the bottom of the pan with a round of parchment paper.

3. In a small bowl, whisk together the flour, baking powder, and salt.

4. In a medium bowl, using an electric hand mixer on low, beat the eggs and sugar until light and fluffy. Add the olive oil in a slow, steady stream, mixing until combined. Add the milk and mix until combined. Add the Grand Marnier and vanilla and almond extracts and mix until combined.

5. Gradually add the flour mixture, beating until a smooth batter forms. Pour the batter into the prepared cake pan.

6. Bake for 30 to 35 minutes, until a toothpick inserted into the center comes out clean.

7. Let cool in the pan for 5 minutes. Remove from the pan and let cool completely on a wire rack.

MAKE-AHEAD TIP: The cake can be wrapped tightly in plastic wrap and stored at room temperature for up to 3 days.

INGREDIENT TIP: You can use orange juice in place of the liqueur if preferred.

PER SERVING:

CALORIES: 433; Total Fat: 21g; Saturated Fat: 4g; Protein: 7g; Total Carbohydrates: 52g; Fiber: 1g; Sugar: 28g; Cholesterol: 95mg

Measurement Conversions

Volume Equivalents

	U.S. STANDARD	U.S. STANDARD (OUNCES)	METRIC (APPROXIMATE)
Liquid	2 tablespoons	1 fl. oz.	30 mL
	¼ cup	2 fl. oz.	60 mL
	½ cup	4 fl. oz.	120 mL
	1 cup	8 fl. oz.	240 mL
	1½ cups	12 fl. oz.	355 mL
	2 cups or 1 pint	16 fl. oz.	475 mL
	4 cups or 1 quart	32 fl. oz.	1 L
	1 gallon	128 fl. oz.	4 L
Dry	⅛ teaspoon	—	0.5 mL
	¼ teaspoon	—	1 mL
	½ teaspoon	—	2 mL
	¾ teaspoon	—	4 mL
	1 teaspoon	—	5 mL
	1 tablespoon	—	15 mL
	¼ cup	—	59 mL
	⅓ cup	—	79 mL
	½ cup	—	118 mL
	⅔ cup	—	156 mL
	¾ cup	—	177 mL
	1 cup	—	235 mL
	2 cups or 1 pint	—	475 mL
	3 cups	—	700 mL
	4 cups or 1 quart	—	1 L
	½ gallon	—	2 L
	1 gallon	—	4 L

Oven Temperatures

FAHRENHEIT	CELSIUS (APPROXIMATE)
250°F	120°C
300°F	150°C
325°F	165°C
350°F	180°C
375°F	190°C
400°F	200°C
425°F	220°C
450°F	230°C

Weight Equivalents

U.S. STANDARD	METRIC (APPROXIMATE)
½ ounce	15 g
1 ounce	30 g
2 ounces	60 g
4 ounces	115 g
8 ounces	225 g
12 ounces	340 g
16 ounces or 1 pound	455 g

Resources

CENTERS FOR DISEASE CONTROL AND PREVENTION
- ◆ cdc.gov

DONNA DEROSA FOOD WEBSITE
- ◆ mostlymediterranean.com

DONNA DEROSA LIFESTYLE WEBSITE
- ◆ donnaderosa.com

DONNA DEROSA YOUTUBE CHANNEL
- ◆ youtube.com/user/derosadm

HARVARD STUDY ON ADULT DEVELOPMENT
- ◆ adultdevelopmentstudy.org

THE MAYO CLINIC
- ◆ mayoclinic.org

SEVEN COUNTRIES STUDY
- ◆ sevencountriesstudy.com

UNESCO
- ◆ en.unesco.org

WORLD HEALTH ORGANIZATION
- ◆ who.int

References

American College of Physicians. "An Indo-Mediterranean Diet Was More Effective Than a Control Diet in Primary and Secondary Coronary Artery Disease Prevention." Accessed on April 30, 2020. acpjc.acponline.org/Content/138/3/issue/ACPJC-2003-138-3-063.htm.

Centers for Disease Control and Prevention. "Heart Disease Facts." Accessed on April 30, 2020. cdc.gov/heartdisease/facts.htm.

Harvard Health Publishing. "Why Nutritionists Are Crazy About Nuts." Accessed on April 30, 2020. health.harvard.edu/nutrition/why-nutritionists-are-crazy-about-nuts.

Harvard T. H. Chan School of Public Health. "Health Professionals Follow-Up Study." Accessed on April 30, 2020. sites.sph.harvard.edu/hpfs.

———. "Nurses Health Studies." Accessed on April 30, 2020. hsph.harvard.edu/nutritionsource/nurses-health-study.

The Mayo Clinic. "The Mediterranean Diet: A Heart-Healthy Eating Plan." Accessed on April 30, 2020. mayoclinic.org/healthy-lifestyle/nutrition-and-healthy-eating/in-depth/mediterranean-diet/art-20047801.

Medical News Today. "Is Red Wine Good for You?" Accessed on April 30, 2020. medicalnewstoday.com/articles/265635.

NutritionFacts.org. "What Is the Healthiest Diet?" Accessed on April 30, 2020. nutritionfacts.org.

Seven Countries Study. "Dietary Patterns and All-Cause Mortality." Accessed on April 30, 2020. sevencountriesstudy.com/dietary-patterns-and-all-cause-mortality.

———. "Four Lifestyle Factors and All-Cause Mortality." Accessed on April 30, 2020. sevencountriesstudy.com/four-lifestyle-factors-and-all-cause-mortality.

———. "Mediterranean Diet." Accessed on April 30, 2020. sevencountriesstudy.com/tag/mediterranean-diet.

———. "What is the Seven Countries Study?" Accessed on April 30, 2020. sevencountriesstudy.com.

Singh, R. B., et al. "Effect of an Indo-Mediterranean Diet on Progression of Coronary Artery Disease in High-Risk Patients (Indo-Mediterranean Diet Heart Study): A Randomised Single-Blind Trial." *The Lancet* 360 (9344) (November 2002). doi: 10.1016/S0140-6736(02)11472-3.

UNESCO Representative List of the Intangible Cultural Heritage of Humanity. "Mediterranean Diet." Accessed on April 30, 2020. ich.unesco.org/en/RL/mediterranean-diet-00884.

Waldinger, Robert. "What Makes a Good Life? Lessons from the Longest Study on Happiness." TEDTalk. Accessed on April 30, 2020. ted.com/talks/robert_waldinger_what_makes_a_good_life_lessons_from_the_longest_study_on_happiness.

World Health Organization. "Healthy Diet." Accessed on April 30, 2020. who.int/news-room/fact-sheets/detail/healthy-diet.

Index

A

Albóndigas (Spanish Meatballs), 93
Alcohol, 5. *See also* Beverages
Alfalfa sprouts
  Veggie Club Sandwich, 222
Algerian Carrot Slaw, 78
Algerian Vegetable Couscous, 149
Almond butter
  Basil Pesto with Almond Butter, 256
  Red Pesto, 257
Anchovies
  Kalamata Spread, 258
  Olive Tapenade, 227
  Spaghetti with Anchovy Sauce, 135
Aperol Spritz, 241
Appetizers. *See also* Dips
      and spreads; Snacks
  Albóndigas (Spanish Meatballs), 93
  Arancini (Italian Stuffed
      Rice Balls), 98–99
  Caponata, 89
  Cauliflower Bites, 86
  Charcuterie Board with
      Red Onion Jam, 88
  Eggplant Roll-Ups, 85
  Moroccan Sardines on Toast, 95
  Pancetta-Wrapped Shrimp, 97
  Patatas Bravas, 87
  Quinoa and Cheese Stuffed
      Mushrooms, 101
  Ricotta-Stuffed Endive
      with Vegetables, 91
  Spicy Calabrian Shrimp, 84
  Spicy Lamb Meatballs, 100
  Stuffed Hot Peppers, 90
  Toasted Polenta with
      Mushrooms, 94
  Tomato Bruschetta, 212
  Tunisian Brik Pastries, 96
  White Bean Crostini, 213
Apricots, dried
  Lamb and Vegetable Stew, 202
Arancini (Italian Stuffed
      Rice Balls), 98–99
Artichoke and Spinach Dip, 234
Arugula
  Arugula and White Bean Salad, 74
  Baked Eggs with Polenta and
      Fontina Cheese, 36

Mussels and Clams in
      White Wine, 181
  Seafood Risotto, 139
  Shrimp Scampi, 177
  Summer Rainbow Salad, 73
Asparagus with Herbs, 115
Avgolemono (Greek Chicken
      and Rice Soup), 52
Avocados
  Avocado Toast, 42
  Chickpea and Avocado Salad, 164
  Cool Cucumber, Avocado,
      and Radish Soup, 56
  Mediterranean Quinoa Salad, 81
  Shrimp Margarita, 178
  Veggie Club Sandwich, 222

B

Baba Ghanoush, 260
Baked Chicken Paella, 141–142
Baked Eggs with Polenta and
      Fontina Cheese, 36
Baked Eggs with Roasted
      Red Peppers, 34
Baked Fish Fingers, 176
Baked Flounder with Parmesan
      and Herbs, 174
Baked Rice with Swordfish
      and Mussels, 143
Baking, 16
Bananas
  Banana "Ice Cream," 267
  Polenta Bowl with Fruit
      and Honey, 43
Barley
  Barley Risotto with Vegetables, 147
  Mushroom Barley Soup, 61
Basil
  Barley Risotto with Vegetables, 147
  Basil Pesto with Almond Butter, 256
  Ciambotta (Neapolitan
      Ratatouille), 109
  Classic Tomato Soup, 57
  Eggplant Towers, 112
  Herbed Salmon with Mashed
      Potatoes, 168
  Lemon Linguine, 133
  Mediterranean Chopped Salad, 69
  Mediterranean Stuffed
      Chicken, 189

Mushrooms Parmigiana, 116
  Olive Tapenade, 227
  Panzanella, 67
  Potenza-Style Chicken, 191
  Radicchio Stuffed with Goat
      Cheese and Salmon, 232
  Red Pesto, 257
  Roasted Tomato Sauce
      with Pasta, 131
  Sicilian Eggplant with
      Israeli Couscous, 148
  Stuffed Cherry Tomatoes, 235
  Tomato Bruschetta, 212
  Tuna Puttanesca, 172
Beans, 3
  Arugula and White Bean Salad, 74
  Barley Risotto with Vegetables, 147
  Black Beans with Cherry
      Tomatoes, 158
  Collard Green Wraps, 113
  Eggplant "Meatballs," 122
  Gigante Beans in Tomato
      Sauce, 155
  La Dolce Vita Wrap, 217
  Mashed Fava Beans, 156
  Mediterranean Stuffed
      Peppers, 105
  Pasta e Fagioli (Pasta and
      Bean Soup), 59
  Red Swiss Chard with
      White Beans, 106
  Spicy Borlotti Beans, 157
  Three-Bean Salad, 154
  Tuscan Tuna Salad, 68
  Vegetarian Chili, 161
  White Bean Alfredo Pasta, 136
  White Bean Crostini, 213
  White Bean Dip, 152
  White Bean Soup, 53
  Zuppa di Farro (Farro Soup), 50
Beef
  Albóndigas (Spanish Meatballs), 93
  Flank Steak with Italian
      Salsa Verde, 197
  Kibbeh (Lebanese Croquettes), 230
Beets and beet greens
  Collard Green Wraps, 113
  Fish en Papillote, 175
  Roasted Beets with Oregano
      and Red Pepper, 107

Berries
  Banana "Ice Cream," 267
  Greek Yogurt Parfait, 41
Beverages
  Aperol Spritz, 241
  Sparkling Spa Water, 243
  Vin Brulé, 242
Black Beans with Cherry
    Tomatoes, 158
Black-Eyed Peas with Mint, 163
Blanching, 16
Boiling, 16
Branzino, Whole, with Garlic
    and Herbs, 169
Breads
  Focaccia (Italian Flatbread), 207–208
  Pesto Vegetable Bread, 211
  Rosemary–Sea Salt Crackers with
    Lemon-Parsley Dip, 233
  Sardinian Flatbread, 206
  Spiced Baked Pita Chips, 237
  Taralli (Pugliese Bread
    Knots), 209
  Testaroli (Etruscan Pancakes), 210
  Tomato Bruschetta, 212
  White Bean Crostini, 213
Broccoli
  La Dolce Vita Wrap, 217
  Pasta Primavera, 132
  Vegetable Rice Bake, 140
Broccoli rabe
  Broccoli Rabe with Red
    Pepper Flakes, 110
  Pesto Vegetable Bread, 211
Broiling, 16
Bruschetta Pizza, 215
Bulgur
  Kibbeh (Lebanese Croquettes), 230
  Tabbouleh (Lebanese Parsley
    and Bulgur Salad), 79
  Vegetable Bulgur, 125

C

Cabbage
  La Dolce Vita Wrap, 217
Capers
  Caponata, 89
  Kalamata Spread, 258
  Olive Tapenade, 227
  Panzanella, 67
  Tuna Puttanesca, 172
  Tunisian Brik Pastries, 96
  Tuscan Tuna Salad, 68

Caponata, 89
Carrots
  Algerian Carrot Slaw, 78
  Algerian Vegetable Couscous, 149
  Black-Eyed Peas with Mint, 163
  Chicken in a Pot, 192
  Creamy Carrot Soup with
    Rosemary, 51
  La Dolce Vita Wrap, 217
  Lamb and Vegetable Stew, 202
  Mediterranean Chopped Salad, 69
  Moroccan Cod, 173
  Moroccan Lentil Soup, 160
  Pasta e Fagioli (Pasta and
    Bean Soup), 59
  Pasta Primavera, 132
  Roasted Root Vegetables, 108
  Root Vegetable Soup, 54
  Sicilian Pork Ribs in
    Tomato Sauce, 203
  Spicy Roasted Carrots, 117
  Tortellini in Brodo (Tortellini
    in Broth with Shrimp), 63
  Vegetable Cassola, 121
  Vegetable Rice Bake, 140
  Warm Lentil Salad, 159
  Zuppa di Farro (Farro Soup), 50
Catfish
  Fishcake Sliders, 219
Cauliflower Bites, 86
Cauliflower Soup with Onion
    and Thyme, 55
Celery
  Caponata, 89
  Chicken in a Pot, 192
  Game Hens Stuffed with Wild
    Rice and Mushrooms, 193
  Lamb and Vegetable Stew, 202
  Mediterranean Chopped Salad, 69
  Moroccan Lentil Soup, 160
  Pasta e Fagioli (Pasta and
    Bean Soup), 59
  Polenta with Wild Greens, 145
  Roasted Butternut Squash Soup, 60
  Root Vegetable Soup, 54
  Shrimp Salad, 71
  Sicilian Pork Ribs in
    Tomato Sauce, 203
  Stuffed Tomatoes, 111
  Tortellini in Brodo (Tortellini
    in Broth with Shrimp), 63
  Tuscan Tuna Salad, 68
  Warm Potato Salad, 72
  Zuppa di Farro (Farro Soup), 50

Celery Root with Yogurt Sauce, 120
Charcuterie Board with Red
    Onion Jam, 88
Cheese. See also Cream
    cheese; Mascarpone
    cheese; Ricotta cheese
  Albóndigas (Spanish Meatballs), 93
  Arancini (Italian Stuffed
    Rice Balls), 98–99
  Baked Eggs with Polenta and
    Fontina Cheese, 36
  Baked Eggs with Roasted
    Red Peppers, 34
  Baked Flounder with Parmesan
    and Herbs, 174
  Barley Risotto with Vegetables, 147
  Basil Pesto with Almond
    Butter, 256
  Bruschetta Pizza, 215
  Charcuterie Board with
    Red Onion Jam, 88
  Cheese Plate with Fruit
    and Crackers, 231
  Chickpea and Avocado Salad, 164
  Eggplant Towers, 112
  Farro with Porcini Mushrooms, 144
  Figs with Pecorino and Honey, 270
  Fusilli Arrabbiata, 134
  Greek Sheet Pan Chicken, 187
  Kalamata Spread, 258
  Lamb Loin Chops with Spaghetti
    in Tomato Sauce, 201
  Layered Hummus Dip, 229
  Lemon Linguine, 133
  Mediterranean Antipasto
    Skewers, 236
  Mediterranean Breakfast Wrap
    with Roasted Vegetables, 39
  Mediterranean Snapper with
    Olives and Feta, 170
  Mushroom Barley Soup, 61
  Mushrooms Parmigiana, 116
  Pasta Primavera, 132
  Peas and Tubetti with
    Pancetta, 165
  Pizza Bianca with Spinach, 216
  Portobello Mushroom
    Sandwich, 218
  Quinoa and Cheese Stuffed
    Mushrooms, 101
  Radicchio Stuffed with Goat
    Cheese and Salmon, 232
  Red Pesto, 257
  Risi e Bisi (Italian Rice and Peas), 58

Cheese (*continued*)
  Roasted Tomato Sauce
    with Pasta, 131
  Shrimp and Polenta, 146
  Spaghetti with Garlic, Olive
    Oil, and Red Pepper, 130
  Spicy Calabrian Shrimp, 84
  Spicy Lamb Meatballs, 100
  Spinach and Artichoke Dip, 234
  Spring Greek Salad, 66
  Stuffed Hot Peppers, 90
  Stuffed Tomatoes, 111
  Tortellini in Brodo (Tortellini
    in Broth with Shrimp), 63
  White Bean Alfredo Pasta, 136
Chicken
  Avgolemono (Greek Chicken
    and Rice Soup), 52
  Baked Chicken Paella, 141–142
  Chicken in a Pot, 192
  Chicken Paisano, 186
  Chicken Souvlaki Skewers, 188
  Chicken Stuffed with Leeks, 190
  Deconstructed Chicken
    Cacciatore, 195–196
  Greek Sheet Pan Chicken, 187
  Lime Chicken and Shrimp, 194
  Mediterranean Stuffed
    Chicken, 189
  Potenza-Style Chicken, 191
Chickpeas
  Baked Chicken Paella, 141–142
  Chickpea and Avocado Salad, 164
  Classic Hummus, 153
  Falafel in Pita, 221
  Mediterranean Chopped Salad, 69
  Moroccan Potatoes with
    Chickpeas, 38
  Spicy Chickpeas, 228
  Three-Bean Salad, 154
Chicory
  Spring Greek Salad, 66
Chiles
  Harissa, 251
  Moroccan Sardines on Toast, 95
  Spicy Borlotti Beans, 157
  Sweet Potato Cakes, 126
  Tortellini in Brodo (Tortellini
    in Broth with Shrimp), 63
  Vegetarian Chili, 161
  White Bean Soup, 53
Chocolate Red Wine Cake, 273
Ciambotta (Neapolitan
  Ratatouille), 109

Cilantro
  Celery Root with Yogurt Sauce, 120
  Chickpea and Avocado Salad, 164
  Lamb and Vegetable Stew, 202
  Moroccan Lamb with
    Couscous, 199–200
  Moroccan Sardines on Toast, 95
  Shrimp Margarita, 178
  Spicy Roasted Carrots, 117
  Sweet Potato Cakes, 126
Citrus Granita, 269
Clams
  Mussels and Clams in
    White Wine, 181
  Seafood Risotto, 139
Classic Hummus, 153
Classic Italian Olive Oil Cake, 275
Classic Niçoise Salad, 77
Classic Tomato Soup, 57
Cod
  Baked Fish Fingers, 176
  Moroccan Cod, 173
Collard Green Wraps, 113
Cooking methods, 16
Cool Cucumber, Avocado,
  and Radish Soup, 56
Corn
  Vegetable Rice Bake, 140
Couscous
  Algerian Vegetable Couscous, 149
  Morning Couscous with Raisins,
    Nuts, and Honey, 47
  Moroccan Lamb with
    Couscous, 199–200
  Sicilian Eggplant with
    Israeli Couscous, 148
Cream cheese
  Rosemary–Sea Salt Crackers with
    Lemon-Parsley Dip, 233
  Sardine Pâté, 183
Creamy Carrot Soup with
  Rosemary, 51
Cucumbers
  Cool Cucumber, Avocado,
    and Radish Soup, 56
  Cucumber and Red
    Onion Salad, 80
  La Dolce Vita Wrap, 217
  Mediterranean Chopped Salad, 69
  Mediterranean Quinoa Salad, 81
  Panzanella, 67
  Stuffed Cherry Tomatoes, 235
  Stuffed Tomatoes, 111
  Tzatziki Sauce, 247

Vegetable Bulgur, 125
Veggie Club Sandwich, 222

D
Dairy products, 4
Dandelion greens
  Polenta with Wild Greens, 145
  Sautéed Bitter Greens
    with Fennel, 114
Deconstructed Chicken
  Cacciatore, 195–196
Desserts
  Banana "Ice Cream," 267
  Citrus Granita, 269
  Classic Italian Olive Oil Cake, 275
  Figs with Pecorino and Honey, 270
  Peach Galette, 271
  Pistachio Ricotta Cookies, 268
  Polenta Cake, 266
  Red Wine Chocolate Cake, 273
  Red Wine–Poached Pears, 272
Deviled Eggs with Spanish
  Smoked Paprika, 239
Dill
  Baked Fish Fingers, 176
  Herbed Salmon with Mashed
    Potatoes, 168
  Spicy Lamb Meatballs, 100
Dips and spreads
  Baba Ghanoush, 260
  Basil Pesto with Almond
    Butter, 256
  Classic Hummus, 153
  Harissa, 251
  Kalamata Spread, 258
  Layered Hummus Dip, 229
  Lemon Aioli, 259
  Olive Tapenade, 227
  Red Pesto, 257
  Roasted Red Pepper Dip, 238
  Rosemary–Sea Salt Crackers with
    Lemon-Parsley Dip, 233
  Sardine Pâté, 183
  Spinach and Artichoke Dip, 234
  Sweet Hot Cherry Pepper
    Relish, 252
  Tahini, 255
  White Bean Dip, 152

E
Easy Rice Pilaf, 137
Eggplants
  Baba Ghanoush, 260
  Caponata, 89

Ciambotta (Neapolitan
	Ratatouille), 109
Eggplant "Meatballs," 122
Eggplant Roll-Ups, 85
Eggplant Towers, 112
Pesto Vegetable Bread, 211
Sicilian Eggplant with
	Israeli Couscous, 148
Vegetable Cassola, 121
Eggs
Avgolemono (Greek Chicken
	and Rice Soup), 52
Baked Chicken Paella, 141–142
Baked Eggs with Polenta and
	Fontina Cheese, 36
Baked Eggs with Roasted
	Red Peppers, 34
Baked Rice with Swordfish
	and Mussels, 143
Classic Niçoise Salad, 77
Deviled Eggs with Spanish
	Smoked Paprika, 239
Mediterranean Breakfast Wrap
	with Roasted Vegetables, 39
Shakshuka, 45
Southern Italian Pepper and
	Egg Sandwich, 37
Stuffed Tomatoes, 111
Warm Potato Salad, 72
Endive
Mediterranean Quinoa Salad, 81
Ricotta-Stuffed Endive
	with Vegetables, 91
Equipment, 16–17
Escarole
Spring Greek Salad, 66
Exercise, 7–8

F

Falafel in Pita, 221
Farro
Farro with Porcini Mushrooms, 144
Zuppa di Farro (Farro Soup), 50
Fennel
Algerian Carrot Slaw, 78
Fennel and Orange Salad, 75
Lamb and Vegetable Stew, 202
Mediterranean Chopped Salad, 69
Pesto Vegetable Bread, 211
Sautéed Bitter Greens
	with Fennel, 114
Figs
Cheese Plate with Fruit
	and Crackers, 231
Figs with Pecorino and Honey, 270

Fish, 3
Baked Fish Fingers, 176
Baked Flounder with Parmesan
	and Herbs, 174
Baked Rice with Swordfish
	and Mussels, 143
Classic Niçoise Salad, 77
Fishcake Sliders, 219
Fish en Papillote, 175
Herbed Salmon with Mashed
	Potatoes, 168
Mediterranean Snapper with
	Olives and Feta, 170
Moroccan Cod, 173
Moroccan Sardines on Toast, 95
Radicchio Stuffed with Goat
	Cheese and Salmon, 232
Spaghetti with Anchovy Sauce, 135
Spanish Salmon with
	Smoked Paprika, 171
Stuffed Tomatoes, 111
Tuna Puttanesca, 172
Tunisian Brik Pastries, 96
Tuscan Tuna Salad, 68
Whole Branzino with Garlic
	and Herbs, 169
Flank Steak with Italian
	Salsa Verde, 197
Flounder, Baked, with Parmesan
	and Herbs, 174
Focaccia (Italian Flatbread), 207–208
Fruits, 5, 15. *See also specific*
Charcuterie Board with
	Red Onion Jam, 88
Oatmeal with Seasonal Fruit, 40
Frying, 16
Fusilli Arrabbiata, 134

G

Game Hens Stuffed with Wild
	Rice and Mushrooms, 193
Gigante Beans in Tomato Sauce, 155
Grains, 3. *See also specific*
Mediterranean Chopped Salad, 69
Greek Sheet Pan Chicken, 187
Greek Veggie Burgers, 223
Greek Yogurt Parfait, 41
Green beans
Classic Niçoise Salad, 77
Green Bean and Potato Salad, 70
Green Bean Fritters, 127
Green Beans with Prosciutto, 118

H

Harissa, 251
Heart health meal plan, 24–27
Algerian Carrot Slaw, 78
Arugula and White Bean Salad, 74
Avocado Toast, 42
Basil Pesto with Almond Butter, 256
Black Beans with Cherry
	Tomatoes, 158
Broccoli Rabe with Red
	Pepper Flakes, 110
Chickpea and Avocado Salad, 164
Classic Hummus, 153
Classic Niçoise Salad, 77
Classic Tomato Soup, 57
Cool Cucumber, Avocado,
	and Radish Soup, 56
Deconstructed Chicken
	Cacciatore, 195–196
Eggplant Towers, 112
Farro with Porcini Mushrooms, 144
Fish en Papillote, 175
Gigante Beans in Tomato
	Sauce, 155
Greek Veggie Burgers, 223
Harissa, 251
Italian Herb Blend, 262
Jazzed-Up Olives, 226
Kalamata Spread, 258
Mediterranean Breakfast Wrap
	with Roasted Vegetables, 39
Mediterranean Quinoa Salad, 81
Mediterranean Snapper with
	Olives and Feta, 170
Moroccan Cod, 173
Moroccan Potatoes with
	Chickpeas, 38
Moroccan Sardines on Toast, 95
Mushroom Barley Soup, 61
Olive Tapenade, 227
Pan con Tomate (Spanish-Style
	Toast with Tomato), 46
Pasteli (Greek Sesame Bars), 35
Polenta with Wild Greens, 145
Quinoa and Cheese Stuffed
	Mushrooms, 101
Red Swiss Chard with
	White Beans, 106
Roasted Beets with Oregano
	and Red Pepper, 107
Roasted Root Vegetables, 108
Sautéed Bitter Greens
	with Fennel, 114
Shakshuka, 45

Heart health meal plan (*continued*)
Shrimp Salad, 71
Spanish Salmon with
Smoked Paprika, 171
Spicy Borlotti Beans, 157
Spicy Chickpeas, 228
Spicy Roasted Carrots, 117
Tabbouleh (Lebanese Parsley
and Bulgur Salad), 79
Toasted Polenta with
Mushrooms, 94
Tomato Bruschetta, 212
Tuna Puttanesca, 172
Tunisian Brik Pastries, 96
Tuscan Tuna Salad, 68
Vegetable Bulgur, 125
Vegetarian Chili, 161
White Bean Alfredo Pasta, 136
Whole Branzino with Garlic
and Herbs, 169
Za'atar, 263
Herbed Salmon with Mashed
Potatoes, 168
Herb-Roasted Potatoes
with Shallots, 104
Herbs, fresh, 12–13, 21. *See
also specific*
Hot Sauce, 253
Hummus
Classic Hummus, 153
La Dolce Vita Wrap, 217
Layered Hummus Dip, 229
Mediterranean Breakfast Wrap
with Roasted Vegetables, 39

I

Italian Herb Blend, 262
Italian Salsa Verde, 246

J

Jazzed-Up Olives, 226

K

Kalamata Spread, 258
Kibbeh (Lebanese Croquettes), 230

L

La Dolce Vita Wrap, 217
Lamb
Kibbeh (Lebanese Croquettes), 230
Lamb and Vegetable Stew, 202
Lamb Loin Chops with Spaghetti
in Tomato Sauce, 201
Moroccan Lamb with
Couscous, 199–200
Spicy Lamb Meatballs, 100
Layered Hummus Dip, 229
Leeks
Chicken in a Pot, 192
Chicken Stuffed with Leeks, 190
Root Vegetable Soup, 54
Vegetarian Chili, 161
Legumes, 3. *See also specific*
Lemon Aioli, 259
Lemons
Avgolemono (Greek Chicken
and Rice Soup), 52
Citrus Granita, 269
Lemon Aioli, 259
Lemon-Dijon Vinaigrette, 254
Lemon Linguine, 133
Rosemary–Sea Salt Crackers with
Lemon-Parsley Dip, 233
Lentils
Moroccan Lentil Soup, 160
Vegetarian Chili, 161
Warm Lentil Salad, 159
Lettuce
Classic Niçoise Salad, 77
Falafel in Pita, 221
La Dolce Vita Wrap, 217
Portobello Mushroom Sandwich, 218
Summer Rainbow Salad, 73
Lifestyle, 7–9
Limes
Citrus Granita, 269
Lime Chicken and Shrimp, 194

M

Marjoram
Herbed Salmon with Mashed
Potatoes, 168
Whole Branzino with Garlic
and Herbs, 169
Mascarpone cheese
Figs with Pecorino and Honey, 270
Sardine Pâté, 183
Seafood Risotto, 139
Mashed Fava Beans, 156
Meal plans
heart health, 24–27
overall wellness, 28–31
weight loss, 20–23
Meat, 4. *See also specific*
Charcuterie Board with
Red Onion Jam, 88
Mediterranean Antipasto
Skewers, 236
Mediterranean Antipasto
Skewers, 236
Mediterranean Breakfast Wrap
with Roasted Vegetables, 39
Mediterranean Chopped
Salad, 69
Mediterranean diet, 2–9
Mediterranean Quinoa Salad, 81
Mediterranean region, 6
Mediterranean Snapper with
Olives and Feta, 170
Mediterranean Stuffed Chicken, 189
Mediterranean Stuffed Peppers, 105
Mint
Black-Eyed Peas with Mint, 163
Moroccan Lamb with
Couscous, 199–200
Quinoa and Cheese Stuffed
Mushrooms, 101
Spicy Lamb Meatballs, 100
Tabbouleh (Lebanese Parsley
and Bulgur Salad), 79
Vegetable Bulgur, 125
Vegetable Cassola, 121
Morning Couscous with Raisins,
Nuts, and Honey, 47
Moroccan Cod, 173
Moroccan Lamb with
Couscous, 199–200
Moroccan Lentil Soup, 160
Moroccan Potatoes with
Chickpeas, 38
Moroccan Sardines on Toast, 95
Mushrooms
Algerian Vegetable Couscous, 149
Chicken Paisano, 186
Deconstructed Chicken
Cacciatore, 195–196
Farro with Porcini Mushrooms, 144
Game Hens Stuffed with Wild
Rice and Mushrooms, 193
Greek Veggie Burgers, 223
Mediterranean Antipasto
Skewers, 236
Mushroom Barley Soup, 61
Mushrooms Parmigiana, 116
Portobello Mushroom
Sandwich, 218
Quinoa and Cheese Stuffed
Mushrooms, 101
Toasted Polenta with
Mushrooms, 94
Tuscan Tuna Salad, 68
Mussels

Baked Rice with Swordfish
    and Mussels, 143
Mussels and Clams in
    White Wine, 181
Mussels in Tomato Sauce
    with Pastina, 182
Seafood Risotto, 139
Mustard greens
    Sautéed Bitter Greens
        with Fennel, 114

N

Nuts, 4
    Charcuterie Board with
        Red Onion Jam, 88
    Cheese Plate with Fruit
        and Crackers, 231
    Eggplant Roll-Ups, 85
    Game Hens Stuffed with Wild
        Rice and Mushrooms, 193
    Greek Yogurt Parfait, 41
    Morning Couscous with Raisins,
        Nuts, and Honey, 47
    Moroccan Lamb with
        Couscous, 199–200
    Oatmeal with Seasonal Fruit, 40
    Pistachio Ricotta Cookies, 268
    Roasted Acorn Squash with
        Sage and Pistachios, 123
    Romesco Sauce, 249

O

Oatmeal with Seasonal Fruit, 40
Olive oil, 13
Olive Oil Dipping Sauce, 248
Olives
    Algerian Carrot Slaw, 78
    Caponata, 89
    Charcuterie Board with
        Red Onion Jam, 88
    Cheese Plate with Fruit
        and Crackers, 231
    Classic Niçoise Salad, 77
    Jazzed-Up Olives, 226
    Kalamata Spread, 258
    Layered Hummus Dip, 229
    Mediterranean Antipasto
        Skewers, 236
    Mediterranean Snapper with
        Olives and Feta, 170
    Olive Tapenade, 227
    Spring Greek Salad, 66
    Stuffed Tomatoes, 111
    Tuna Puttanesca, 172

Onions
    Cauliflower Soup with
        Onion and Thyme, 55
    Charcuterie Board with
        Red Onion Jam, 88
    Chicken Souvlaki Skewers, 188
    Cucumber and Red Onion Salad, 80
    Kibbeh (Lebanese Croquettes), 230
    Roasted Root Vegetables, 108
Oranges
    Fennel and Orange Salad, 75
    Polenta Cake, 266
    Red Wine–Poached Pears, 272
Overall wellness meal plan, 28–31
    Albóndigas (Spanish Meatballs), 93
    Algerian Vegetable Couscous, 149
    Aperol Spritz, 241
    Arancini (Italian Stuffed
        Rice Balls), 98–99
    Avgolemono (Greek Chicken
        and Rice Soup), 52
    Baked Chicken Paella, 141–142
    Baked Eggs with Polenta and
        Fontina Cheese, 36
    Baked Fish Fingers, 176
    Baked Rice with Swordfish
        and Mussels, 143
    Black-Eyed Peas with Mint, 163
    Bruschetta Pizza, 215
    Charcuterie Board with
        Red Onion Jam, 88
    Cheese Plate with Fruit
        and Crackers, 231
    Chicken Paisano, 186
    Chicken Souvlaki Skewers, 188
    Classic Italian Olive Oil Cake, 275
    Collard Green Wraps, 113
    Deviled Eggs with Spanish
        Smoked Paprika, 239
    Easy Rice Pilaf, 137
    Eggplant Roll-Ups, 85
    Figs with Pecorino and Honey, 270
    Flank Steak with Italian
        Salsa Verde, 197
    Focaccia (Italian Flatbread), 207–208
    Fusilli Arrabbiata, 134
    Greek Sheet Pan Chicken, 187
    Green Bean and Potato Salad, 70
    Green Bean Fritters, 127
    Green Beans with Prosciutto, 118
    Herbed Salmon with Mashed
        Potatoes, 168
    Herb-Roasted Potatoes
        with Shallots, 104

Hot Sauce, 253
    Italian Salsa Verde, 246
    Kibbeh (Lebanese Croquettes), 230
    Lamb and Vegetable Stew, 202
    Lamb Loin Chops with Spaghetti
        in Tomato Sauce, 201
    Lemon Aioli, 259
    Lemon-Dijon Vinaigrette, 254
    Lemon Linguine, 133
    Lime Chicken and Shrimp, 194
    Mediterranean Antipasto
        Skewers, 236
    Mediterranean Stuffed
        Chicken, 189
    Morning Couscous with Raisins,
        Nuts, and Honey, 47
    Moroccan Lamb with
        Couscous, 199–200
    Mussels and Clams in
        White Wine, 181
    Mussels in Tomato Sauce
        with Pastina, 182
    Olive Oil Dipping Sauce, 248
    Pancetta-Wrapped Shrimp, 97
    Panzanella, 67
    Pasta e Fagioli (Pasta and
        Bean Soup), 59
    Patatas Bravas, 87
    Peach Galette, 271
    Peas and Tubetti with Pancetta, 165
    Peas with Pancetta, 119
    Pistachio Ricotta Cookies, 268
    Pizza Bianca with Spinach, 216
    Pizza Dough, 214
    Polenta Bowl with Fruit
        and Honey, 43
    Polenta Cake, 266
    Red Pesto, 257
    Red Wine Chocolate Cake, 273
    Red Wine–Poached Pears, 272
    Risi e Bisi (Italian Rice
        and Peas), 58
    Roasted Tomato Sauce
        with Pasta, 131
    Romesco Sauce, 249
    Rosemary–Sea Salt Crackers with
        Lemon-Parsley Dip, 233
    Sardine Pâté, 183
    Sardinian Flatbread, 206
    Seafood Risotto, 139
    Shrimp and Polenta, 146
    Shrimp Fra Diavolo, 179
Overall wellness meal
    plan (*continued*)

Shrimp Scampi, 177
Sicilian Pork Ribs in
    Tomato Sauce, 203
Southern Italian Pepper and
    Egg Sandwich, 37
Spaghetti with Anchovy Sauce, 135
Spaghetti with Garlic, Olive
    Oil, and Red Pepper, 130
Spiced Baked Pita Chips, 237
Spicy Calabrian Shrimp, 84
Spicy Lamb Meatballs, 100
Stuffed Hot Peppers, 90
Sweet Potato Cakes, 126
Taralli (Pugliese Bread Knots), 209
Testaroli (Etruscan Pancakes), 210
Tortellini in Brodo (Tortellini
    in Broth with Shrimp), 63
Turkish Garlic Yogurt Sauce, 261
Tzatziki Sauce, 247
Vin Brulé, 242
Warm Potato Salad, 72
White Bean Dip, 152

P

Pancetta
    Pancetta-Wrapped Shrimp, 97
    Peas and Tubetti with
        Pancetta, 165
    Peas with Pancetta, 119
    Shrimp and Polenta, 146
    Zuppa di Farro (Farro Soup), 50
Pan con Tomate (Spanish-Style
    Toast with Tomato), 46
Pantry stables, 12–13
Panzanella, 67
Parboiling, 16
Parsley
    Albóndigas (Spanish Meatballs), 93
    Algerian Carrot Slaw, 78
    Asparagus with Herbs, 115
    Baba Ghanoush, 260
    Baked Flounder with Parmesan
        and Herbs, 174
    Caponata, 89
    Eggplant "Meatballs," 122
    Falafel in Pita, 221
    Farro with Porcini Mushrooms, 144
    Game Hens Stuffed with Wild
        Rice and Mushrooms, 193
    Italian Salsa Verde, 246
    Kalamata Spread, 258
    Mediterranean Quinoa Salad, 81
    Mediterranean Snapper with
        Olives and Feta, 170

Moroccan Cod, 173
Moroccan Lentil Soup, 160
Moroccan Sardines on Toast, 95
Mushroom Barley Soup, 61
Pasta Primavera, 132
Root Vegetable Soup, 54
Rosemary–Sea Salt Crackers with
    Lemon-Parsley Dip, 233
Shakshuka, 45
Shrimp and Polenta, 146
Spaghetti with Anchovy Sauce, 135
Spaghetti with Garlic, Olive
    Oil, and Red Pepper, 130
Spanish Salmon with
    Smoked Paprika, 171
Spicy Lamb Meatballs, 100
Tabbouleh (Lebanese Parsley
    and Bulgur Salad), 79
Toasted Polenta with
    Mushrooms, 94
Tunisian Brik Pastries, 96
Vegetable Bulgur, 125
Vegetable Cassola, 121
White Bean Alfredo Pasta, 136
Parsnips
    Roasted Root Vegetables, 108
    Root Vegetable Soup, 54
Pasta
    Deconstructed Chicken
        Cacciatore, 195–196
    Fusilli Arrabbiata, 134
    Lamb Loin Chops with Spaghetti
        in Tomato Sauce, 201
    Lemon Linguine, 133
    Mediterranean Stuffed Peppers, 105
    Mussels in Tomato Sauce
        with Pastina, 182
    Pasta e Fagioli (Pasta and
        Bean Soup), 59
    Pasta Primavera, 132
    Peas and Tubetti with Pancetta, 165
    Roasted Tomato Sauce
        with Pasta, 131
    Shrimp Fra Diavolo, 179
    Spaghetti with Anchovy Sauce, 135
    Spaghetti with Garlic, Olive
        Oil, and Red Pepper, 130
    Tortellini in Brodo (Tortellini
        in Broth with Shrimp), 63
    White Bean Alfredo Pasta, 136
Pasteli (Greek Sesame Bars), 35
Patatas Bravas, 87
Peach Galette, 271
Pears, Red Wine–Poached, 272

Peas
    Pasta Primavera, 132
    Peas and Tubetti with Pancetta, 165
    Peas with Pancetta, 119
    Risi e Bisi (Italian Rice and Peas), 58
Peppers
    Baked Chicken Paella, 141–142
    Baked Eggs with Roasted
        Red Peppers, 34
    Baked Rice with Swordfish
        and Mussels, 143
    Chicken Paisano, 186
    Ciambotta (Neapolitan
        Ratatouille), 109
    Deconstructed Chicken
        Cacciatore, 195–196
    Fishcake Sliders, 219
    Fish en Papillote, 175
    Fusilli Arrabbiata, 134
    Harissa, 251
    Hot Sauce, 253
    Mediterranean Antipasto
        Skewers, 236
    Mediterranean Chopped Salad, 69
    Mediterranean Stuffed
        Chicken, 189
    Mediterranean Stuffed Peppers, 105
    Panzanella, 67
    Pasta Primavera, 132
    Pesto Vegetable Bread, 211
    Potenza-Style Chicken, 191
    Quinoa and Cheese Stuffed
        Mushrooms, 101
    Red Pesto, 257
    Ricotta-Stuffed Endive
        with Vegetables, 91
    Roasted Red Pepper Dip, 238
    Romesco Sauce, 249
    Shakshuka, 45
    Southern Italian Pepper and
        Egg Sandwich, 37
    Spanish Salmon with
        Smoked Paprika, 171
    Spicy Borlotti Beans, 157
    Spring Greek Salad, 66
    Stuffed Hot Peppers, 90
    Stuffed Tomatoes, 111
    Sweet Hot Cherry Pepper
        Relish, 252
    Vegetable Bulgur, 125
    Vegetable Cassola, 121
    Vegetable Rice Bake, 140
Pesto
    Basil Pesto with Almond Butter, 256

Pesto Vegetable Bread, 211
Red Pesto, 257
Pistachio Ricotta Cookies, 268
Pizzas
  Bruschetta Pizza, 215
  Pizza Bianca with Spinach, 216
  Pizza Dough, 214
Polenta
  Baked Eggs with Polenta and
    Fontina Cheese, 36
  Polenta Bowl with Fruit
    and Honey, 43
  Polenta Cake, 266
  Polenta with Wild Greens, 145
  Shrimp and Polenta, 146
  Toasted Polenta with
    Mushrooms, 94
Pork. See also Pancetta;
    Prosciutto; Sausage
  Albóndigas (Spanish Meatballs), 93
  Sicilian Pork Ribs in
    Tomato Sauce, 203
Portion control, 7
Portobello Mushroom Sandwich, 218
Potatoes. See also Sweet potatoes
  Chicken in a Pot, 192
  Ciambotta (Neapolitan
    Ratatouille), 109
  Classic Niçoise Salad, 77
  Creamy Carrot Soup with
    Rosemary, 51
  Green Bean and Potato Salad, 70
  Herbed Salmon with Mashed
    Potatoes, 168
  Herb-Roasted Potatoes
    with Shallots, 104
  Lamb and Vegetable Stew, 202
  Moroccan Cod, 173
  Moroccan Potatoes with
    Chickpeas, 38
  Patatas Bravas, 87
  Roasted Root Vegetables, 108
  Root Vegetable Soup, 54
  Warm Potato Salad, 72
Potenza-Style Chicken, 191
Poultry, 4
Prosciutto
  Green Beans with Prosciutto, 118
  Stuffed Hot Peppers, 90
Pumpkin seeds
  Pasteli (Greek Sesame Bars), 35

Q
Quinoa

Mediterranean Quinoa Salad, 81
Quinoa and Cheese Stuffed
  Mushrooms, 101

R
Radicchio
  Fish en Papillote, 175
  Radicchio Stuffed with Goat
    Cheese and Salmon, 232
  Sautéed Bitter Greens
    with Fennel, 114
  Summer Rainbow Salad, 73
Radishes
  Charcuterie Board with
    Red Onion Jam, 88
  Cool Cucumber, Avocado,
    and Radish Soup, 56
  Green Bean Fritters, 127
  Pesto Vegetable Bread, 211
  Veggie Club Sandwich, 222
Raisins
  Algerian Vegetable Couscous, 149
  Morning Couscous with Raisins,
    Nuts, and Honey, 47
Recipes, about, 17
Red Pesto, 257
Red Swiss Chard with
  White Beans, 106
Red Wine Chocolate Cake, 273
Red Wine-Poached Pears, 272
Refrigerator staples, 14
Rice
  Arancini (Italian Stuffed
    Rice Balls), 98–99
  Avgolemono (Greek Chicken
    and Rice Soup), 52
  Baked Chicken Paella, 141–142
  Baked Rice with Swordfish
    and Mussels, 143
  Easy Rice Pilaf, 137
  Game Hens Stuffed with Wild
    Rice and Mushrooms, 193
  Risi e Bisi (Italian Rice
    and Peas), 58
  Seafood Risotto, 139
  Shrimp Margarita, 178
  Vegetable Rice Bake, 140
Ricotta cheese
  Eggplant Roll-Ups, 85
  Greek Veggie Burgers, 223
  Pistachio Ricotta Cookies, 268
  Ricotta-Stuffed Endive
    with Vegetables, 91

Stuffed Cherry Tomatoes, 235
Risi e Bisi (Italian Rice and Peas), 58
Roasted Acorn Squash with
  Sage and Pistachios, 123
Roasted Beets with Oregano
  and Red Pepper, 107
Roasted Butternut Squash Soup, 60
Roasted Red Pepper Dip, 238
Roasted Root Vegetables, 108
Roasted Tomato Sauce
  with Pasta, 131
Roasting, 16
Romesco Sauce, 249
Root Vegetable Soup, 54
Rosemary
  Cheese Plate with Fruit
    and Crackers, 231
  Chicken Stuffed with Leeks, 190
  Creamy Carrot Soup with
    Rosemary, 51
  Focaccia (Italian Flatbread),
    207–208
  Lamb Loin Chops with Spaghetti
    in Tomato Sauce, 201
  Mashed Fava Beans, 156
  Radicchio Stuffed with Goat
    Cheese and Salmon, 232
  Roasted Butternut Squash Soup, 60
  Rosemary–Sea Salt Crackers with
    Lemon-Parsley Dip, 233
  White Bean Soup, 53
Rutabagas
  Roasted Root Vegetables, 108

S
Sage
  Game Hens Stuffed with Wild
    Rice and Mushrooms, 193
  Roasted Acorn Squash with
    Sage and Pistachios, 123
  White Bean Dip, 152
Salads
  Algerian Carrot Slaw, 78
  Arugula and White Bean Salad, 74
  Caponata, 89
  Chickpea and Avocado Salad, 164
  Classic Niçoise Salad, 77
  Cucumber and Red Onion Salad, 80
  Fennel and Orange Salad, 75
  Green Bean and Potato Salad, 70
Salads (continued)
  Mediterranean Chopped Salad, 69
  Mediterranean Quinoa Salad, 81
  Panzanella, 67

Shrimp Salad, 71
Spring Greek Salad, 66
Summer Rainbow Salad, 73
Tabbouleh (Lebanese Parsley
    and Bulgur Salad), 79
Three-Bean Salad, 154
Tuscan Tuna Salad, 68
Vegetable Bulgur, 125
Warm Lentil Salad, 159
Warm Potato Salad, 72
Salmon
    Fish en Papillote, 175
    Herbed Salmon with Mashed
        Potatoes, 168
    Radicchio Stuffed with Goat
        Cheese and Salmon, 232
    Spanish Salmon with
        Smoked Paprika, 171
Sandwiches. See also Wraps
    Avocado Toast, 42
    Falafel in Pita, 221
    Fishcake Sliders, 219
    Greek Veggie Burgers, 223
    Pan con Tomate (Spanish-Style
        Toast with Tomato), 46
    Portobello Mushroom Sandwich, 218
    Southern Italian Pepper and
        Egg Sandwich, 37
    Veggie Club Sandwich, 222
Sardines
    Moroccan Sardines on Toast, 95
    Sardine Pâté, 183
Sardinian Flatbread, 206
Sauces
    Basil Pesto with Almond Butter, 256
    Hot Sauce, 253
    Italian Salsa Verde, 246
    Lemon Aioli, 259
    Lemon-Dijon Vinaigrette, 254
    Olive Oil Dipping Sauce, 248
    Red Pesto, 257
    Romesco Sauce, 249
    Turkish Garlic Yogurt Sauce, 261
    Tzatziki Sauce, 247
Sausage
    Albóndigas (Spanish Meatballs), 93
    Baked Chicken Paella, 141–142
    Baked Rice with Swordfish
        and Mussels, 143
    Spicy Lamb Meatballs, 100
Sautéed Bitter Greens
    with Fennel, 114
Sautéing, 16
Seafood Risotto, 139

Seasonal eating, 15
Seasonings
    Italian Herb Blend, 262
    Za'atar, 263
Seeds, 4. See also specific
Sesame seeds
    Classic Hummus, 153
    Pasteli (Greek Sesame Bars), 35
    Tahini, 255
    Za'atar, 263
Shakshuka, 45
Shallots, Herb-Roasted
    Potatoes with, 104
Shellfish, 3
Shrimp
    Lime Chicken and Shrimp, 194
    Pancetta-Wrapped Shrimp, 97
    Seafood Risotto, 139
    Shrimp and Polenta, 146
    Shrimp Fra Diavolo, 179
    Shrimp Margarita, 178
    Shrimp Salad, 71
    Shrimp Scampi, 177
    Spicy Calabrian Shrimp, 84
    Tortellini in Brodo (Tortellini
        in Broth with Shrimp), 63
Sicilian Eggplant with Israeli
    Couscous, 148
Sicilian Pork Ribs in Tomato
    Sauce, 203
Simmering, 16
Snacks, 29. See also Appetizers;
    Dips and spreads
    Cheese Plate with Fruit
        and Crackers, 231
    Deviled Eggs with Spanish
        Smoked Paprika, 239
    Jazzed-Up Olives, 226
    Kibbeh (Lebanese Croquettes), 230
    Mediterranean Antipasto
        Skewers, 236
    Radicchio Stuffed with Goat
        Cheese and Salmon, 232
    Rosemary–Sea Salt Crackers with
        Lemon-Parsley Dip, 233
    Spiced Baked Pita Chips, 237
    Spicy Chickpeas, 228
    Stuffed Cherry Tomatoes, 235
Snapper with Olives and Feta,
    Mediterranean, 170
Soups
    Avgolemono (Greek Chicken
        and Rice Soup), 52

Cauliflower Soup with
    Onion and Thyme, 55
Classic Tomato Soup, 57
Cool Cucumber, Avocado,
    and Radish Soup, 56
Creamy Carrot Soup with
    Rosemary, 51
Moroccan Lentil Soup, 160
Mushroom Barley Soup, 61
Pasta e Fagioli (Pasta and
    Bean Soup), 59
Risi e Bisi (Italian Rice
    and Peas), 58
Roasted Butternut Squash Soup, 60
Root Vegetable Soup, 54
Tortellini in Brodo (Tortellini
    in Broth with Shrimp), 63
Vegetarian Chili, 161
White Bean Soup, 53
Zuppa di Farro (Farro Soup), 50
Southern Italian Pepper and
    Egg Sandwich, 37
Spaghetti with Anchovy Sauce, 135
Spaghetti with Garlic, Olive Oil,
    and Red Pepper, 130
Spanish Salmon with Smoked
    Paprika, 171
Sparkling Spa Water, 243
Spiced Baked Pita Chips, 237
Spicy Borlotti Beans, 157
Spicy Calabrian Shrimp, 84
Spicy Chickpeas, 228
Spicy Lamb Meatballs, 100
Spicy Roasted Carrots, 117
Spinach
    Baked Chicken Paella, 141–142
    Black-Eyed Peas with Mint, 163
    Greek Veggie Burgers, 223
    Mediterranean Breakfast Wrap
        with Roasted Vegetables, 39
    Mediterranean Chopped Salad, 69
    Moroccan Potatoes with
        Chickpeas, 38
    Pizza Bianca with Spinach, 216
    Spinach and Artichoke Dip, 234
    Veggie Club Sandwich, 222
Spring Greek Salad, 66
Squash
    Roasted Acorn Squash with
        Sage and Pistachios, 123
    Roasted Butternut Squash Soup, 60
Stress management, 8
Stuffed Cherry Tomatoes, 235
Stuffed Hot Peppers, 90

Stuffed Tomatoes, 111
Summer Rainbow Salad, 73
Sunflower seeds
    Pasteli (Greek Sesame Bars), 35
Swaps, 25
Sweet Hot Cherry Pepper Relish, 252
Sweet potatoes
    Roasted Root Vegetables, 108
    Sweet Potato Cakes, 126
Swiss chard
    Moroccan Potatoes with
        Chickpeas, 38
    Polenta with Wild Greens, 145
    Red Swiss Chard with
        White Beans, 106
Swordfish and Mussels,
    Baked Rice with, 143

T

Tabbouleh (Lebanese Parsley
    and Bulgur Salad), 79
Tahini, 255
Taralli (Pugliese Bread Knots), 209
Testaroli (Etruscan Pancakes), 210
Three-Bean Salad, 154
Thyme
    Cauliflower Soup with
        Onion and Thyme, 55
    Celery Root with Yogurt
        Sauce, 120
    Cheese Plate with Fruit
        and Crackers, 231
    Chicken Stuffed with Leeks, 190
    Classic Niçoise Salad, 77
    Classic Tomato Soup, 57
    Eggplant Roll-Ups, 85
    Fish en Papillote, 175
    Game Hens Stuffed with Wild
        Rice and Mushrooms, 193
    Herbed Salmon with Mashed
        Potatoes, 168
    Jazzed-Up Olives, 226
    Mushroom Barley Soup, 61
    Pesto Vegetable Bread, 211
    Quinoa and Cheese Stuffed
        Mushrooms, 101
    Roasted Root Vegetables, 108
    Root Vegetable Soup, 54
    Rosemary–Sea Salt Crackers with
        Lemon-Parsley Dip, 233
    Sparkling Spa Water, 243
    Vegetable Cassola, 121
    White Bean Soup, 53

Whole Branzino with Garlic
    and Herbs, 169
Za'atar, 263
Toasted Polenta with Mushrooms, 94
Tomatoes
    Albóndigas (Spanish Meatballs), 93
    Algerian Carrot Slaw, 78
    Baked Eggs with Polenta and
        Fontina Cheese, 36
    Barley Risotto with Vegetables, 147
    Black Beans with Cherry
        Tomatoes, 158
    Bruschetta Pizza, 215
    Caponata, 89
    Charcuterie Board with
        Red Onion Jam, 88
    Chicken Paisano, 186
    Chicken Souvlaki Skewers, 188
    Ciambotta (Neapolitan
        Ratatouille), 109
    Classic Niçoise Salad, 77
    Classic Tomato Soup, 57
    Deconstructed Chicken
        Cacciatore, 195–196
    Falafel in Pita, 221
    Fish en Papillote, 175
    Fusilli Arrabbiata, 134
    La Dolce Vita Wrap, 217
    Layered Hummus Dip, 229
    Mediterranean Chopped Salad, 69
    Mediterranean Quinoa Salad, 81
    Mediterranean Snapper with
        Olives and Feta, 170
    Mediterranean Stuffed
        Chicken, 189
    Mushrooms Parmigiana, 116
    Mussels in Tomato Sauce
        with Pastina, 182
    Pan con Tomate (Spanish-Style
        Toast with Tomato), 46
    Panzanella, 67
    Pasta Primavera, 132
    Portobello Mushroom
        Sandwich, 218
    Potenza-Style Chicken, 191
    Red Pesto, 257
    Red Swiss Chard with
        White Beans, 106
    Ricotta-Stuffed Endive
        with Vegetables, 91
    Roasted Tomato Sauce
        with Pasta, 131
    Shakshuka, 45
    Shrimp Fra Diavolo, 179

Shrimp Margarita, 178
Sicilian Eggplant with
    Israeli Couscous, 148
Sicilian Pork Ribs in
    Tomato Sauce, 203
Spanish Salmon with
    Smoked Paprika, 171
Spicy Borlotti Beans, 157
Stuffed Cherry Tomatoes, 235
Stuffed Tomatoes, 111
Tabbouleh (Lebanese Parsley
    and Bulgur Salad), 79
Tomato Bruschetta, 212
Tuscan Tuna Salad, 68
Vegetable Bulgur, 125
Vegetable Cassola, 121
Vegetarian Chili, 161
Veggie Club Sandwich, 222
Zuppa di Farro (Farro Soup), 50
Tortellini in Brodo (Tortellini in
    Broth with Shrimp), 63
Tuna
    Classic Niçoise Salad, 77
    Stuffed Tomatoes, 111
    Tuna Puttanesca, 172
    Tunisian Brik Pastries, 96
    Tuscan Tuna Salad, 68
    Tunisian Brik Pastries, 96
Turkish Garlic Yogurt
    Sauce, 261
Turnips
    Roasted Root Vegetables, 108
    Root Vegetable Soup, 54
    Vegetable Rice Bake, 140
    Tuscan Tuna Salad, 68
Tzatziki Sauce, 247

V

Vegetable Bulgur, 125
Vegetable Cassola, 121
Vegetable Rice Bake, 140
Vegetables, 2–3, 15. *See also specific*
    Mediterranean Breakfast Wrap
        with Roasted Vegetables, 39
    Summer Rainbow Salad, 73
Vegetarian Chili, 161
Veggie Club Sandwich, 222
Vin Brulé, 242

W

Warm Lentil Salad, 159
Warm Potato Salad, 72
Water frying, 16

Watermelon
  Sparkling Spa Water, 243
Weight loss meal plan, 20–23
  Asparagus with Herbs, 115
  Baba Ghanoush, 260
  Baked Eggs with Roasted
      Red Peppers, 34
  Baked Flounder with Parmesan
      and Herbs, 174
  Banana "Ice Cream," 267
  Barley Risotto with Vegetables, 147
  Caponata, 89
  Cauliflower Bites, 86
  Cauliflower Soup with
      Onion and Thyme, 55
  Celery Root with Yogurt Sauce, 120
  Chicken in a Pot, 192
  Chicken Stuffed with Leeks, 190
  Ciambotta (Neapolitan
      Ratatouille), 109
  Citrus Granita, 269
  Creamy Carrot Soup with
      Rosemary, 51
  Cucumber and Red Onion Salad, 80
  Eggplant "Meatballs," 122
  Falafel in Pita, 221
  Fennel and Orange Salad, 75
  Fishcake Sliders, 219
  Game Hens Stuffed with Wild
      Rice and Mushrooms, 193
  Greek Yogurt Parfait, 41
  La Dolce Vita Wrap, 217
  Layered Hummus Dip, 229
  Mashed Fava Beans, 156
  Mediterranean Chopped Salad, 69
  Mediterranean Stuffed Peppers, 105
  Moroccan Lentil Soup, 160
  Mushrooms Parmigiana, 116

Oatmeal with Seasonal Fruit, 40
Pasta Primavera, 132
Pesto Vegetable Bread, 211
Portobello Mushroom
    Sandwich, 218
Potenza-Style Chicken, 191
Radicchio Stuffed with Goat
    Cheese and Salmon, 232
Ricotta-Stuffed Endive
    with Vegetables, 91
Roasted Acorn Squash with
    Sage and Pistachios, 123
Roasted Butternut Squash Soup, 60
Roasted Red Pepper Dip, 238
Root Vegetable Soup, 54
Shrimp Margarita, 178
Sicilian Eggplant with
    Israeli Couscous, 148
Sparkling Spa Water, 243
Spinach and Artichoke Dip, 234
Spring Greek Salad, 66
Stuffed Cherry Tomatoes, 235
Stuffed Tomatoes, 111
Summer Rainbow Salad, 73
Sweet Hot Cherry Pepper
    Relish, 252
Tahini, 255
Three-Bean Salad, 154
Vegetable Cassola, 121
Vegetable Rice Bake, 140
Veggie Club Sandwich, 222
Warm Lentil Salad, 159
White Bean Crostini, 213
White Bean Soup, 53
Zuppa di Farro (Farro Soup), 50
Wellness meal plan. See Overall
    wellness meal plan
White Bean Alfredo Pasta, 136

White Bean Crostini, 213
White Bean Dip, 152
White Bean Soup, 53
Whole Branzino with Garlic
    and Herbs, 169
Wine, 5. See also Beverages
Wraps
    La Dolce Vita Wrap, 217
    Mediterranean Breakfast Wrap
        with Roasted Vegetables, 39

Y

Yogurt
    Baked Fish Fingers, 176
    Celery Root with Yogurt Sauce, 120
    Greek Yogurt Parfait, 41
    Moroccan Lentil Soup, 160
    Radicchio Stuffed with Goat
        Cheese and Salmon, 232
    Rosemary–Sea Salt Crackers with
        Lemon-Parsley Dip, 233
    Spicy Lamb Meatballs, 100
    Spinach and Artichoke Dip, 234
    Sweet Potato Cakes, 126
    Turkish Garlic Yogurt Sauce, 261
    Tzatziki Sauce, 247

Z

Za'atar, 263
Zucchini
    Barley Risotto with Vegetables, 147
    Ciambotta (Neapolitan
        Ratatouille), 109
    Vegetable Cassola, 121
    Zuppa di Farro (Farro Soup), 50

Acknowledgments

Special thanks to my family for all of their love and support, and especially to my brother, James, for his willingness to test recipes, and for listening to me read the entire book out loud numerous times. Thank you to Anne Lowrey for showing me the way through this process and for her fine editing skills. Thank you to Katherine Green for bringing clarity to my recipes. Thank you to Mohammed Munsifzadah for sending this opportunity my way and allowing me to share my passion with the world. I want to thank everyone at Callisto Media who worked on this book. I'd also like to thank Dr. Sharon McLaughlin for her continued support and inspiration. And thanks to Dr. Christopher Sun for encouraging me to eat more vegetables.

About the Author

DONNA DEROSA is a journalist and food writer specializing in the Mediterranean lifestyle. She runs a self-titled YouTube channel through which she shares recipes and Italian lifestyle tips. Learn more at DonnaDeRosa.com.

CPSIA information can be obtained
at www.ICGtesting.com
Printed in the USA
JSHW031509100820
7155JS00001B/1

9 781647 392611